SCALING
THE
IVORY
TOWER

Lionel S. Lewis

The Johns Hopkins University Press Baltimore and London

SCALING THE IVORY TOWER

Merit and Its Limits in Academic Careers

Copyright © 1975 by The Johns Hopkins University Press
All rights reserved. No part of this book may be
reproduced or transmitted in any form or by any means,
electronic or mechanical, including photocopying,
recording, xerography, or any information storage and
retrieval system, without permission in writing
from the publisher.

Manufactured in the United States of America.

The Johns Hopkins University Press, Baltimore, Maryland 21218
The Johns Hopkins University Press Ltd., London

Library of Congress Catalog Card Number 75-11358
ISBN 0-8018-1734-x

Library of Congress Cataloging in Publication data
will be found on the last printed page of this book.

Reputation is an idle and most false imposition; oft got without merit and lost without deserving.

Othello

Contents

Preface

This book is about university professors. It is in part a summation and reformulation of some of my research of the past ten years on the sociology of higher education and academic culture.

Until very recently systematic inquiry into academic life had been mostly neglected by social scientists. Now, after a decade of unsettling change on campus, so much is being written about scholars, from freshmen to distinguished scientists, that yet another book on the subject might seem to require some justification or explanation. However, after one sets aside accounts limited to the condemnation or romanticization of contemporary manifestations of Sturm und Drang, research underwritten by organizations whose vast economic resources and touching faith in the putative achievements of universities has not been matched by a wealth of ideas and a vision of the promise of higher learning, and exquisite but subjective alarums about the impending collapse of universities, high culture, and Western civilization, there really is not that much that informs us about the world of work of professors. This is not to deny the value of what a number of other investigators have been and are presently doing; my extensive use of their work, particularly in chapters 2 and 5, indicates that a body of data has begun to accumulate about the species *academic man* (*and woman* has not yet been added). It is only to suggest that the academic profession has been studied too little rather than too much.

No attempt is made in this volume to examine all aspects of the life, on and off campus, of all types of academic men; its purpose and scope, the examination in detail of the effects of the principle of merit on the careers of university faculty, are not at all comprehensive. Attention is given only to those facets of academic culture which touch upon the precept that in the last analysis university professors are judged primarily by the quality of their work. Few are not convinced that merit, more than anything else, is central to the professional assessments professors make of each other. To be sure, there have always been some who have been skeptical of this assumption, and although their observations may have been met with a nod and knowing smile, they are seldom taken very seriously. The time is well past to examine a proposition first advanced by Thorstein Veblen when the modern American university was beginning to take shape:

> A member of the staff may render his tenure more secure, and may perhaps assure his due preferment, by a sedulous attention to the academic social amenities, and to the more conspicuous items of his expense account; and he will then do well in the same connection also to turn his best attention in the day's work to administrative duties and schoolmasterly discipline, rather than to the increase of knowledge. Whereas he may make his chance of preferment less assured, and may even jeopardize his tenure, by a conspicuously parsimonious manner of life, or by too pronounced an addiction to scientific or scholarly pursuits, to the neglect of those polite exhibitions of decorum that conduce to the maintenance of the university's prestige in the eyes of the (pecuniarily) cultured laity.[1]

The intention here is not to trace out the implications and validity of every tenet of this assertion but only to determine where the truth lies relative to it—and relative to its antithesis that little else besides merit counts in scaling the ivory tower.

After a brief review in chapter 1 of how the principle of merit has evolved with the university tradition in America, chapter 2 focuses on the seemingly endless complications involved in assessing the work of academic men, that is, determining their merit. Through an examination of letters of recommendation written by academics appraising other academics in chapters 3 and 4, inferences can be drawn about what faculty hold to be the normal course of conduct for one who desires a not irregular career. Chapter 5 considers how extraneous, nonprofessional criteria, particularly sex, influence the acceptance of a person and his or her work. In chapter 6, attention is given to how the intrusion of factors peripheral to the search for the truth gives rise to disputes over academic freedom, which results in some having an irregular (or truncated) career. In chapter 7, the issue of how academic bureaucracy impedes the possibility of finding and advancing the best people is examined.[2] In the final chapter, the case is made that the principle of merit is indispensable to institutions of higher learning if they are to be a civilized and civilizing force in society.

The body of evidence presented in the following chapters indicates that there is less attention given to excellence in research and, as is more commonly acknowledged, in teaching than most persons both within and outside the university seem to believe. The contention that the evaluation and advancement of academics turns on merit is simply untrue.

Some might see the case being made here as one-sided, polemical, and potentially harmful to the professoriate. I can only respond that the argument is unbalanced because the evidence is unbalanced, that the thesis appears strident because it questions some commonly held beliefs, and that, to the degree that anyone takes what is written here seriously, what can be learned from the chapters that follow can only benefit academics by helping them know themselves better. It hardly needs to be said that knowledge in itself is not bad, although what some people make of it sometimes is.

The insights that these findings may give to other professors, both those who also care about the higher learning and those heretofore devoted to more secular idols, hopefully can be applied to making the reality of academic life more consistent with the ideal. The understanding they give to the remainder of the intended audience—the general public—of the complexities and ambiguities confronting even the most utopian, committed, and well-intended academic in his attempt to hold true to his students, his work, and himself should strike a sympathetic chord that may lead interested citizens to resist asking universities to be something other than universities. Perhaps as a result they can better do what they must—discover, preserve, and transmit knowledge, engage in idle curiosity, and demonstrate how the life of the mind can enrich the human experience (and the human spirit).

Jackson I. Cope, Leo S. Bing Professor of English at the University of Southern California, and Reece J. McGee, professor of sociology and master teacher at Purdue University, read most of a very ragged, early draft of the manuscript. I greatly profited from their comments and criticism and am most grateful to them. The editors of the *AAUP Bulletin, New Society*, the *Journal of Higher Education*, and *Social Problems* have generously given me the permission to reanalyze and reuse in chapters 3, 4, and 6 some materials previously published by me in their journals, and I appreciate this courtesy.

Finally, I would like to dedicate this book to my wife, Ann Winifred Lewis—a wise and trusty scout.

Buffalo, New York
March 1975

1

Higher Education in America and the Principle of Merit

It has long been customary for Americans to criticize academics. This is not because higher learning has not been taken seriously but rather because it has been taken all too seriously. In general, what has inspired these attacks, past and present, has been the belief either that the professoriate is too committed to sacred matters or that it is too committed to secular affairs. In earlier times the concern was with either excessive piety or heterodoxy; in recent years it has been with too much idealism, or theorizing, on the one hand, or engaging in research too applied (or practical) or careerism, on the other. Regardless of what is being said about men of learning—dispraise or praise about dissipation or achievement through reverie or pragmatism or mischief—there seems to be little doubt in people's minds that they are hard at work and that those who reach out the furthest travel the furthest. This notion is seldom looked at very closely. It is the relationship between the professional activities of academics and their chances of occupational success that is the subject of this study.

AMERICAN INSTITUTIONS AND THE
EUROPEAN HERITAGE

The contemporary American university is an amalgam borrowed from western Europe, most particularly England and Germany. The assumptions underlying the undergraduate curriculum were originally

1

English, while graduate education is grounded in German scholarship and science. The English influence can be dated from the founding of the first college in colonial America, Harvard, in 1636, while the German influence did not take hold until more than two centuries later. Even the idea that an essential function of universities is to serve the state, usually thought to be so peculiarly American, is not particularly new. In his analysis of scholastic America, the English statesman and historian James Bryce noted that by utilizing public universities to improve the common welfare this country had merely "returned to the conception of the functions of the State which prevailed in the Greek republics of antiquity. . . ."[1] Even the debatable idea that faculty should be instruments of state and corporate interests seems to have been borrowed from the French Enlightenment, which in general stressed the utility of institutions.

The influence of English higher education on the colonial colleges of New England and Virginia went a good deal deeper than external organization: it affected the curriculum. To produce a learned clergy, cultivated gentlemen, and a lettered ruling class, higher learning in England was based on a liberal arts curriculum grounded in the classics. The emphasis was on students, teaching, and order rather than on scholarship, study, and learning, as was the case in Germany. Thus, the essential ingredient of early American academic life was the residential unit of students and teachers. Designed to mold character and impart an aristocratic life style to the wellborn, colleges resembled secondary schools as much as they did institutions of higher learning. Since the core of the English university system, Oxford and Cambridge, was of and for the elite, scholarly standards were not high: the life of the mind simply was not relevant to the elite.

The English contribution to college life, with the accent on high culture and the leisurely pursuit of the humanities, has given the American system of higher education the vitality and balance to carry on the most precious traditions of Western civilization, in spite of incessant lapses of public support. Yet by adopting the English collegiate model, the American college also laid the foundation for many of the nonintellectual purposes, especially those surrounding what are broadly referred to as extracurricular activities, that plague institutions of higher learning even to this day. The result of these facts is that even the present American multiversity is more an outgrowth of the English college than of the German university: the Germanic tradition never really surpassed the collegiate way; it was merely appended to it. As Talcott Parsons and Gerald Platt put it, "though the graduate school differentiated from the undergraduate college, it did not displace it

. . . though graduate faculties exist, they are far from having become the dominant structural pattern."[2]

Unlike the English, Americans from the earliest days have been possessed by the frantic desire continually to create new colleges. Originally, this was mostly the work of divines of evangelical fervor motivated by denominational competition. Although England was relatively free of the numerous religious schisms that characterized America, higher learning was for the most part under denominational control, since one of the primary functions in both countries was to train young men for the religious calling. In the seventeenth century more than half of all college graduates in the New World became ministers, and it was not until near the end of the eighteenth century that this figure decreased to less than 20 percent. Most college professors were clergymen or at least were trained in theology. In fact, well into the eighteenth century the primary criterion for appointment for college faculty was religious conformity; religious nonconformists simply were not given professorial appointments. Before the Civil War almost all college presidents were ministers. Harvard appointed its first lay president in 1869; Yale in 1899; and Princeton, Amherst, and Dartmouth did not do so until after the turn of this century. Moreover, it is estimated that in the 1860s between 30 and 40 percent of all college trustees were clergymen, and this number decreased only to about 25 percent by 1900. But by 1930 the figure had dropped to less than one in ten.[3]

From the time Harvard was established until after the Civil War, higher learning in America was a facsimile of English academic culture, and the colleges were of modest intellectual caliber. The English curriculum based on medieval studies with its tradition of scholasticism had hardly changed in its journey across the Atlantic. Christianity and the humanities were blended into a program devised to instill mental discipline and build character. The colleges worked to preserve and transmit existing truths rather than to advance knowledge. The emphasis was quite clearly on teaching. Even as late as 1857, a committee of the Columbia College board of trustees attributed the poor quality of the college to the fact that three professors "wrote books."[4]

As America's ties with England and the force of European traditions weakened, the dominant influence of orthodox religion on college life waned. Consequently, not only was more attention paid to the liberal arts—a shift from theology to ethics—but the way was left open for academic life to become more comprehensive. Professors could turn their attention to matters other than daily recitation, corporal punishment, and, in general, parietal nuisances. The time was ripe for the colleges, with their ministerial faculties, classical curriculums, daily lessons, upper-class student bodies, and bachelor's degrees, to be challenged by the spirit of university life, marked by a deep-rooted professionalism, utilitarian programs, and an enthusiasm for advanced learning that depended on research, seminars, and dissertations.

From 1815, when George Ticknor, who is believed to have been the first American to pursue advanced studies in Germany, enrolled at the University of Göttingen, until 1900, more than nine thousand Americans studied in German universities. Before 1850 the total was a little over two hundred; in the decade of the 1880s enrollment had grown to more than two thousand;[5] and during the academic year 1895–96 alone, over five hundred Americans were matriculated in German universities.

Whether a budding scholar studied at Göttingen, Berlin, Halle, Leipzig, Heidelberg, Bonn, or Munich, he encountered what to Americans was the alien notion that what was important to higher learning was scholarship, not monitoring students. Of those who recorded their impressions, almost all were overawed by what against American practices were high standards of scholastic achievement, freedom for both teacher and student (the ideas of *Lernfreiheit* ["freedom of learning"] and *Lehrfreiheit* ["freedom of teaching"]), and the German academic's consuming interest in higher learning. James Morgan Hart, for one, eulogized that the object of the German university was the "ardent, methodical, independent search after truth in any and all its forms, but wholly irrespective of utilitarian applications."[6] Not surprisingly, these young converts returned home passionately determined to change the course of the American college, which was already writhing from the conflicting pressures from an antiquated curriculum and the still experimental and orderless elective system, away from that of a custodial and socializing institution in the direction of a productive research organization. This was quite consistent with the development of a notion that has become central to the American dream, namely, that unremitting production is the consummate symbol of economic success.

In the beginning, admission standards for those studying science were lower than admission standards for those seeking the conventional bachelor's degree. In addition, the course of study for scientists lasted three years rather than the four years of study normally necessary to complete the undergraduate curriculum. At both Harvard and Yale, students studying science were considered second-class citizens and were treated with condescension; at Yale, for example, they were not permitted to sit with regular students in chapel. As the curriculum broadened, this type of discrimination gradually diminished.

One obvious consequence of the growing body of academic Germanophiles was the founding of a number of institutions, most notably Johns Hopkins, Clark, Chicago, and Stanford, making use of the newly discovered Teutonic Model. Hopkins, established in 1876, was the first, and it was there that the ideal of research was the most successful. At other prominent institutions, such as Harvard, Columbia, and Wisconsin, research became progressively important but was still considered merely one among a number of contending distractions. Due to inadequate support, Clark University, originally solely a research institution, suffered crippling financial setbacks; Stanford University experienced many years of precarious finances—at one time Mrs. Leland Stanford had to offer her personal assets as security to stave off bankruptcy.

One clear indication that the mission of American institutions of higher learning was broadening to include the advancement of knowledge, as well as its conservation, was the establishment of university presses to disseminate, in Nicholas Murray Butler's words, "marked activity" in original research. Only two years after it opened its doors Johns Hopkins had a press; the second oldest university press to continue without a break, the University of Chicago Press was in operation less than twelve months after the school's first students enrolled. With Daniel Coit Gilman's declamation that "it is one of the noblest duties of a university to advance knowledge, and to diffuse it not merely among those who can attend the daily lectures—but far and wide," the Johns Hopkins Press commenced publication of the *American Journal of Mathematics* (1878) and the *American Chemical Journal* (1879). In 1891, its first year, the University of Chicago Press inaugurated three journals—the *Journal of Political Economy*, the *Journal of Geology*, and the *Journal of Near Eastern Studies* (originally *Hebraica*)—which are still in print today.

When Johns Hopkins was conceived, it was anything but universally celebrated among the leaders of higher learning. Presidents Charles William Eliot of Harvard and Andrew D. White of Cornell urged that this radical idea of pure research be put aside and that practical education be accentuated instead. Eliot still held to his inaugural remarks made in 1869 that "the prime business of American professors in this generation must be regular and assiduous class teaching."[7] Even many years later such opinions were not at all atypical: as late as 1910, the president and trustees at the University of Minnesota took the position that a chemistry professor's research was "his own private business, much like playing the piano or collecting etchings."[8]

It soon became clear, however, that the brightest young men choosing academic careers were more interested in the laboratory and the seminar than in teaching. The disinterested pursuit of truth through original investigation undercut the faculty's concern with undergraduate teaching and, by focusing course materials on a professor's particular interests, played havoc with a standardized curriculum. The solid hold of the pedagogue and disciplinarian was consequently weakened by those steeped in Germanic scholarship. Within less than two decades, the graduate school was clearly established as an influential component in institutions of higher learning in America. In 1900, there were 5,668 students enrolled in graduate schools throughout the country; by 1930, the figure was 47,225. In 1909, a little more than fifty years after Henry Tappan's failure to establish a "System of Public Instruction . . . copied from the Prussian" at the University of Michigan,[9] Cornell University established the first research chair in the United States. (The first professor in America was appointed at Harvard in 1722.)

Although there is no denying that graduate education, marked by research and the advancement of the individual scholar, was securely entrenched, nonetheless, it was for the most part superimposed on the English-style college. As Bernard Berelson has noted:

> though the graduate school was "on top" of the college, it was really subordinate to it for many years and in some respects it still is. Again, this is partly due to the economics of the situation: the larger and less costly undergraduate unit helps to support the smaller and more costly graduate program.[10]

In the late nineteenth century, science at last came of age in American institutions of higher learning. First, scientific courses began to be widely taught and soon, in fact, became prominent. Moreover, the scientific approach was adopted by heretofore soft disciplines: social studies became the social sciences; the emphasis of literary studies became technical and philological; psychology abandoned philosophy and began to study rats, monkeys, and fish; philosophy itself looked toward positivism for ultimate answers. Berelson has observed

> that the graduate school came into being under the pressures of science and . . . it has lived its whole life in an increasingly scientific and technological age. . . . In an important way, the institution has from the start been a scientific institution, and it is today.[11]

One stimulus for this was the Morrill Acts of 1862 and 1890, which provided substantial financial assistance in developing research, both pure and applied, and hence graduate facilities.

TEACHING VERSUS RESEARCH

Prior to the Civil War, the academic man was evaluated primarily on the basis of, in earlier days, religious orthodoxy and, later, moral character. But with the introduction of scientific work as a legitimate and essential activity for a growing proportion of individuals and of the more widely accepted definition of professors as professionals, it was not long before new criteria were introduced: institutions of higher learning felt a need to spread about news of a faculty laden with Ph.D.'s, presumably assiduously engaged in research.[12] As late as 1884, of a faculty of 189 at Harvard University only nineteen had earned research degrees, that is, Ph.D.'s; the figure at the University of Michigan was six of eighty-eight.[13] Twenty-five years later more than half the Michigan faculty held Ph.D.'s. By 1904, the City College of New York mandated that all professors hold Ph.D.'s;[14] the University of Illinois took this step the following year.[15] Although not every institution required an advanced degree, there were few who did not require some graduate work for a permanent appointment.

The next short step, of course, was the necessity of publications for advancement. In 1892, William Rainey Harper, Thorstein Veblen's prototype of the captain of erudition, announced to his board of trustees at the University of Chicago that faculty promotion would henceforth depend on scholarly research rather than on teaching. First he introduced the relatively light teaching load—less than ten hours a week. Two years later he told his faculty: "The University . . . will be patient, but it expects from every man honest and persistent effort in the direction of contribution to the world's knowledge."[16] Later in the same decade, the faculty at the University of Pennsylvania were warned against putting too much time into teaching at the expense of research. Those who insisted on draining their energy in the classroom rather than in a library, laboratory, or study were advised to go elsewhere.[17] Yale University, in 1901, advocated "productive work" for its staff in order to help establish "a national reputation."[18] By 1905, one could hear a dean complaining at a meeting of the Association of American Universities that "a man can hardly expect to get an appointment of a higher grade than instructor upon his record as a teacher alone."[19]

A few years later Abraham Flexner was warning that the university had sacrificed teaching on the altar of research.[20] In fact, he went beyond this simple dehortation when he reported in the *Atlantic*

Monthly the following conversation regarding the fortunes of an excellent and popular teacher:

"What is his rank?"
"Assistant Professor."
"When will his appointment expire?"
"Shortly."
"Will he be promoted?"
"No."
"Why not?"
"He hasn't *done* anything!"[21]

The day of research had arrived; and even when the twentieth century was still embryonic, there was little doubt that this dazzling process was firmly entrenched as a method of gaining institutional prestige. Thus, with Harper's announcement that "it is proposed in this institution to make the work of investigation primary, the work of giving instruction secondary,"[22] it was not long before the belief was widely held that academics lived by the code of publish or perish; that men of learning were judged only according to the merit of their research; that at least the university, unlike the college, was one institution (perhaps the last) in American society where there was substantial recognition and recompense for individual initiative. To many, this was all to the good. Liberal culture, the life of leisure, and the life of the mind were synonymous with laziness. Why pursue a useless muse such as idle curiosity anyway, when tangible products—papers and books—could be produced?

In the remainder of this essay the question of how firmly meritorious principles have taken hold of faculty culture is examined. It is the theme of this book that the case has been somewhat overstated: the professoriate are not necessarily judged on the basis of the quality of their research or teaching, that is, they are not necessarily judged according to how well they perform the central academic functions, which is the meaning of merit; other factors less vital to the discovery or dissemination of knowledge are as important to the careers of university professors.

MERITOCRACIES

The term "meritocracy," although still generally not found in dictionaries, has been part of our language since the late 1950s, when Michael Young published his droll essay depicting English society in the twenty-first century. Meritocracies are organizations in which people are assigned tasks and responsibilities and successive power, prestige, and rewards, on the basis of competence. Although there is no presupposition of positional equality, there is an assumption of equality of opportunity and also of a clear relationship between an individual's tasks, responsibilities, power, prestige, and rewards. It is taken for granted that evaluation, placement, and advancement are decided in terms of performance: achievement rather than ascription holds sway. The better qualified an individual, the more elevated his rank, so that under ideal conditions, the best qualified exercise the most control. The criteria for advancement are thus clearly evident: competence, performance, and achievement.

Unlike C. Northcote Parkinson or, more recently, Laurence J. Peter, Young in his flight of fancy accents what appear to be less perverse social processes in the transformation of social institutions, though the impact of these mutations on human affairs is no less bizarre than Parkinson's ominous administrative aberrations or Peter's celebrated incompetence. Extrapolating from what is generally regarded as the sound practice of all contemporary, complex societies of emphasizing ability and effort in the evaluation and eventual placement of individuals in the class structure, Young sketches the effects of a "redistribution of ability between the classes" on the family, on education, in politics, and on the economy.[23] The oligarchy of Young's future, which rewards intelligence, training, experience, and hard work, is a fine caricature of what we are told is today the common practice of giving "the talented . . . the opportunity to rise to the level which accords with their capacities. . . ."[24]

Here in part is Young's description of English society in the 2030s.

The ranks of the scientists and technologists, the artists and the teachers, have been swelled, their education shaped to their high genetic destiny, their power for good increased. Progress is their triumph; the modern world their monument.[25]

As a consequence

the world beholds for the first time the spectacle of a brilliant class, the five per cent of the nation who know what five per cent means. Every member is a tried specialist in his own sphere. Mounting at a faster and faster rate, our knowledge has been cumulative from generation to generation. In the course of a mere hundred years we have come close to realizing at one stroke the ideal of Plato, Erasmus, and Shaw.[26]

Hopefully, all of this is more a parody than a consummation of what Young sees as the present drift.

Yet, in discussing present-day trends, and sounding more ideological than sober, the controversial Harvard psychologist R. J. Herrnstein writes:

> While Sunday supplements and popular magazines crank out horror stories about genetic engineering, our society may be sorting itself willy-nilly into inherited classes. What troubles [one] most about this prospect is that the growth of an increasingly hereditary meritocracy will arise out of the successful realization of contemporary political and social goals.[27]

Perhaps Young's narrative is more descriptive than portentous. After all, Herrnstein contends, "simple arithmetic tells us that removing the higher I.Q.'s from the lower classes must reduce the average score of those remaining. Whatever else this accomplishes, it will also increase the I.Q. (hence, the genetic) gap between upper and lower classes. . . ."[28]

To question or be baffled by the conclusions of such a curious utopian is not to dispute the fact that the social structure in all modern, industrial countries is fluid. It is doubtful whether the United States would have earned its reputation as the land of opportunity and would still be regarded as such if the outlines of these sorts of descriptions were not in part founded on fact. Even the most vehement critics of American society would probably acknowledge that there is indeed considerable upward and downward social mobility and that some of this at least has been brought to pass by men of considerable ability or with gross incapacities. What those who celebrate and those who scoff at the American dream disagree about is how much mobility there is; how much of this is occasioned by the extraordinarily competent and incompetent; what the cumulative effects of ability or its complete lack are as against luck, kinship ties, other ascribed traits, and the capacity to smoothly interact with others; and how much mobility goes beyond movement simply to an adjacent class.

In the last quarter of the century, students of social stratification have shed some light on the question of relative mobility, but what they have found has in large part been determined by the particular ideology of the individual researcher—some find the bottle half full, others find it half empty—and little has been done to moderate the debate.

Partially on the basis of widely distributed government statistics, most observers would acknowledge that it is more difficult for an Horatio Alger to climb the success ladder today in the world of commerce with a limited stake from his savings from years as an apprentice, and with pluck, virtue, and an open mind and heart than, say, fifty years ago. Large sums of capital may be necessary so that one can purchase expensive and complex technology to compete with agri-business, multinational corporations, conglomerates, and industries with large governmental subsidies. The mom-and-dad's corner store, the independent service-station operator, the unfranchised roadside or quick-order restaurant, and the twenty-unit motel are becoming anomalies; many enterprises that survive the competition of chain-store merchandising are at best financially marginal. The self-made man is not a relic of the good old days, but more often than in the past he has gotten where he is through real-estate speculation, holding the patent on an invention that a large corporation needs, judicious investments on Wall Street, or establishing a company that does 80 percent of its business with the Department of Defense. Success is usually defined as getting a college education, starting at the bottom of a large organization in the management-training program, slowly but systematically advancing to more responsible administrative positions, and working one's way into top management in order to become eligible for stock options, a six-figure salary, company credit cards, and access to the executive dining room, elevator, men's room, and sauna.

Presumably, there are still institutions in American society where *ability* and *effort* are of particular importance, and most commonly mentioned among these, in fact, is the university. Although distended by bureaucracy, the university is still assumed to be one of the last frontiers of individualism, of hard work, where excellence is cultivated —where merit is rewarded.

That a pervasive equity—in spite of a great deal of bad faith and bad manners—persists in universities is taken for granted by nearly all students of academic life. Thus, a few years ago when Christopher Jencks and David Riesman published their *The Academic Revolution,* wherein they attempted to demonstrate that the professional, technical, and mindless training which had permeated the undergraduate curriculum was suffocating the true purpose of higher learning, the intelligentsia squabbled over a number of issues that they raised: Are parochial institutions that parochial? Are Negro colleges that inferior? Are professional schools really that dominant? Is social mobility that closely related to higher education? However, almost no one challenged their description of the dynamics of academic life, which in large part has won its stability through the unswerving trust that in the long run those with the most talent will surface through a sort of natural selection.

Jencks and Riesman believe that meritocracy is playing an increasingly important part in the American experience. As a consequence of the spreading influence of distinctive values prevailing in institutions of higher learning, our life style is becoming more cosmopolitan, moderate, universalistic, and legalistic.[29]

> These changes in the character of American society have inevitably been accompanied by changes in higher education. The most basic of these changes has been the rise of the university. . . . College instructors have become less and less preoccupied with educating young people, more and more preoccupied with educating one another by doing scholarly research which advances their discipline.[30]

Later:

> The universities, especially their graduate professional schools, have become pacesetters in the promotion of meritocratic values. In Talcott Parsons' terms, they are "universalistic," ignoring "particularistic" and personal qualities in their students and professors. This means that they choose professors almost entirely on the basis of their "output" and professional reputation. Students in the graduate professional schools are selected by similar criteria: by their ability to write good examinations and do good academic work. The claims of localism, sectarianism, ethnic prejudice and preference, class background, age, sex, and even occupational plans, are largely ignored.[31]

Thus, we are told, faculty are judged "almost entirely on the basis of the one set of standards almost all its members accept: professional performance."[32]

> The academic routines of today's graduate schools place a high premium on certain virtues, such as clarity of thought, skepticism, precision, and a capacity to organize one's time and energy. But there are other virtues, which the present system ignores or positively discourages, such as tact, practicality, social inventiveness—and even faith, hope, and charity.[33]

In a separate article, Riesman contends that with the movement toward meritocracy, qualities such as tenacity and the willingness to learn new things become more important while others, such as gregariousness and ingratiation, become less so; where intelligence and skill are important, manners and charm are not.[34]

Although it is frequently asserted that an elite organized along technocratic lines rules the roost in American universities, such a statement must be carefully examined before it is taken in faith: institutions of higher learning may or may not turn on merit and accomplishments. Zbigniew Brzezinski is one among many Ivy League professors successful in the world of affairs who claims to see a new meritocratic elite who are, among other things, "utilising the universities" as they are "taking over American life."[35] Because the social order is rational, those who are any good rise to the top. Since it is believed that scholarship and even teaching are tangible products, easily amenable to objective assessment, the circulation and placement of the able and less able into positions befitting their talent is uncomplicated, predictable, and relatively precise. As in all human affairs, there is slippage in the system, and many exceptions to the rule can be found. Yet, chance, caprice, and other wanton factors are held to a minimum. Once excellence is ascertained—a relatively easy task—it can be and is readily rewarded. The simplicity and straightforwardness of it all leaves one with the distinct impression that a certain logic and sanity prevail in academia.

In fairness it must be noted that the work of other relatively perceptive observers of the latter-day academic scene—Jacques Barzun,[36] Pierre van den Berghe,[37] and Theodore Caplow and Reece McGee[38] —begins or ends with this same undisputed premise. We seem to be dealing with a received doctrine. However, some acute reflection about the muddle of the academic world cannot help but make one mindful that this quaint picture is somewhat overdrawn. There are more than a few charlatans who have achieved academic acclaim; there are more than a few injustices perpetrated in every department in every institution to vitiate a more sanguine picture of academic life. The talented and the hack can be found in the most prestigious institution and in the most provincial two-year community college, though clearly able people are more concentrated in the former.

Thus, the principle of merit perhaps does not guide academic men any more than it does those in other occupations. Sometimes ability is central in the assessment and rewarding of academic men, and sometimes other factors hold sway. It is not the purpose in the pages that follow to establish unequivocally Iago's comment to Cassio, with which this book started; the intention is more modest: to demythologize the image of academic man as a lucid, reasonable, goal-directed automaton seeking the truth and acting in all facets of his professional life on the basis of that truth. The argument is that academics are only human; they, like everyone else, respond from their strengths and weaknesses, pride and prejudices, to new facts and old, with passion and dispassion, with affection and enmity.

To shed as much light as possible on the question of the place of merit in academic culture, an examination will be made of a wide assortment of materials, mostly of a statistical nature, from numerous national studies, letters of recommendation written by academics for colleagues and students, and all of the cases involving contested dismissals reported in the *American Association of University Professors Bulletin* over a fifty-year period.

A university is conventionally defined as an institution that stresses graduate education, grants advanced degrees in a number of fields, and has at least two professional schools. Obviously, the term is used by some institutions that do not meet these criteria, although the Office of Education of the Department of Health, Education, and Welfare does not officially categorize them as universities. Furthermore, while some liberal arts colleges do offer master's degrees, their primary emphasis is on undergraduate instruction, and they, therefore, are not classified as universities.

In light of the marked differences between the functions of the university and those of the college, it hardly needs to be said that since the genus faculty in the United States ranges from the Nobel laureate and highly regarded government consultant seldom seen on campus, never by undergraduates, to the instructor in a rurally located two-year community college with a fifteen-hour teaching load and countless advisees and parietal responsibilities, it is meaningless to make sweeping statements about faculty behavior, values, and attitudes. Inasmuch as those who teach in universities are the pacesetters and the most influential in establishing academic norms, when available, reports and accounts about them will be referred to and utilized throughout the volume. Although a study of some aspect of the faculty of the English department at Johns Hopkins may, in reality, be no more generalizable to the academic world than a complete survey of the entire faculty of Niagara County Community College, the former is usually taken as a more accurate reflection of academic life.

INSTITUTIONS AND ACADEMICS: SOME STATISTICS

In 1970, of the 2,556 institutions of higher education in the United States,[39] 159 were classified by the Department of Health, Education, and Welfare as universities, 1,506 were classified as other four-year institutions, and the remaining 891 were two-year colleges. The enrollments for these three categories were 2,996,506; 3,291,690; and 2,209,921, respectively. It might be mentioned here that the number of institutions of higher learning in the United States has expanded markedly in the past two decades: in 1950, there were but 1,851; in 1960, there were 2,008; and in 1970, the number had grown to the 2,556 figure. For the 1971–72 academic year, this figure had increased again to 2,626.

Of the 185,626 faculty members with the rank of full-time instructor or above teaching in all types of four-year institutions in the fall of 1963, the last year for which such statistics were readily available, 90,567 were placed in universities; 60,166 were in liberal arts colleges; 18,414 were in teachers colleges; 8,705 were in technological schools; 2,940 were in theological and religious schools; 1,128 were in schools of art; and 3,706 were in other professional schools. If one adds the 18,935 instructors who taught full-time in that year in those schools with something less than a four-year program, then it can be concluded that something less than 50 percent of those on the faculties in institutions of higher learning are located in universities.[40]

Most surveys, in fact, suggest that the number of academics with university appointments is closer to one-third than to one-half. For example, in the early 1960s Elbridge Sibley found that of the 75 percent of sociologists with academic positions who had the Ph.D. degree one-third were located in major universities, members of the Association of American Universities.[41] Of the some twenty-five thousand physicists in the United States in 1970, only a little more than two thousand, or less than 10 percent, were employed by one of the leading eighty-six Ph.D.-producing departments (that is, departments that granted at least one Ph.D. in each of the years between 1952 and 1962); and about four hundred, or less than 2 percent, were in the ten most distinguished departments.[42] And according to the Carnegie Commission on Higher Education, which categorized institutions of higher learning in terms of both function and quality, 12.5 percent of 432,482 individuals with regular academic appointments in 1969 were located in high-quality universities, and 18.1 percent were located in medium-quality universities.[43]

And, obviously, professional expectations for faculty are a function of the type of institution where one has an appointment. For example, in the spring of 1969, 64 percent of the faculty of universities held medical degrees, Ph.D.'s, Ed.D.'s, or other doctorates; 43.7 percent who taught in four-year colleges possessed one of these degrees; while only 7.5 percent of the faculty in two-year colleges held doctorates.[44]

In 1971–72, only 35.4 percent of the 2,626 institutions of higher learning awarded a degree higher than the baccalaureate. Seventy-six offered the first professional degree, 438 awarded only the master's degree, 105 gave a degree beyond the master's but less than the doctorate, and 312 (11.9 percent) had doctoral programs. The largest number of the 2,626 were 943 two-year colleges—a gain of over fifty from the previous year.[45] As is evident from the first set of statistics given above, these figures do not mean that there are almost three times as many persons teaching in community or junior colleges as there are teaching and doing research in institutions that award a doctorate. The average enrollment at the former type of institution is somewhere around one-tenth the enrollment at the latter; sometimes the differences are much greater than this. The point being made is that any way one wants to count, it is clear that between one-third and one-half of all full-time faculty of instructors, assistant professors, associate professors, or professors teach in universities; the rest are in the liberal arts colleges, teachers colleges, technological schools, theological seminaries, art schools, specialized professional schools, and two-year colleges. This ratio appears to have been relatively stable at least since World War II. Thus, there seems little question that of the approximately 350,000 full-time faculty at the rank of instructor or above in four-year institutions of higher learning during the 1971–72 academic year, less than half were subject to rigid professional academic norms that assumed scholarly research and productivity, as well as excellence in teaching. Put another way, at least half of the faculty were not operating in the type of system under which a manifold principle of merit held sway—they were tutors rather than professors.

In a study looking at some characteristics of university faculty, carried out in 1969 by the Carnegie Commission on the Future of Higher Education and the American Council on Education,[46] it was found that less than 5 percent had only a bachelor's degree, and almost 23 percent held a master's. For those with a higher degree, it took almost three-fifths of them five or more years of advanced study to earn it. Less than 7 percent had received their highest degree before 1939, and almost 56 percent had obtained theirs in the past ten years.

Slightly more than one-fourth of the sample of 17,610 were full professors, and slightly less than one-fourth were associate professors. Almost 30 percent held the rank of assistant professor, and most of the remaining one-fifth were instructors (15.1 percent) and lecturers (2.9 percent). About half of the appointments carried tenure. Only one in eight had his degree in the social sciences, more than 18 percent had theirs in fine arts or humanities, and 22 percent were scientists. Over one-third specialized in the professional fields, and one in eight did not have a degree in an academic specialty.

As far as salient characteristics of family background are concerned, the fathers of 26 percent had completed eight grades of school or less, almost 31 percent had high-school diplomas, 24 percent had begun or graduated from college, and almost 19 percent had some graduate school or advanced degrees. The survey of the family lives of university faculty shows that 83 percent are married; 4 percent are divorced, separated, or widowed; and almost 13 percent have never been married. Almost one-third have no children, while over two-fifths have one or two, and more than one-fourth have three or more.

Finally, regarding other personal characteristics, half were forty-one years of age or older, almost 98 percent were white, almost 90 percent were native-born, and 95 percent were American citizens. Two-thirds were raised as Protestants, 13 percent as Catholics, and one in ten as Jewish. Their current religious affiliations were: less than 50 percent Protestant, less than 10 percent Catholic, and 7 percent Jewish. Almost 24 percent claimed no religious affiliation.

All in all, there is little in these data to indicate that university faculty are much different from other professionals: like most, they are white; their social origins are less impressive than physicians' but clearly middle-class; they are less religious than most subcultures (even significantly less so than two-year college teachers, of whom less than 14 percent claim no current religion). Figures on salary means, mediums or modes, have not been included, as their modulation from year to year is such as to make them too unstable for analysis, which would preclude the development of almost any generalization. It can be said, however, that in the early 1970s the overwhelming majority of university full professors earned between $20,000 and $30,000 a year—enough to guarantee them a comfortable suburban home furnished with a mélange of antiques, Danish modern, and junk, perhaps two automobiles, some mutual funds, an annual vacation (or two), an orthodontist, and a pervasive belief in the American way of life. The country has been good to them, and it would be beyond expectation for them to fail to appreciate this fact. It would not be beyond expectation for the behavior of academics to resemble that of professionals who staff other types of institutions.

If merit is to obtain on any campus, the assessment of individuals must be in accordance with their performance. The difficulties attendant to evaluating the professoriate's primary functions, teaching and scholarship, are the subject of the next chapter.

2

The
Evaluation
of Teaching
and
Publication

As a first step in determining the pervasiveness of the principle of merit in the American university, this chapter reviews what other researchers have learned about the judgmental processes affecting the professional activities of academics. The discussion begins by threading through the jumble that surrounds what has proven to be an elusive concept, that of teaching effectiveness, and then moves on to examine how seriously even the much publicized scientific and scholarly products of academics are taken in advancing a university career. Special attention is given to the potency of the putative indispensability of publication—an unadulterated manifestation of merit—for helping individuals succeed, not as scholars or scientists but occupationally. In general, what is found does not support the thesis, central to essentially all studies of academic life in America, that the work of faculty is evaluated along narrow professional lines, or as Parsons and Platt put it: "Faculty members review each other's publications, teaching, and service on the basis of cognitive standards. . . ."[1]

ASSESSING TEACHING EFFECTIVENESS

The question of assessing the teaching effectiveness of academic men is such a tangled skein that the more it is held up to examination, the more it seems that those who would have us ignore what goes on between faculty and students possess a sort of primeval wisdom. The

first point of difficulty is that, from a survey of numerous review articles summarizing well over a thousand studies which have attempted
to measure teaching effectiveness, it is evident that researchers have
never really adequately sorted out the various connotations of this
concept. Many investigators have equated effective teaching with
good teaching—which, since, for example, one can inspire students to
learn much trivia well, may or may not be the case—and have let it go
at that. If we were to grant that these two concepts are synonymous,
this still begs the question; What is a good teacher? someone with an
outgoing and pleasant personality? someone who is popular and well-
received? someone who is knowledgeable? someone who motivates
good students? One cannot begin to answer these and countless other
queries until what is meant by *outgoing, pleasant, popular, well-
received, knowledgeable, motivate*, and so forth, is explained.

The philosopher of education Harry Broudy sees both the complexity and the simplicity of this question of explicitness:

> Why is a definition of good teaching so elusive? In one sense it is not
> elusive at all. You can define good teaching any way you like. Simply take
> any outcome, process, or quality that seems desirable, and then define
> good teaching as whatever something called a teacher does to bring it
> about efficiently. Even a cursory fishing in the literature will net such
> definitions by the dozen. Good teaching has been defined as what the
> "teacher" does to produce inspired pupils, excited pupils, interested pupils,
> creative pupils; pupils who are good citizens, who can read, do arithmetic
> problems and write grammatical English essays. Among other desiderata
> used to define good teaching are critical thinking, subject matter mastery,
> ideals, love of freedom, respect for law and order, universal brotherhood,
> various attributes of character, a love of learning and a devotion to the
> arts. I am sure one can add another hatful of items to this list.[2]

But, again, what do *inspired, excited, interested, creative*, and so on,
mean? Moreover, as Broudy points out in the next paragraph of his
article, "such definitions . . . tell us nothing about the factors which
produce these results." For the most part, as the mental gyrations
become more involved, the notion of teaching effectiveness floats further from our grasp, becoming less specific and verifiable and more
ecclesiastical than scientific.

Because effective teaching is not easily conceptualized, it is not easily measured. Even the most simple and direct approach is fraught
with pitfalls. For example, to argue that to assess what is transmitted is
to assess effectiveness, although straightforward enough, is far from
satisfactory. To know what is transmitted is not to know what is received. And when do we assess what reaches the student's ears? at the

end of a class period? at the end of the course? three months later? when the student graduates from college? five, ten, or fifteen years later? But more important, is what is communicated really a valid mark of effectiveness? Is the end of higher learning to stuff the student —as one would stuff a Thanksgiving turkey—with facts and figures? Is teaching only communication, the sharing of knowledge, or is it more? Is the goal of education comprehension? changing values? developing critical thinking? educating the whole man? making him more civilized or humane? Or should there be a combination of some or all of these goals? In sum, the objective of a course might be the understanding of basic concepts and principles; the development of an appreciation of a discipline; the learning of factual material; the acquisition of values; the fostering of critical thinking; the cultivation of specific skills; or any combination of these. This is what makes the task of course evaluation so complex. In more than a half-century of surveying what goes on in the college classroom, researchers have not progressed beyond making more reliable a number of tests (the validity of which is questionable) of teaching effectiveness. As more than one authority on this topic has observed: "Though they are worth seeking, precise before and after measures of teaching effectiveness are hard to envision."[3]

Given the level of our understanding of teaching effectiveness, the most that can be said regarding how it is best measured is that it would depend on what is being taught (geometry or literature), what the caliber of the students is (well prepared or ill prepared), and what the instructor hopes to accomplish (to teach specific scientific laws or to instill appreciation of the life of the mind). Or, as one scholar in the field has put it: "*Some* teachers can use *some* techniques with *some* students when dealing with *some* subjects."[4] To put all of this another way, there is no theory of learning because of the complex interaction of the many variables affecting its progress and outcome. How, then, can we evaluate the teaching role, that is, how can we judge teaching effectiveness?

We do know that class size affects the amount of learning that goes on, in that the number of students with which the instructor must interact in part dictates the teaching method employed; and retention, the ability to solve problems, the probability that class material will be applied in other contexts, change of attitude, the desire to continue learning, and factual learning are all a function of how the subject matter is presented. Thus, one of the few statements we can make with some certainty is that class size and method are determinants of what is commonly agreed to be the most valid measure of effectiveness —learning. On the other hand, we also know that although most students prefer seminars to large lectures and democratic instructors to martinets, there is little difference (given similar modes of presentation) in the amount of learning that takes place under such diverse conditions, at least as measured by standardized tests.

Teaching method, of course, also depends on the purpose of the class, on characteristics of students besides their number, and on the special skills of the teacher. In general, then, we have a situation in which, for the most part, we do not know what students learn. Nor do we know how faculty contribute to that learning that does occur or what conditions facilitate this eventuality. If the point had to be pressed, one could conclude with some assurance that teaching effectiveness is, at least, a combination of knowledge of one's subject, hard work, enthusiasm, common sense, and skill in handling others.

Although all of this may provide insight into the difficulties involved in carrying out meaningful research in assessing the conduct of education, more importantly and to the point, such complexities lay bare the immediate problem of evaluating teaching performance. They strongly suggest that at bottom it is a worthless task; that teaching is too much of a personal activity to be defined or measured; that it is an art, a noncommunicable technique. But the dependence on such a recondite term as "art" may only be a reflection of bewilderment or ignorance about the process of teaching. One cannot help believing that if learning, and not teaching, were seen as the logical product of faculty-student exchanges, we could concentrate on it and abandon the futile attempt to determine teaching effectiveness. Still,

> the most difficult kind of data to obtain is that which shows an actual, verifiable, relationship, positive *or* negative, between student learning and teaching performance. The measures we commonly use to judge either student learning or faculty teaching effectiveness are none too accurate. Grades, performance on examinations, subjective assessments of teachers, performance criteria are limited measures of student learning. Student ratings, self-evaluations, visiting of classes by peers or supervisors, informal feedback are similarly limited.[5]

Moreover, pursuing this tack of calculating the extent to which learning takes place might only lead to the same kinds of indeterminable questions already raised in the preceding paragraphs. However, even if it were acknowledged that learning may be a subjective, personal experience, would it not be possible to estimate the amount that occurs by simply asking those who are doing the learning to rate their courses? Thus, individual differences and singular expectations of students and instructors could be discounted. Such factors are more or less beside the point if one is interested in the question of learning (as assessed by those most directly involved) per se.

Many institutions—the estimates range from 25 percent to more than 50 percent—have some type of administratively sanctioned questionnaire that enables students to express their opinions about the courses they complete. Yet, in spite of research by Costin and his associates which concludes that in general student ratings are reliable, valid, and useful ("a review of empirical studies indicates that students' ratings can provide reliable and valid information on the quality of courses and instruction"),[6] there is considerable resistance to utilizing this information in the evaluation of faculty. The arguments of those opposed to relying on this technique are varied, but the two most commonly heard are that students, who are expected to understand theoretical physics or Chaucer, lack the experience and maturity to pass judgment on their (learned) elders and that the questionnaires used in these procedures may be invalid. Items about an instructor's sense of humor or appearance, which can be found in many evaluation forms, certainly suggest that curious notions as to what is important in institutions of higher learning abound. However, the concern expressed by many faculty members about such matters is ill spent: these questionnaires are rarely used to assess faculty teaching performance when decisions are being made regarding promotions, salary increases, and the granting of tenure.

Findings from a single extensive study can be used to demonstrate the manner in which judgments are made about teaching, since all other research on this topic is relatively consistent with these data. In 1966, the American Council on Education tabulated the responses of 1,100 deans to the question of how their faculty's undergraduate teaching was evaluated.[7] The responses from those deans of colleges of arts and sciences that were units of large universities (a total of 110) are of particular interest because of the expectation that meritocratic principles are well-implanted in these particular settings. In almost all of these colleges, 98.2 percent, the chairman's evaluation was a primary source of information about classroom performance. Next in importance as a source, in 71.8 percent of the colleges, was an assessment made by the dean himself. Where a dean in a large college in a large university obtained his information about individuals of a faculty that numbered perhaps three hundred, perhaps six hundred, was not specified. In 70.0 percent of these colleges, scholarly research and publications were used to determine teaching skill in all or most departments. Presumably the reasoning here is that if a man knows his field well enough to push beyond its frontiers and be creative, then he obviously knows enough to be a tolerably good teacher. Needless to say, it has never been empirically established that there is a positive relationship between ability to do research and teaching competence. In 62.0 percent of these colleges, colleague opinion was considered. In only 35.0 percent of the colleges was informal student opinion utilized as evidence in weighing teaching competence. Finally, only 2.0 percent used classroom visits, and 1.0 percent practiced a long-term follow-up of students.[8]

When asked about the importance of various factors in evaluating faculty for promotion, salary increases, and granting tenure, 93.6 percent of the 110 deans mentioned classroom teaching, 92.7 percent specified research, 83.3 percent indicated publication, and 55.2 percent referred to supervision of graduate study.[9] It is obvious that teaching is considered a central function for academics in even the most prestigious institutions. Yet, what is evaluated, and how this is done, leaves something to be desired. As a leading psychologist has noted: "We do not know the effects of misinformation, amount of information presented, level of abstraction, emphasis upon cognition versus motivation, analysis versus synthesis, didactic versus problem-solving approaches, or deductive versus inductive styles [on learning]."[10]

Furthermore, it is evident that at least in the colleges of arts and sciences of leading universities little precise information about the teaching of individual faculty is secured. To the contrary, there is evidence that what is known about someone's classroom performance is fabricated from gossip, rumor, ex parte evidence, and other random and unreliable means of intelligence. For example, in 1960 the Committee on College Teaching of the American Council on Education began an analysis of "policies and practices in faculty evaluation" and obtained completed questionnaires from, among others, sixty-eight private universities and sixty-two state universities. Responses from the sixty-eight private universities revealed that student opinions (not ratings) and chairman evaluation were the principal sources of data gathered for evaluating classroom teaching.[11] For the sixty-two state universities in the sample, the chairman's evaluation was primary, and the opinions of students were secondary. The report notes:

> Since classroom teaching was universally cited as the most important single factor in evaluating faculty members, one might therefore assume that a good bit of attention had been paid to sources of information about it. Instead, what was found made it apparent that next to nothing has been done in this area. With but one or two exceptions, the most frequently cited sources of information can be described simply as *hearsay*.[12]

Few faculty visit each other in the classroom. To do so, we are told, is to infringe on someone's academic freedom, that is, the right to teach as poorly as one wishes. Moreover, since many individuals do not formally prepare for the teaching function and others have only desultory experience in practice teaching, data on which to make even the roughest predictions about future performance are simply not available.

All in all, there is little information about how faculty teach, and the few tidbits that are relied upon are tangential and of doubtful value. What, specifically, does "informal student opinion" mean? the complaints from those whose marks were lower than they had anticipated? the dissatisfaction of those who thought their assignments too difficult? the veneration of those flattered by being put on the honor system? the gratification of others who appreciated the practice of self-grading? Are such students a self-selected sample of those with whom an instructor has had contact? It is all inexact—and immaterial. And although few would dispute this point, reliance on these sources continues. After all, what better information do we have? It makes just as little sense to hold, as many senior faculty and administrators apparently do, that the capacity to do research necessarily goes hand in hand with the capacity to teach. It might be noted as a final paradox that the less likely an institution is to use teaching to evaluate faculty performance, the more likely it is to have some sort of outstanding-teacher award.[13]

In light of all of this, it is likely that most would agree that to arrive at the value of an academic man by assessing his teaching is at best problematic. However, it would be erroneous to conclude that, because teaching effectiveness is not generally evaluated as adequately as it might be and because our best measures of teaching effectiveness are perhaps invalid, we should not try to distinguish the good, fair, and bad classroom performers. John Gustad, who has spent many years studying faculty, addresses himself to this issue:

> The evaluation of faculty members, particularly of their teaching, is indeed an extremely complex matter, not likely soon to be susceptible of precise, quantitative solution. . . . A perfectly reliable and valid system of evaluation may, in fact, be for the foreseeable future unattainable; nevertheless, the history of learning, particularly of science, would seem to support the notion that, given time, effort, and the kind of critical appraisal that identifies blind alleys, reasonable approximations to a goal *can* be attained.[14]

In a more general way, Joseph Seidlin has remarked:

> No applied science or technology or art marks time until all that is ever to be known is known: until mythical exact measurement becomes available. As rational human beings, we must put into practice whatever knowledge, whatever measuring instruments are available at any given time.[15]

Thus, it seems reasonable to use the best measures of teaching effectiveness we now have at least to weed out the totally incompetent pedagogue. This situation is analogous to the problem of measuring intelligence. Although nobody has satisfactorily defined intelligence and we are unsure what I.Q. tests are tapping, we can be pretty certain that someone who scores 130 on one of these instruments is more mentally adroit than someone with a score of 90.[16]

ASSESSING PUBLICATION

Even in the assessment of scholarly and scientific writing, to which we now turn, uniform, cold, and objective standards are not necessarily often applied. A great deal of subjectivity and inaccuracy find their way here too. ("This paper is good" means "I like this paper"; and "He has made important contributions to his field" means "he has a number of publications" or "he has published in prestigious journals.") Some results from one survey clothe in a scientific veneer what probably every academic knows to be the true case.

In the study summarized above, which included 130 universities, it was reported that the faculty résumé was most often reviewed when "data [were] gathered for evaluating research." Second in importance in judging research in private universities were both faculty committees' and chairmen's evaluations, and only the latter by itself was second in importance in state universities. In interpreting this finding, the report's author writes: "A less polite way of describing this would be 'yardage' or the publications list." The faculty résumé was also the "principal basis" in evaluating publication.[17] What is written often is not read but counted. The section of this report concerned with these procedures concludes:

> To call what is typically collected or adduced to support evaluative decisions "evidence" is to stretch the meaning of that honored word beyond reason. Certainly, if anyone presumed to support a thesis in the published literature with evidence of this quality, he would be ruled off the course forthwith.[18]

And the account ends on a note bordering on despair:

It was not assumed, when this study was planned, that the situation with respect to faculty evaluation would be found to be good. It was no great surprise, therefore, to find it as it was. What *was* somewhat surprising was the extent and depth of the chaos. The majority of institutions [both universities and colleges] studied said that they place principal weight on teaching ability, but no even approximately effective method of evaluating this seems to be in use. Scholarship is evaluated by bulk rather than by quality. Other factors are evaluated on a hit-or-miss basis.[19]

On the subject of ascertaining quality, Caplow and McGee report that in the course of evaluation, "publications are not generally read."

The dialogue below is a fair sample of what happens to them . . . , if anything happens at all.

Q: Are the men's publications read?
A: Oh, yes!
Q: By whom?
A: By the tenure members, at least.
Q: All of them?
A: Yes.
Q: Did you read them?
A: Yes.
Q: Did you read those of the man you finally hired?
A: Yes.
Q: What was the one which you remember best about?
A: Well . . . I didn't read it, exactly. I looked it over. It was in a good journal. Nothing trashy gets in there.
Q: What do you mean by you "looked it over"?
A: Well, I looked at it, looked at his references, read his abstract.
Q: Is that the way the rest of the committee handles the publications, do you think?
A: I think so, yes, they look them over.[20]

PUBLISH OR PERISH: REALITY OR MYTH?

Even if it were not so readily acknowledged that the whole business of teaching effectiveness was an empirical wasteland and if the truth regarding the assessment of journal articles and books were more widely known, it is unlikely that the former would in any case become a signal factor in decisions regarding promotions, salary increases, and tenure—protestations of both faculty and administrators to the contrary. Because positivism is so pervasive on campus and in American society in general, many believe that something more concrete than a subjective factor such as the reaction of others, which is the essence of judging classroom performance, is necessary to determine competence —the more tangible the factor, the better. Harry Newburn points out that "productivity is emphasized not only because of the positive belief of many officials that it is the most important element . . . but also for the negative reason that it can be evaluated more readily than another important quality—namely, teaching."[21]

In the second place, teaching is a local activity, in that one's reputation in this endeavor is generally restricted to the school where one holds forth. Who in the chemistry department at the University of Minnesota can name the superior teachers in his discipline at the state university in neighboring Wisconsin? Who in the multiversity in Bloomington, Indiana, knows of the master teachers at her sister school, Purdue? Since fame attracts endowment, institutions of higher learning are keen to secure as much visibility—which is equated with prestige—as possible. Little is gained by cultivating a stable of quality classroom performers. Something that will spread the name of a school abroad is necessary.

For the lay public, a championship football or basketball team or administrators or individual faculty members who have illustrious records as cold war freedom fighters can achieve this; if nothing else, they are an asset in the competition for funds from both the public and private sectors. Intramurally, leading scientists and scholars in various disciplines are essential. Simply put, there is widespread consensus among departmental members that as a body they can only achieve professional prominence if their ranks are filled with men who appear to be industrious—a not surprising inference, given the typical American concern with tangible labor. (It is of some interest that although at one level academics may realize that they need colleagues who are talked about on other campuses, they may not always be eager to make the hard decisions to recruit such persons.) An individual may hope to improve his chances of reaching immortality through publication; one's students pass on, but one's publications are preserved, protected, and mostly untouched, in libraries. Thus, publication, read and unread, good and bad, useful and useless, creative and banal, is reified. Quantity and quality are equated, and as a result there is a nearly universal belief, on and off the campus, that academic men must publish or perish. This dictum, we are told, compels students to mutiny, causes parents to complain about being shortchanged for the staggering tuition they must lay out, and rends the minds and souls of those who are prepared and able to teach but are unwilling to do penance in professional journals. Because academics must publish or perish, it is said, everybody and everything suffers: students, faculty, education, and the level of societal culture.

It is worth noting that although academics prefer that their colleagues publish, from time to time one hears tales of negative sanctions directed against the rate-buster: "he's too superficial"; "he's really not saying much that's new, he's been hitting the same theme for years"; "no serious scholar publishes in the *AAUP Bulletin*—not twice at any rate"; "only one of his 22 papers had been in the *American Anthropologist* [the rest, ipso facto, are worthless]." Sometimes, in fact, the observation that a particular department abides by the canon of publish or perish is made with disdain to suggest that the entire faculty are overachievers.

The contention that a publish-or-perish doctrine has a solid and sinister grip on the whole of the academic community comes from nearly all quarters. A widely read and respected textbook on the history of higher education in America states:

> Advance in academic rank and salary for the most part went to those with long lists of publications rather than those successful in the classroom. Perhaps the college or university administration rewarded research activities because it thought them more worth while, or perhaps because published research was a more tangible and therefore less controversial measure of appraising professional worth.[22]

Both seasoned and budding academics assume the authenticity of the publish-or-perish maxim. A cosmopolitan sociologist of education asserts:

> In the leading state universities, faculty are recruited and retained primarily on the basis of scholarly achievement or promise. It is a commonplace (and often a reproach) that in a large state university, publication and the reputation that publication earns carry the heaviest weight in promotion and tenure decisions.[23]

A social anthropologist who has unmercifully parodied the professor as priest and conjuror holds that "tenure and promotion at the better universities depend in good part on publication and on some test of professional recognition outside the home campus."[24] Jacques Barzun is also persuaded that "the reality of 'publish or perish' . . . [is] the slogan of the profession."[25] In "An Open Letter to the Academic Profession," seven young scholars completing their studies at Princeton University express their concern "over what seems to us an unfortunate and inflexible situation in our chosen profession, namely its overemphasis on publication." These earnest novices are troubled by the fact that "the single vision of the overwhelming majority of institutions remains that of the teacher-scholar equally productive in both fields."[26]

One even reads in "intellectual" magazines that "each spring, faculty members on hundreds of campuses are dismissed or denied promotion for the same reason . . . [the failure to fulfill] 'the promise of scholarly publication. . . .' [Institutions of higher learning] continue to promote or retain faculty members largely on the basis of publications . . . [so that] a top-flight teacher is held back if he does not publish."[27] In a more moving passage, a young instructor of English in a large state university writes in a student publication:

> Now in order to be an exciting and effective lecturer you must spend a great deal of time digesting your subject matter and carefully planning how you will present this material to your students. Very soon, however, it is made clear to you that you will lose your job if you do not use your time for something else: i.e., the writing of articles or books. . . . The articles are to be written so that you will make yourself and your department famous. The articles are to be written so that you can avoid being fired. The articles are written so that you can provide money for rent and food (for yourself, and probably also for a wife and children). In short, the articles are written so that you can survive.[28]

Even those who discern one variation or another to a simple publish-or-perish theme and see a modified system in operation do not deny its pervasiveness. Arguing that it was really a "celebrity policy" and not a publish-or-perish policy that did a colleague in (or out), a philosopher contends:

> In "publish or perish" contexts the junior scholar knows what he must do to earn the academic freedom and economic security which tenure represents. There is, of course, the evident danger that his teaching will suffer, rather than his research, since it is the latter which will earn him his place. It is nevertheless clear what the rules of the game are.[29]

Caplow and McGee, who seem more informed about the underlife of academic culture than most, are aware that: "if [one] is able to publish at all, however, he is not impossibly handicapped, since the actual number of publications necessary to meet tenure requirements at most universities is not large."[30] Yet, on the page following this observation they write: "It is neither an overgeneralization nor an oversimplification to state that in the faculties of major universities in the United States today [1958], the evaluation of performance is based almost exclusively on publication of scholarly books or articles in professional journals as evidence of research activity."[31] It is indeed a rather grim picture.

The assumption that academics must either publish or perish, however, has not been incontrovertible.[32] Near the end of his long career as a university and foundation president, Logan Wilson concluded: "The much-discussed publish-or-perish dictum, however, is in actuality more fiction than fact in the average institution. . . . [I]n all except a few leading institutions less than 10 percent of the faculty accounts for more than 90 percent of all published research."[33] Allan Cartter, who has also had a career in both the university and a foundation, states that "except in a small number of leading universities, 'publish-or-perish' is largely a myth popularized by the few poor teachers who, lacking the one credential for tenure appointment, did indeed perish when found lacking in the other."[34] These, however, are not widely held views. In fact, it would appear from the weight of academic opinion that the tenet of publish or perish is a crude—even somewhat cruel—firmly-rooted mechanism to introduce meritocratic principles into faculty culture. However, as the materials reviewed in the remainder of this chapter indicate, there is little evidence that such a rule is generally applied, and perhaps it is in large part an elaborate fiction.

In the first place, it should be reiterated that, as the statistics in the preceding chapter show, more than half of the academic men in the country do not even teach in universities, those institutions where there is a putative emphasis on scholarship. In fact, from time to time one hears tales that this or that backwater college explicitly discourages scholarly research and publication in the belief that it detracts from a man's teaching or undermines his loyalty to the institution.[35] But, again, let us look mainly at universities and see how much publication there really is, what academics in these institutions feel about the relative importance of teaching and research, and what the payoff is for those who amass an extensive bibliography.

HOW MUCH PUBLICATION?

As early as the 1920s, various studies revealed that less than 20 percent of American Ph.D.'s produced significant research after completing their dissertations.[36] An analysis of the scholarship of historians in 1927 attributed their lack of productivity to "the low social value placed on scholarship in the United States as compared with European countries."[37] A study released in 1935 showed that 80 percent of those receiving doctorates in mathematics published no significant research beyond their doctoral theses.[38]

Moreover, research conducted prior to World War II, when universities were supposedly becoming more professional, that is, moving toward a publish-or-perish standard, suggests that those with the greatest scholarly productivity did not necessarily receive the greatest rewards. A study examining the factors leading to promotion at Indiana University between 1885 and 1937 revealed an "apparent lack of relationship between publication and rapidity of promotion . . .":

> The period of service before promotion for both instructors and assistant professors who demonstrated their ability for independent intellectual activity outside of teaching was slightly longer before they were promoted than for those who did not publish. On the average, the associate professor who published has had to wait slightly more than one semester longer before promotion than the man who did nothing outside the classroom. The same generalization holds for the few irregular promotions that did not follow the normal rank to rank channels. Clearly, there has been no close relation between promotion and publication. Furthermore, on the average, the person who has reported on a piece of research or formulated some creative or interpretive writing and has either published or had it accepted for publication has not been promoted as rapidly as the person who confined his activities to classroom teaching and social affairs.[39]

Moving ahead to the 1950s and 1960s, once more the evidence indicates that the publication record of most academics is rather skimpy. In their study of 2,451 social scientists, Paul Lazarsfeld and Wagner Thielens, Jr., found that only 1,377 of them had published three or more papers and that only 861 had published a book, aside from their dissertations.[40] Again, an analysis of the scholarly productivity of 262 sociologists ten years or more after receiving their Ph.D.'s revealed that 155 had published fewer than three articles in professional journals.[41] A paper published a decade later found that for individuals promoted to senior-level positions in 1970 or 1971 in the top thirty-three sociology departments in the country, over one-eighth of those in the "top nineteen" departments and almost one-third of those in the fourteen "good" or "adequate plus" departments had published at most one article. Moreover, only 37.9 percent in the leading departments and 30.0 percent in the other two categories had authored or coauthored one book. From twenty additional departments randomly chosen from the more than one hundred other graduate departments of sociology, 47.5 percent of those promoted had published at most one article, and only 12.5 percent had written a book.[42] Further, in a survey of 486 faculty members at a large state university, it was found that only 207 had published at least one professional book, monograph, or article each year.[43]

A sample survey published by the Carnegie Commission Study on the Future of Higher Education and the American Council on Education in 1970 revealed that almost 30 percent of university faculty reported that they had published no professional articles, and about the same percentage reported that they had only published between one and four papers. Just over 14 percent had between five and ten publications, while 26.6 percent had seen eleven or more of their papers in print. There were no data on books or monographs.[44]

Logan Wilson found in his study of the faculties of three large institutions in a university system that on one campus 71 percent of the faculty had never published an article, and 90 percent had not published a book. On the second campus, 40 percent of the faculty had never published an article, and 90 percent had not published a book; and on the third campus, 29 percent of the faculty had yet to publish an article, and 66 percent a book.[45] In addition, he reports that in his examination of one thousand faculty—all from large universities in a different state system—32 percent had no published articles, and 71 percent had no published books.[46]

In David Brown's study of over ten thousand mobile professors in the mid-1960s, the percentage of individuals in each discipline who had no publications as contrasted with those who had at least one book or ten journal articles, art objects included, are as follows:[47]

	No publications	Big publishers
Anthropology	29	17
Art	11	49
Biochemistry	14	13
Biology (general)	71	10
Botany (general)	41	5
Chemistry	24	9
Earth science and geology	31	20
Economics	60	11
Education, secondary	60	5
Engineering, chemical	22	15
Engineering, civil	43	1
Engineering, electrical	29	16
Engineering, mechanical	36	8
English and literature	70	11
French	70	18
History	60	12
Mathematics	66	6
Microbiology	23	14
Music	64	11
Physical and health education	71	8
Physics	29	16
Physiology	29	11
Political science	55	16
Psychology, clinical	37	20
Psychology, counseling	47	12
Psychology, experimental	20	16
Sociology	45	14
Zoology (general)	42	10

In a paper by Kenneth Nelson, presented at a meeting of the American Association for the Advancement of Science in 1964, it was shown that while as many as 85 percent of his sample in the biological sciences had "any published article," the figures for other disciplines are 77 percent for physical sciences, 74 percent for psychology, 69 percent for health fields, 61 percent for engineering, 61 percent for social sciences, 58 percent for education and related fields, 52 percent for religion and philosophy, 50 percent for business and commerce, 46 percent for English and journalism, 46 percent for foreign language and literature, 43 percent for mathematics, 36 percent for fine arts, and 32 percent for physical education.[48]

All of this is consistent with generalizations of Derek de Solla Price, who has examined the publication picture throughout the world. He notes

> that the publication rate of scientific papers is one-half a paper per scientist per year [700,000 scientists produced 350,000 papers]. . . . Defining scientific manpower as publishing scientists, the world supply totals 700,-000, with the United States' portion pegged at about 30% or 200,000 [publishing scientists]. This is about half the 400,000 scientists generally considered to be engaged in research in the U.S., as shown in the Central Register.[49]

In other words, the work of one-half of America's research scientists is finding its way into scientific journals every year. Many of these articles are coauthored, which might lead some to conclude that the 50 percent figure is low; but this might be offset by the fact that some individuals get their names into print more than once a year. As Price points out:

> The greatest difficulty in any measurement of scientific manpower, however, is that comparatively large numbers of persons trained in science and technology are not really working on the research front. A frequent estimate for total scientific and technical manpower in the United States is about 800,000. The figure of 200,000 publishing scientists suggests that about one-quarter of this total U.S. technical manpower is on the research front, the remaining three-quarters is concerned with applied research and development [and college teaching?].[50]

Elsewhere, Price develops the thesis that productivity is a function of an inverse-square law. This means that for every one hundred authors who write but a single paper, twenty-five write two, eleven write three, six write four, four write five, three write six, two write seven, two write eight, one writes nine, and so on. Looking at this in another way, it could be predicted that 165 men would turn out 586 plus papers and that the top two men would produce nearly one-quarter, ten men would produce more than 50 percent, 75 percent of the men would produce but one-quarter, with an average of 3.5 papers per man.[51] According to Price, the output of most scientists who publish is very meager. He estimates that well over half of the scientists who publish at all contribute only one paper in their lifetime, that ten percent of publishing scientists author well over one-third of the papers in print, and that only three percent of all scientists are "highly prolific, major contributors."[52] The regularity of these figures over time is testimony that a rule of publish or perish could not be expected to hold under any condition.

Bernard Gustin also has concluded that "a large proportion of the scientific community publishes very little."[53] And the rate of publication for those not in the hard sciences is generally lower. Consistent with this conclusion, a study completed by the American Psychological Association found that only 2,200 out of approximately 27,000 psychologists (obviously, not all with university appointments) had published at least one paper per year between 1959 and 1963.[54]

In 1940, the Modern Language Association reported that its 2,500 members published 2,200 books, articles, and reviews. The comparable figure in 1950 was 4,095 publications for 6,480 members; in 1960, 10,435 publications for 13,757 members; and in 1964, 16,303 publications for 19,256 members. The number of publications per member for the four dates over the twenty-four-year period are .88, .63, .76, and .85, respectively—clearly no indication that there has been more pressure to publish, at least in the humanities, since World War II than before.

Even in instances when the case is being made that most people publish, the figures are not generally impressive. Berelson, for example, in 1957–58 examined the publication records of individuals who had received their doctorates in 1947–48 in nine disciplines and argued that "the score on publication is quite high." He based this conclusion on the following data:[55]

Discipline	Published one or more titles other than the dissertation (in percent)	Average number of publications per recipient	Publications with single author (in percent)
Chemistry	87	6.1	17
Biology	77	5.7	30
Physics	77	4.9	33
Psychology	72	5.4	53

Discipline	Published one or more titles other than the dissertation (in percent)	Average number of publications per recipient	Publications with single author (in percent)
Mathematics	61	4.0	85
Philosophy	59	2.8	95
English	57	2.2	97
Education	51	2.4	80
History	19	0.5	96

It can be concluded from these figures that more Ph.D.'s publish than do not publish, but on the average they do not publish a great deal—less than one title every two years (in the sciences most are coauthored) for the first ten years after receiving their degrees. Berelson also listed the institutional affiliation of contributors of articles to the major learned journals in 1958, and his findings again indicate that even in the most prestigious schools not everyone is compulsively publishing. Here is a partial summary of his data:[56]

Institutions	Number of authors per 100 faculty members
Top twelve universities (e.g., Harvard, California, Columbia, Yale)	12.0
Next ten universities (e.g., Pennsylvania, Minnesota, Stanford, U.C.L.A.)	5.5
Other members of Association of Graduate Schools (e.g., Brown, Duke, Texas, Washington at St. Louis)	5.2
Other universities	2.5

Moreover, when Orlans reanalyzed some of Berelson's data, he found that the number of authors in 1958 per one hundred full-time faculty in his Group I institutions (twelve universities that received large sums of money from the federal government), Group II institutions (twelve universities that received more modest funds), and Group III institutions (good liberal arts colleges) were 10.5, 6.7, and 3.6, respectively.[57] Although those in major universities are more active in publishing than those in less renowned institutions, even their productivity is not particularly impressive.

THE BALANCE BETWEEN TEACHING, RESEARCH, AND OTHER FACTORS

Not all university faculty seem haunted by the need to pursue research. First of all, lack of scholarly productivity does not appear to have an adverse effect on the self-perceptions of very many people. In the study by the Carnegie Commission and the American Council on Education, referred to above, 26.3 percent of the university faculty rated their careers as very successful, and over two-thirds thought they were fairly successful. Less than 6 percent, a significantly smaller proportion than those who had not published, felt unsuccessful.[58]

When university faculty were asked by the Carnegie Commission about their relative interest in teaching and research, almost twice as many (65 percent, as compared with 35 percent) indicated an interest in the former over the latter. Only 6 percent responded that they were "heavily" interested in research, while an additional 29 percent leaned toward research; conversely, 28 percent responded that they leaned "heavily" toward teaching, and an additional 37 percent leaned somewhat toward teaching.[59] Finally, when Brown asked a sample of chemists, physicists, biochemists, sociologists, and economists if they spent more time teaching and counseling or researching and writing, slightly more than one in eight indicated the latter; fewer than one in sixteen of those in English, music, physical and elementary education, and general biology and zoology answered likewise.[60]

However, university faculty are not overwhelmed with teaching responsibilities. In the study just cited, it was found that 11.5 percent had no contact hours with students, 21.0 percent were in the classroom between one and four hours a week, 32.6 percent did between five and eight hours of teaching, 22.8 percent had a teaching load of between nine and twelve hours per week, and the remaining 12.1 percent taught 13 or more hours weekly. Slightly over 55 percent of the sample taught less than fifty students a semester.

Other figures show that about one-fifth (19.2 percent) of those with university appointments instruct only graduate students, while a somewhat larger number (27.8 percent) teach only undergraduates.[61] The generally heavier commitment to undergraduate teaching suggests that there is more interest in transmitting knowledge than in creating it. It can be added here that according to a survey by the American Council on Education, the average young scholar of English literature spends 15 percent of his time on administrative tasks, time forfeited as far as academic work is concerned, while his senior colleague spends an average of 21 percent of his time on such tasks. In physics, the corresponding figures are 8 percent and 20 percent, respectively.[62]

Over the years, academics and academic-administrators have expressed views that indicate that they are not necessarily bound by a publish-or-perish dogma. In an examination of the internal factors influencing promotion at Indiana University between 1926 and 1937 (teaching, scholarship, administrative work, and service), teaching ability was rated by deans and department heads to be more important than productive scholarship.

> There is an inverse relation between the proportionate share teaching has played in promotion and the rank to which a person was advanced. The higher the rank, the less influence it has had; nevertheless, it remains the main conditioner, even from associate professor to professor.[63]

These findings parallel what was found at the University of Minnesota in the early decades of the century. In the promotions made between 1913 and 1931, the most important factors were: "teaching, 43.4 percent; productive scholarship, 27.6 percent; student counseling, 11.6 percent; administrative work, 11 percent; and public service, 6.4 percent."[64] And through the 1960s, the emphasis—at least on the verbal level—on productive scholarship, if anything, seems to have decreased, not increased. The 1960 study by the Committee on College Teaching of the American Council on Education showed that for the 130 universities in the sample, classroom teaching was ranked first in "factors considered in evaluating faculty members."[65] For the sixty-eight private universities, "other"—"such items as cooperation, loyalty, Christian character, church membership and activity, and compatibility"[66]—ranked second, research was third, while publications ranked fourth. For the sixty-two state universities, research was second, "other" was third, and publications ranked fourth.[67] In what may be a surprise for some, Brown reports that "our Southeastern study indicates that the higher prestige universities are at least equally concerned with good classroom teaching. . . . Time was taken to investigate candidates' teaching ability almost three times as often by top quality departments as by lowest quality ones."[68]

A national sample of 6,087 university faculty and administrators from 242 institutions revealed that for the most part academics still overwhelmingly believed more weight should be given to teaching effectiveness than to research activity and publication record when promotion was under consideration. When respondents were classified according to rank, and the institutions according to size and type of control, the largest percentage who believed that a man's publication record should be the primary criterion in promotion was 13.8 (1,846 respondents from institutions with enrollments over 10,000, for promotion from associate to full professor).[69]

This latter finding corresponds with the results of a questionnaire study of 3,440 sociologists, in which the researchers found that only 26.3 percent agreed with the statement that "the best indicator of a man's professional worth is his professional publications," while 65.4 percent disagreed. Again, only 43.0 percent agreed that "it is understandable that those who do the most and best research should have greater prestige than the man who simply teaches well," while 48.1 percent disagreed.[70]

In another study, over two-thirds of the respondents felt that teaching effectiveness, not publication, should be the primary criterion for promotion of faculty. Yet, although 64.0 percent admitted that "in my department it is very difficult for a man to achieve tenure if he does not publish," it seems clear that the English influence on American higher education is still quite potent.

Perhaps some individuals are paying lip service to teaching and these statistics overstate its influence in the assessment of university faculty. Yet, it seems clear that factors other than publications affect who in universities is rewarded, and it is this point that must be emphasized. It is as if there were a different set of ground rules for each decision regarding promotion, the granting of tenure, or the acknowledgment of merit. A finding by Fred Luthans, reported in 1967 from his study of promotion policies and practices in business schools of forty-six large state universities, is germane here: although both faculty and administrators were of the opinion that promotion was based on research activity, advancement in rank was not always preceded by publication, and in almost two-fifths of the cases when men moved to the rank of associate or full professor, they could do so with three or fewer articles and no books.[71] Further, in 1970, Donald P. Hoyt was unable to find significant relationships between rates of faculty promotion and merit increases and either performance in teaching or publishing.[72]

Although it is a prominent tenet of academic mythology, there is little evidence to support the contention that remuneration and performance are closely related. In one study of "the determinants of faculty salaries and promotions" of eleven departments in "a large highly ranked public university," "whether or not a professor had an administrative assignment" was the factor which most significantly influenced his 1969–70 salary. Being female, teaching in the humanities, and having gone to an unprestigious institution as an undergraduate all had strong negative effects on salary level. The total number of articles published and a ranking among the top 50 percent of all instructors by students were inconsequential to the reward system.[73] In fact, "of all variables included in the regression, student evaluations of teachers were the least predictive of salary."[74] A second highly quantitative study, this one of the forty-five man economics department at the University of Wisconsin (Madison) to test the hypothesis "that research and teaching performance will be positive and significant variables affecting faculty salaries," produced some results which closely parallel these findings. Most important, the publishing of monographs was not related to an individual's salary level, while holding a major administrative position, such as that of departmental chairman or research institute director, was "worth" over five thousand dollars. On the other hand, an article in one of the six national, general journals had a value of $392, an article in a specialty journal had a value of $345, each additional year of experience had a value of $253, and quality teaching as determined by student ratings had a value of $732.[75]

In his study of "Book Productivity and Academic Rank at Twenty-six Elite Universities," Richard Doering found that

> the correlation between number of books in print and number of years before attainment of full professorship is −.12. Professors with more than 2.5 books in print achieved full professor status 9.5 years after finishing the Ph.D., while professors with no books in print achieved full professor status 10.9 years following receipt of the degree . . . the difference is significant at the .13 level. [Although] when the variables were reversed, fast climbers—persons who achieved full professorship less than 7 years after receiving a Ph.D. (N = 31)—had a mean of 2.4 books in print; slow climbers—persons who did not become full professors until more than 13 years after acquiring a Ph.D. (N = 41)—had only 1.5 books in print. This difference is significant at the .05 level. . . .[76]

At most, this suggests that, whatever the limited rewards for publishing, one who publishes may prosper. In sum, it would appear that the assertion that academics must publish or perish is a gross overstatement.

Occasionally, an odd case is given considerable coverage by the mass media because some exotic factor seems to make it newsworthy. A talented and renowned mountain climber who is the grandson of a former president of the United States is fired from Tufts; A Jewish philosopher is denied tenure at one of the last refuges of the WASP, Yale, in spite of a reasonably creditable publication record; a somewhat leftist economist whose father, a titan in the world of advertising, has served the federal government with distinction as undersecretary of state and ambassador to India is sacked at Harvard. Popular teachers who refuse to be dismissed quietly from prestigious schools make good press. The common reaction to such situations is that if such solidly connected individuals can be affected by the publish-or-perish dictum, then certainly more ordinary academics must really feel its harshness. But this may not be the case. One could just as easily argue that persons with upper-class or old-family ties are more likely to suffer discrimination and negative sanctions at the hands of their mostly middle-class colleagues. It may be that many academics would feel less pain in ridding themselves of the grandson of a president rather than the son of a lawyer or engineer—persons with whom they could more easily identify. Both positions are equally tenable.

This is not to deny that there are instances in which people who have failed to meet very minimal publication norms have been fired. William Stallings and Sushila Singhal, for example, found a relationship between their Research Productivity Index and academic rank in two midwestern universities. They attribute this to the " 'publish or perish' selection process," although the variance could be simply explained by age—older people have had more time to get themselves in print, as well as promoted.[77]

THE FUNCTION OF THE PUBLISH-OR-PERISH THREAT

The man who publishes absolutely nothing will almost assuredly find himself downwardly mobile from a major university, and the man whose name appears often in reputable journals can expect to receive some rewards, although these could indeed be marginal. But for 80 or 90 percent of those who pursue a university career, except in a dozen or so prestigious institutions—Harvard, Yale, Columbia, Chicago, Berkeley—the threat of publish or perish is empty. It is well to remember that about 90 percent of all major publications originate in the top twenty-five doctorate-granting departments in each field and that one-quarter of the doctorate-granting departments turn out less than one article a year.[78] Thus, academic men can publish or not publish, and few will perish. Of course, the myth's widespread acceptance keeps many at their desks, the library, or laboratory and the computer center open twenty-four hours a day. And to the degree that men publish because they are fearful that if they do not they will perish, the fiction becomes a somewhat accurate expression of life in the university.

In most academic departments there are oligarchs who act as gate-keepers in the determination of promotion or tenure. A common char-acteristic of oligarchies is loyalty to predecessors and peers. A young man in a department is judged as to how well he fits into things. Does he adhere to the set of ideological biases which is in fashion in the department? Does he recognize as legitimate the existing distribution of authority within the department? If he seems to be malleable and gracious, he may be groomed for a position within the oligarchy. Otherwise, because he could well endanger the existing order, he is left to make his own career.

For the dissenting scholar there are four possible outcomes. First, he may voluntarily leave the department. Second, if he fails to engage in any scholarly activity, he may be asked to leave, regardless of his skill in the classroom. Third, he may become an industrious scholar, put a minimum amount of effort into his teaching and other departmental responsibilities, and be harassed, or treated unfairly; eventually he may leave to maintain his self-respect. Fourth, he may become a pro-ductive scholar and a skilled teacher, and since his senior colleagues would be flagrantly violating academic norms by denying promotion or tenure, he can expect eventually to receive either or both.

The rule of publish or perish is operative only in the second and fourth examples, and its consequences are injurious solely in the for-mer instance. Since many of the most uncontrollables probably do not make it through graduate school, the disruptive force of the publish-or-perish doctrine is not as overwhelming as we are led to believe. The mechanisms of social control in a university generally function to re-fute the Durocherian principle "nice guys finish last." Although publi-cation may be held up as the ideal in the academic world, in over 99 percent of the institutions of higher learning it is limited—it is neither necessary nor sufficient for scaling the ivory tower. So many factors other than the quantity or quality of articles or books enter into deci-sions departments make about those who are accepted or rejected as members that it is humbug when the question of someone's productiv-ity is raised.

Thus, the publish-or-perish dogma is largely a fraud, perpetuated by the notoriety of a few cases. But it is no accident that in a society marked by pragmatism its pervasiveness is acknowledged. First, it is an easily grasped justification for what are sometimes complicated departmental or institutional decisions. Put another way, it is a protec-tive device to conceal the true reasons why someone is forced to leave a department. Second, it keeps those who are fearful of losing their position in check; research and writing (even if a good deal of it is useless) diverts their attention from departmental affairs and helps maintain the status quo. Third, it promotes the idea that an objective standard is utilized in arriving at decisions which are made subjectively. David Riesman has discerned that "people like to think that the system under which they operate is more rational than in fact it is because that quiets anxiety even if in their own case they are the victims of arbitrariness."[79]

The idea that academics must publish or perish sounds clear and unequivocal. Academics are, after all, scientists and scholars and should not be faulted for arriving at their decisions using explicit and fair criteria. And what better defense for institutions that are thought to harbor too many nonconformists than the inspired argument that they are there because of objectifiable criteria?

THE PROFESSOR AT WORK

If nothing else, the body of data examined in this chapter leaves one with the incontrovertible impression that university faculty are not overburdened with staggering teaching and research commitments. This should not be taken to mean, however, that they are not tangibly busy, that they fritter away their days lolling about; applying their minds to daytime television; reading the newspaper from headlines to want ads; gamboling with children, pets, or spouses; or, excogitating about trivia. Some of this goes on, without doubt, but, on the whole, academic men find themselves constantly and fully occupied. Like most persons, they may not have a great deal to show after an eight-, ten-, or twelve-hour day, but they are putting the time in, and this point must be made. In his study of *Scientists in American Society*, Walter Hirsch asked a colleague to write an account of a fairly typical day, and after some delay in getting around to it, the following journal was submitted:[80]

A DAY IN THE LIFE OF A SCIENTIST-PROFESSOR

7:00 A.M.   Watch *Today* show until 7:30.

8:00 A.M.   Breakfast with wife, two daughters, and son.

8:45 A.M.   Start correcting set of ten exams. This is the third two-hour exam in my course, Genetics, given to undergraduates this semester— also the last. Finals are next.

9:50 A.M.   Call the office to tell my secretary that I will be half an hour late.

10:15 A.M.   Arrive at my office at the University. As I enter the laboratory, graduate student A corners me immediately to tell me that he must discuss his research program today. I say, "Yes, will see you later." Now call in secretary and tell her how to file away advertisements for instruments, chemicals, glassware, etc., which have accumulated in the several months before she began this job. She does not know any of the technical names and it will take some time for her to cope with this job with understanding. Then I show her how to punch the author classification into my Keysort Type Card File System. Unfortunately I cannot ask her to punch the subject classification; this must be done by myself or by a scientist who is familiar with the field covered by the card. Literature evaluation is too technical for a person without advanced science training. I use the cards to make notes from technical literature or from scientific lectures. The Keysort System eliminates the need for cross-filing cards by subject and author, as well as cross-filing for several subjects. This is my own personal stab at the problem of coping with the staggering information explosion in genetics and molecular biology. Now I show her how to fill in a university order blank, to pay a bill for photographic work.

11:45 A.M.   Go to lunch with graduate student A. He tells me proudly how carefully he performed a difficult experiment. All techniques worked well. Unfortunately the new results seem to conflict with earlier data. If the new result is true, the key experiment for his dissertation (which he wishes to finish before May) might not be achievable. After lengthy discussion we devise an experiment that will show how the new and old data are related. This experiment involves a technique that has just been developed by a young, able research associate in our laboratory. Would it infringe on her discovery to use it? I think not. Student A can go ahead with planning this experiment, and I will talk with her about using her technique. Scientific discussion now concluded, we get into a conversation about graduate student morale. In a recent colloquium discussion between faculty and graduate students on "The Duties of the Faculty toward the Graduate Students and the Duties of the Graduate Students toward the Faculty," the morale of the graduate students was described as very depressed. This was a surprise to me, and I now ask A whether this description is accurate. A explains that it is. Reason: Several graduate students have been asked to leave after having spent considerable time in the department. He describes in detail the role of one faculty member in one of these dismissals. This account contains several items of information that are new to me, and quite shocking.

1:00 P.M.   Return from lunch. Graduate student B stops me in hallway, saying he must see me today. I tell him "later." Finish correcting exams and record these grades and laboratory grades that have been submitted by the graduate student laboratory instructors.

1:30 P.M.   Call in graduate student B to discuss his latest experiments. This student works hard; usually, however, successive experiments do not have the same results. By Herculean labors and with detailed coaching he seems to be approaching believable data. Today he is elated—a crucial experiment seems to have worked. I look over the data with care. I note that one set of results was recorded twice. Apparently this is due to incorrect transfer of data from rough record to final record. The rough record is fortunately retrieved from the waste basket. The data indeed look promising. We (I) devise a new experiment—mostly a repeat of the present one. Although this student is diligent and very cooperative, he'll probably be asked to leave with a "terminal Master's"; he just doesn't have the ability to do independent work. This will be another blow to graduate student morale.

2:00 P.M.   Secretary comes in with several orders for glassware, chemicals, and equipment. I check them. As happens rather often, something was being ordered that was not really needed. I cross it off. One of the orders is for a major item. I call up the purchasing office and then the grants and contracts office to find out (a) whether I can now charge this item to my NIH grant, which was scheduled to start on January 1 but for which the award papers have not been sent to the university (a routine kind of delay: I have yet to meet up with a grant that was available for use on the starting date!), and (b) whether the award papers have arrived. They have not. We therefore charge the new orders to the National Science Foundation grant and only the expensive order and less pressing items to the National Institutes of Health grant to await the availability of the money in a few days.

3:00 P.M.   Call up a colleague to ask if she has arranged dinner for the invited speaker next Friday. Yes, she has, but some of the guests still need to be invited by me. (I am chairman of the seminar committee—actually there is no committee—each faculty member has the privilege of inviting two or three speakers in his area of interest; I do the coordination and the paper work.)

3:05 P.M.   Call up a chairman of a department in the medical school. Can he suggest someone to give a lecture on the evolution of the kidney for a course on evolution that I am organizing together with my wife (an anthropologist) at her university? The intent is, perhaps, to collect the various lectures in a book. Answer: Well, he or a colleague might be willing to do it. Could I call back in two days? Yes.

3:10 P.M. I see graduate student C in the laboratory. I call him in to tell him he has been assigned to assist in my graduate course (a departmental assignment in which I did not play a direct role), which starts in about two weeks. I know he does not like it because assisting in my course is a lot of work for anyone—and he is lazy, although capable. He asks me to try to get someone else to help him. Maybe I will—if I do, he'll shift the responsibility to that person, but if I don't there is danger that the laboratory won't be prepared properly. The conversation now shifts to a discussion of his research project. A paper has just been published that has beautifully solved an important part of his dissertation project—before he even got started on it. His response is to want to repeat the same experiment by a different, less laborious, and less informative technique. So far, his aim is to get a degree, not to produce a good piece of research (he is over forty—time to get a union card!)—of which he is perfectly capable. I tell him he has to work on other aspects of the problem, that the exact sequence in which the experiments are done doesn't matter, but for heaven's sake to get to *work!*

3:30 P.M. I leave my office, toting my lecture notes for the semester and some old exams to the library. There I sit at a desk for 2½ hours to compose a final exam.

6:15 P.M. Drive home, listening to the news.

6:40 P.M. Arrive at home. Wife is not yet home; she had called to say that she could not get detached from the office. Have to have dinner without her. Son is asleep in front of TV set. Daughters, maid, and I have dinner immediately. Daughters are in high spirits about adventures in school—the errant ways of teachers, the new way in which the school day is subdivided, and the foibles of their classmates.

7:15 P.M. End of dinner. Daughter No. 1 gives demonstration of what she learned in gym today—on Persian rug in the living room. Not a bad performance. I retire to browse through newspaper.

8:00 P.M. Telephone call from Dr. Walter Hirsch: What happened to my intention to send him an account of "A Day in the Life of a Scientist"? Why haven't I written it? He asked me to do it three weeks ago. Chastised, I say I will do it right away, and begin to write up this account.

10:15 P.M.   Wife arrives. Gave exam this evening. (She is an anthropologist.) Gives brief account of day. I continue to write this account.

11:45 P.M.   A quick foray to the outside to cover up the trees that need
protection against immediately impending cold wave.

12:00 A.M.   To bed.

There is little question that this was a long and tedious day and that, moreover, some attention was even paid to academic matters.[81] And perhaps even more time could have been spent in scientific study had he been able to hire an additional secretary with his National Science Foundation grant or another maid with his National Institutes of Health grant.

3

Professional Evaluation and Letters of Recommendation

PURITANISM AND PROFESSIONALISM

As has been indicated from the beginning of this book, an assumption underlying both sympathetic and censorious portraits of American universities is that they operate on austere principles, such as rationality and efficiency, and that there is unremitting labor for the glory of higher learning. Their faculties would seem to be governed by a kind of puritan ethic by which individuals are evaluated and rewarded for boundless effort, as well as concrete achievements. Notwithstanding a wide range of discordant and less flattering conceptions and a general acknowledgment that the professoriate fall short of this ideal, it is believed that at the nub of academic life this puritan ethic founded on hard work and self-discipline holds sway. Indeed, one commonly hears university life pictured in terms quite similar to those used by Richard Tawney to describe Puritanism:

> What it showed was a picture grave to sternness, yet not untouched with a sober exultation—an earnest, zealous, godly generation, scorning delights, punctual in labor, constant in prayer, thrifty and thriving, filled with a decent pride in themselves and their calling, assured that strenuous toil is acceptable to Heaven.[1]

Academic men may forswear such piety but little else in Tawney's inventory.

Given this starting point, it is not surprising that most people, both within and outside the university, are pretty well convinced that at bottom academic men are guided by professional norms. In the last two decades, the proportion of the population who would agree with the contention of Jencks and Riesman cited in chapter 1 that individuals in the university community are judged "almost entirely on the basis of the one set of standards almost all its members accept: professional performance"[2] has grown significantly. The premise that professional norms are central to academic culture has, in fact, been accepted without qualification in the overwhelming majority of published observations about institutions of higher learning over at least the past fifty years.

"Professional" is a multifaceted concept, and there is no precise way of telling what might be meant when it is used with reference to any particular aspect of the university—some may be suggesting that professional norms are omnipresent; others may be suggesting something less. Nevertheless, it is certain that regardless of what is conveyed in one or another context, any usage would encompass the basic elements of professional behavior—disinterestedness, service, commitment to task, excellence, responsibility, rationality. And, most central to the theme of this chapter, all would include the notion of technical competence, which Parsons has described as "one of the principal defining characteristics of the professional status and role."[3] Who would deny that the valuation accorded academic men derives from their expertise?

There is also a popular image of scientists as practical, skillful, active, effective, diligent, and unselfish servants of truth.[4] Social scientists, themselves, have done a great deal to advance this attractive characterization, regardless of whether or not it contradicts everyday experience.

All in all, studies of American university life have maintained that disinterested professional evaluation, rationality, and so on, are invariably encouraged. Sometimes, as in *Who's Afraid of Virginia Woolf?*, *Purely Academic*, *A New Life*, *Pnin*, and other fiction, we get a somewhat different perspective of life on campus. Seldom, however, is any one piece of commentary on the American academic scene balanced, and the narrative is generally one of persons assiduously plying their trade. In addition to Jencks and Riesman, Parsons and Platt[5] have advanced the notions of meritocratic advancement and universalism[6] in their analysis and description of university life. The critic Jacques Barzun, in lamenting "the invidious system of academic promotion, the perversion of the undergraduate curriculum, and (most recent) the professional teacher's contempt of teaching," has attributed this condition to determined endeavor—the "mania for research."[7]

Even more telling, a review by Theodore Roszak and ten other critics of developments in some of the humanities and social sciences in the late 1960s exemplifies the pervasiveness of this thesis. The general theme of these eleven "socially engaged intellectuals" is that scholars in these soft disciplines are for the most part studying such irrelevant questions that they and their work are of no real value to a troubled society and world.[8] There is implicit here a presumption that most academics are busily engaged in scholarship, however misdirected. Thus, both celebrants and critics of the multiversity take for granted a ubiquitous professionalism among faculty. Even to lament the potency of publish or perish, which is blamed for many problems that trouble American universities—academic gamesmanship and career building; disdain for students and teaching, the pursuit of insignificance; complicity with, and concession to, those who can confer rewards, punishment, status, or praise—is to make the assumption that this is the case. For to claim that scholarly activity is necessary for professional advancement is to claim that rational (or pseudorational) criteria significantly affect the decisionmaking process on campus.

All of this is not to suggest that those most informed about academic life are unaware of the importance of subjective factors, which could be inconsistent with a puritan ethic or professionalism, in day-to-day activities. The pertinence of prestige to all aspects of academia is the theme of Logan Wilson's landmark study, *The Academic Man*, published in 1942.[9] More recently, Caplow and McGee recognized the importance of "prestige as a central variable" for understanding the academic marketplace.[10] Furthermore, the distinction commonly made between academic locals, who are oriented to campus affairs, and cosmopolitans, who are oriented to a discipline, is founded on the awareness that the entire range of behavior of academics cannot be understood unless idiosyncratic attitudes such as loyalty are accorded adequate attention.[11] Moreover, as we will see in chapter 5, some research shows not only that extra-academic considerations affect which individuals are finally recruited to the most prestigious departments but even how "the evaluation of scientific articles [by scholarly journals] is affected to some degree by non-scientific factors."[12]

It is obvious to anyone minimally familiar with campus life that both particularistic and universalistic factors influence academic affairs; both are operative at various times and in various places. Surely, most who have pictured one or the other as prevalent recognize the existence of both a puritan and a social ethic. This and the following chapter focus on the extent to which extra-academic elements, many of a subjective and particularistic nature, are injected into a facet of academic life where it is said they are largely ignored, namely, the process of selecting faculty for academic positions. The purpose of this analysis is to delineate the behavioral expectations for those anticipating a normal and happy academic career by those who play some part in affecting that career.

LETTERS OF RECOMMENDATION

The method of inquiry is a content analysis, and the data are information contained in letters of recommendation written on behalf of candidates for academic positions. One might take exception here by making the observation that the purpose of such letters is to obtain information of a personal, not a professional, nature. Such a concern is beside the point. Some personal information may reflect on academic qualifications, some may not. If it were held that letters of recommendation were of special value precisely because they bore on matters not necessarily germane to academic performance, then this sort of review would, of course, be superfluous, but only because it would no longer be necessary to make the case for the importance of extra-academic considerations. To the degree that the intent of such letters is to help establish academic qualifications, the introduction of other kinds of information opens to question the primacy of professional considerations in the recruitment of faculty.

An analysis of letters of recommendation may be challenged on two other counts. First, it may be argued that they are a ritualistic exercise used only to confirm what the reader wants to confirm. If the real purpose of these letters were to evaluate individuals fairly, they would be submitted by strangers, who would be unmoved by personal relationships. This begs the question. True, almost all letters are probably one-sided, in that they heap praise on candidates, and academics are surely not uniformly of such high quality. The point is, however, that recommendations are written with the certainty, perhaps fed by repeated experience, that the various attributes mentioned are important to the reader, and it is this fact that makes them significant data. Even if these letters are not pivotal in the hiring process, as is sometimes argued, this does not diminish their materialness as salient artifacts.

Second, these letters are private documents, not intended for examination by a researcher. With this in mind, care is taken to shift the focus mostly away from the candidates to qualities writers judge to be important to departments seeking to recruit effective faculty. Although it would surely be illuminating, for example, no attempt is made to determine how closely the description of an individual in a letter and his performance coincide. Attention is directed to particular qualities that writers feel should be weighed in acting on an applicant.

If writers consider certain characteristics of importance to another department, it is possible that these characteristics are of importance to their own. We can thus proceed prompted by the presupposition that a letter of recommendation is reflexive, in that it reveals as much about the values of a writer as about the qualities of a candidate. The staleness of many letters indicates that they can be produced without much thought—like an autonomic response. Yet, in the last analysis, not many would deny that they do in fact reveal a good deal about the concerns of academics.

One hundred and eighty-five letters of recommendation written by 167 American sociologists in an eighteen-month period in the late 1960s were read and analyzed. Letters were written to a single department for fifty sociologists seeking standard university appointments to all faculty ranks. The department to which the letters were directed was not one of the most prestigious in the country but would be ranked somewhere in the top fifty. Of the fifty candidates, six were female; between eight and twelve (depending on the criteria used) had some national reputation; and all had or soon expected to receive their Ph.D.'s. There was a single letter for one candidate, and there were from two to seven for the other forty-nine, with a mean of 3.7 letters per candidate. Many writers were widely known sociologists. One or more letters originated from fifteen of the seventeen departments whose graduate faculties in sociology were rated distinguished or strong in a study by Cartter published in 1966.[13]

DELINEATING THE ACADEMIC ROLE

Departments interested in filling a vacancy will request an evaluation of a candidate's "qualifications for teaching, research, and participation as a colleague." And the response to the question of how a candidate might perform in these three dimensions of the academic role is most perfunctory; few persons are not articulate and/or well organized, intelligent and/or competent, congenial, cooperative, pleasant and/or warm.

Information regarding teaching is often qualified with something on the order of "I have no firsthand information, but I would guess from what I have seen [or heard] that. . . ." Qualities most frequently mentioned are those that help to ensure a good performance: fluency and enthusiasm. Attributes related to carrying out the task effectively —degree of organization and preparation, thoroughness, and con-scientiousness—are also emphasized. Some consideration is given to ordinary relationships with students—how much attention they might be spared or how they would be treated. Reference is occasionally made to intellectual qualities, such as knowledge of material, imagination, originality, and thoughtfulness. Seldom specified are interest in and dedication to the teaching enterprise in general. A candidate is always portrayed as having a fervent interest in research; the suspicion that one might devote too much time to teaching at the expense of this is almost never raised.

Almost all attributes attesting to research capacity fall into three categories. First, there is training. When offered, the explanation for the equivocal "competent" specifies knowledgeableness ("well-read"), facility for expression ("writes well"), and work habits ("systematic" or "thorough"). Second, there are qualities of the mind, and it is possible here to construct two quasi scales from the descriptive adjectives. From one, the basic properties of mental capacity (brilliance, brightness, intelligence) can be fixed, while the other establishes one's degree of creativity (ingeniousness, originality, innovativeness). Third, there is tenacity. Excessive energy, high motivation, or delight in hard work are taken as signs of ability to be a successful scholar. Judgment of a candidate is seldom based on his completed research, either because experience, age, or other characteristics preclude his having carried out a project or because a referee is not familiar enough with what he has done to assess its worth. These reasons may also explain why reference to research "on topics which have relevance to the problems within the society" or which is "concern[ed] with a range of human issues" is indeed a rarity, so much so that it would appear that this aspect of a man's work is essentially not germane.

The appeal for an assessment of an academic's participation as a colleague is obviously open to a variety of interpretations: any number of factors may be considered relevant to academic performance, and one could not expect a consensus as to which are truly central and which are not.[14] It is this ambiguity that is of special interest. It is not always a simple matter to determine whether a writer had a purely academic or an extra-academic quality in mind when referring to a candidate, usually because terms are not defined. The many letters stating that a candidate would be a dependable or considerate (reliable, responsible, supportive, helpful) colleague were mostly clear. Those promising a mature, versatile, or stimulating colleague were more difficult to classify. Even more perplexing are those asserting that someone could be expected to be delightful, enjoyable, or attractive.

Interaction

Prominent in the letters is the theme that if an individual is congenial, cooperative, likeable, and/or effective in interaction he will have "no difficulty in fitting into [a] colleague group." Being congenial means being informal, amiable, and in general "a wonderful chap." Being cooperative means being flexible, accommodating, and agreeable, that is, being able to offer "unobtrusive and yet efficient cooperation—in contrast to some young scholars who are clumsy about handling such chores and about their personal relations with the faculty." Being likeable is simply being "a nice guy to have around." Of course, candidates can possess some combination of the preceding traits: "Moreover, he is very likeable and cooperative and will make a good colleague."

The capacity to handle interaction is more complex. It might entail being "easy to live with," being able to form "close colleague relations," being a "pleasant companion," being able to "work smoothly with a research team," being "sensitive to personal and organization obstacles," being "quite pleasant interpersonally," "fitting in" with "a wide variety of types" or "superbly into almost any social situation," being "courteous," being "gregarious," merely "outgoing" or just plain "friendly," being able to establish "excellent rapport," being "fully engaged with others," having an "aptitude for meeting and getting on with people," doing well in developing "interpersonal contacts," or having "social sensitivity." It is a relatively easy matter to decide who has these skills and how they are developed. To be "perceptive of interpersonal relations" it might only be necessary to find the "time to attend all the departmental gatherings," or one might limit oneself to being "active in graduate student social and athletic activities."

Departments must be assured, no matter how meager the evidence, that a candidate can maintain satisfactory social relationships: "This winter quarter [he] taught introductory sociology at ——— [an institution in another state]. The reports on his relations with students and colleagues there have been quite good"; or, as a former professor writes: "I have found [him] a pleasant person to have around and would expect him to get along well with faculty and students."

The issue of a candidate's not wanting or not being able to get on with all colleagues is treated gingerly, and with some embarrassment. Apologies are made for those who, from shyness or wariness, do not seek out others: "[He] is somewhat reserved, but has a sense of humor and a pleasant manner. I would expect [him] to wear well as a colleague"; and, "[He] is also a personable fellow, seemingly a bit shy and retiring. This is somewhat of a façade which quickly fades when he is confronted with an encounter."

If someone might think that a candidate is "coldly rational," he is assured that "if one wishes to look for it he will find underneath something of warmth and receptivity to genuine friendship." Being "a bit on the aggressive side" may be "a trait which makes him a good teacher as well as an interesting individual." Or the writer may take the offensive by asserting that a candidate's frankness only "irritates conservative and less imaginative people."

An even stronger case must be made for someone who is both withdrawn and unlikely to be a "prolific scholar": "He is warm and articulate but not aggressive. He is very well liked by both our faculty and graduate students. I expect that [he] will be a cooperative and valued colleague in whatever department he joins."

Comments about difficulties in interaction were more likely to be made if the candidate had an established reputation as a scholar or recommendations of distinction. One explanation for this is that, given the strength of a candidate in terms of scholarly qualifications, writers possibly felt that a realistic description of personal relationships would not do excessive harm in the search for employment. Further, those who lack some national reputation are possibly still in, or recently out of, graduate school and are unlikely to have forgotten how to ingratiate themselves. A show of pliancy would endear these young scholars to those who write letters on their behalf, so that more features might come in for favorable comment than might otherwise be the case.

A principle operating here is that the weaker the scholarly qualifications, the stronger the candidate should appear along other dimensions. It is evident from the tortuous formulations of some writers that this proposition is uppermost in their minds:

> He has a good capacity for organizing materials and a warm receptive personality. My only doubts about him concern the likelihood that he will make a substantial contribution through research. . . . Moreover, such a small proportion of our colleagues make substantial intellectual contributions that it is uncharitable to demand so much of an apprentice to our field. [He] will be a good and useful departmental member; I recommend him to you on these terms.

It should be mentioned that there seems to be no confusion between intradepartmental and extradepartmental relationships:

> As a person he is very pleasant and restrained in his interaction with others—a bit stiff and self-conscious perhaps. This makes him rather easy to get along with, though not someone whom one might enjoy enormously on a social basis. But as a colleague, whom one needn't enjoy on a social basis, I would suspect he would be most pleasant and helpful.

Here, through a curious metamorphosis, awkwardness, a shortcoming in most settings, becomes a positive academic quality. Of course, as is the case with any characteristic, one must not display excessive group-consciousness: "In task after task he has shown himself to be a good teamworker but with a capacity to work independently on his own." This may be a formula for academic success.

Personality

It is manifest, then, that departments are not interested in recruiting men who will disrupt social relationships and upset the status quo. The distinguishing personality traits needed by a prospective departmental member to indicate that he will not be an irritant are friendliness ("amiable," "warm," "personable," "pleasant" [surely the most common adjective found in the letters]), gentleness ("patient," "modest," "quiet," "easygoing," "relaxed"), and soundness of mind ("stable," "well-adjusted," "balanced," "even-tempered"). Possessing, or seeming to possess, such traits is deemed of greatest importance: "I should add that he is a thoroughly charming and personable guy, and he should make an excellent colleague"; or "In addition, he is a very pleasant person to work with. . . . Finally, he evidences considerable personal maturity and emotional stability, and should fit smoothly into any department."

When these traits are not evident, there are explanations in order to avoid misunderstandings: although "his style" is temperate, "he is basically, however, a warm person." Even when an intradepartmental memorandum is written regarding information received over the telephone about a candidate, these traits, though hearsay, receive substantial attention: "also, he says [the candidate] is as nice a guy as one could wish for." In sum, the central place that the evaluation of personality (mostly of an unmistakable type) has in the letters cannot be overstated. As one writer simply puts it, "I recommend him for his personal and social qualities as well as his promise as a social scientist."

Some candidates seen as being especially tractable came in for extra praise, particularly if they had at one time been employed by or in some way assisted the writer. One of the not unexpected consequences of such relationships was conspicuously laudatory testimony, which in turn resulted in marked discrepancies among writers for such persons, and a tendency to minimize the scholarly shortcomings for those who were "easy." One writer could characterize a candidate as showing "considerable originality," while another thought he was "not highly innovative or ground-breaking"; one could attest that a candidate showed "substantial professional promise," while another had "reservations about [his] research potential"; one could predict that a candidate "will be productive," while another could feel he would not be a "prolific scholar." We will return to this question of contradictory assertions later in the chapter.

There was also an odd assortment of justifications (some probably good and true) for what might be taken as signs of professional insufficiency. Lack of scholarly progress or production was said to be due to working with ideas so complex that they could not be easily expressed, to excessive reflection and rumination, to consuming administrative burdens, to domestic pressures, to involvement in too many projects, to a proclivity for working on problems until they are solved, to spending too much time in the field, and so on.

A correspondent who felt an unusual obligation to a person might even advance his candidacy at the expense of another's. In a postscript to a letter for one candidate, a writer said of another man "who is working for me now": "[He] has a far broader training, is more mature and experienced [than the candidate] . . . [although his] academic record is poor[er]. . . ." The day after sending a highly complimentary letter for his research assistant, a professor made these damaging observations about another candidate for the same department: "[He] tends to come on in a somewhat brash and glib way . . . moreover I suspect this is the defensiveness of both his age and his ambition." These are admittedly rare cases.

WIVES, FEMALES, AND OTHER CONSIDERATIONS

The inoffensive personality, though seen as an essential element in departmental tranquility, is not the only type believed to be helpful in promoting this state. The fact that an individual was "balding [and] pipe-smoking" (apparently mature and thoughtful) might qualify him for the role of peacemaker. A good sense of humor was also considered an attraction. A wife who is "charming," "fits in well," or "is lovely" might be "a distinct asset" or "a distinct 'fringe benefit.'" It may be possible, for example, to smooth over intradepartmental discord in the evenings or on weekends: "He and his charming wife are gracious hosts and the kind of people who make a most favorable impression in any circle." A wife may also directly influence departmental affairs, insofar as she can use her feminine intuition to supplement or corroborate the not always perfect judgment of her spouse: "Intramurally, my wife likes ——— as a person and personality, and I have come to realize that her instincts in matters of interrelationships are, on the whole, good and commonly sounder than mine." Wives might have other functions, but these were not specified in the letters. In no case was it suggested that abrasiveness on the part of a husband could be overlooked because his wife was "a great addition" and would compensate for his deficiencies; a wife is merely to complement her mate so that they will "form an effective team."

Apparently, it is believed that the female candidate poses graver problems to departmental relationships, as special pains are taken to delineate her special assets. She may be described as "a very attractive young woman in her early twenties," "highly decorative," or "petite and personally attractive," and she must unmistakenly satisfy such specifications if she is to proudly "adorn any department of sociology." It would appear that the threat a female presents does not stem from fear of jealousy or favoritism as much as from apprehension of being dominated by a matriarch, and assurances must be given that this will not happen: "She is very articulate although not combative nor aggressive in her exchange with others."

It is noteworthy that the overwhelming majority of extra-academic factors mentioned bore on the question of maintaining equable social relationships in a department. One letter did note that a candidate was "active in Catholic circles"; another noted that a candidate "contributed to [his] community," but such remarks were not common. References to a candidate's orientation to sociology were just as rare. There was but one serious reference to ideological commitment, which, at a time of desperate national tragicomedy, when America was losing a war as well as her honor, was somewhat less than would be anticipated:

> He brings an unusually developed social conscience and humanistic concern to his approach to sociology. He is an excellent representative of the younger group of activists and dissenters who see much to be dissatisfied with in the larger society, in the structure of higher education, and in the field of sociology itself.

However, another referee for this man indicated that he thought "quite highly" of both the candidate and his wife and that the candidate was manifestly "congenial," and it is possible that these comments would mitigate the effect of the first writer's remarks.

One further observation should be made at this point. Essential to complete humanity are those psychological traits referred to as "character." Since academics play a part in the education of the young, it might be expected that a large proportion of the letters would make some reference to character. This was not the case. In only a small minority of the letters is attention given to this facet of a candidate. When there was an allusion to character, comments touched on two themes: decency (generosity, compassion) and honesty (integrity, principles, ethics). Perhaps writers did not feel well enough acquainted with candidates to discuss such a delicate topic; perhaps honorable character is taken for granted; perhaps decency and honesty are not seen as especially salient.

PROFESSIONAL VISIBILITY

The discussion to this point indicates that, in the course of assessing the professoriate, alongside a dependence on extra-academic factors is an uneasiness about a potential faculty member's upsetting the network of social relationships within a department. It could be predicted then that the penchant for order and stability might work to diminish the influence of the puritan ethic. It appears that a department would be willing to pass up the man thoroughly devoted to the continued success of his work on the chance that he would be oblivious to his social responsibilities. It was, therefore, somewhat unexpected that concern about another extra-academic interest and a feature of departments that effects change, visibility (luster, distinction, and the like), also affected the contents of the letters. Apparently the interest of departments in hiring and retaining faculty with high professional visibility is born of the belief that some of this will rub off on all departmental members, hopefully increasing their individual status, as well as that of the collectivity.

It is almost unnecessary to state that letters of recommendation, academic and otherwise, are swollen with exaggeration. The use of hyperbole is said to have many functions: to repay a debt, to reduce guilt, to rid a department of an unwanted member, to incur favor rather than disfavor, to cultivate a friend, to impress others with one's connections, experiences, and insights ("He's the most gifted theorist that I've run across in any of the Big Ten schools"). These purposes and many others are undoubtedly served by the 185 letters at hand. But it would also appear that the overstating of a candidate's qualifications was used to convince the recruiting department that it would be employing someone with extraordinary attributes, attributes which would help him (and them) obtain more visibility than the next man (department).

In order to find the depth of such bombast, it is necessary to go well beyond the blanket of platitudes ("pleasant," "warm," "intelligent"). That one writer described two candidates as "well-trained," "very capable," "bright," able to endure "hard work," "responsible," "mature," "cooperative and valuable colleagues" who "take on their share and more of the chores" and who are "intellectually . . . about even" does not necessarily mean that these letters are simply orgies of praise. Besides words such as "superior," "excellent," "superb," "splendid," "topnotch," and "first-rate," there were terms such as "unusual," "exceptional," "outstanding," "remarkable," "far superior," and "extremely"; and these latter concepts imply a position that sets one apart from and above others. If an individual is in a separate category, he will surely be more visible.

Thus conditions that make individuals exceptional are emphasized: performing well on qualifying, preliminary, or oral examinations; being "one of the brightest and most capable computer programmers on campus"; being a "rare bird"; being one of the best (top 5, 10, 15, 20 percent) in a cohort of graduate students; being the "most sophisticated" in research methodology; being "one of the better sociologists [in his thirties, in his forties] in the country"; having graduated with honors; being one of the "three or four top essayists in our field"; having won an award (Bobbs-Merrill, Phi Beta Kappa); being selected as a teaching assistant; being "one of the three or four best informed sociologists in the country [in his specialty]"; being "among the most productive in research"; doing research which is some of the "more outstanding currently being done"; being well read; "making substantial contributions"; standing out in a seminar; having written a dissertation which is one of the "two or three best." Since everyone has done something that might be counted remarkable, the list is expansive.

In the event that some meritorious accomplishment does not come easily to mind, names of widely known persons with whom the candidate has had some tie can be listed. One letter mentioned thirteen scholars at whose feet a candidate had studied. Or attention can be turned to the future: "I expect a major work within the next half decade, for this is the period in which he will really bloom"; he will be a "prolific publisher"; he "will bring credit to the institution where he is located." For more effect, a letter can begin with a distinguishing clause: "There are few people in sociology I can write about as enthusiastically as I can about ————."

On the face of it, being suitable for a department on the basis of harmoniously settling into established relationships and of being able to bring it some visibility may seem incongruous. But the letters make clear that this is only an illusory difficulty; someone who is "one of the best known names" will not necessarily endanger existing intradepartmental accommodations: "I would expect him to be a pleasant and productive colleague." Yet, the issue is usually handled more positively: "one of the leading sociologists [in his field]" can be "motivated to be a productive sociologist . . . and is a nice guy to have around." It is altogether possible to "be among the best . . . in performance, personality, and future promise." For those who need more explicit assurance, there are declarations that one man is "unduly modest about [his] talents and achievements," that another, although "an ambitious man . . . does not impress me as being opportunistic," or that a third ("one of the better sociologists in the country") was found "to be a very affable and responsible individual, easy to get on with, sensitive to other people's needs and wishes, and not in any way afflicted by neurotic needs either to push others around or to inflate his own worth or any of the other such behavior syndromes which can make trouble in a department."

The Visible and Invisible

The letters for those who promise to add most to the visibility of a department differ from the letters for those whose appointment would not obviously do this. Systematic comparisons of letters for established academics, that is, those with some record of scholarly publication, who are candidates for an appointment at the level of associate or full professor, or who have some national reputation, with an equal number of letters for others without these qualifications reveal differences in both form and content. The letters for the former category are among the very shortest and the very longest. This is perhaps because referees either believe that the accomplishments of the candidates speak for themselves and do not demand elaboration or that such concrete accomplishments deserve labored evaluation. (An alternative explanation might be that the noted sociologists who write these letters feel either that their approval, unspecified, is a sufficient recommendation or that it is incumbent upon them to show their expertise and pontificate about the state of sociology and its practitioners.) An important point, however, is that the same number of comments about extra-academic qualities can be found in all letters, although for tested academics they are more florid—"must remember him with the same affection and respect," "beloved by . . . students," "a luminous, golden man personally." On the other hand, these guarantees for the neophyte are sometimes more lengthy: "[He] has been one of the leaders among his cohorts in graduate school. He should be an excellent colleague. I have found him to be a delightful person. He has his own ideas, but does not force them upon others."

There are also prolix descriptions of candidates who are not recent recipients of a degree and who do not have extensive or conspicuous publications. These accounts sometimes contain both positive and negative elements.

> He suffered somewhat from a lack of confidence in his own ability. . . . This lack of self-confidence led him to be too hesitant in making decisions about his research plans, and also decisions concerning the rapid completion of steps in the doctoral program.
>
> He is also gifted with a pleasing personality, and he has a very cooperative attitude. I would say that he would make a good colleague, one who is stable, helpful, and conscientious.

The uncertainty about someone who has had an opportunity to make an impact on the discipline but has yet to do so sometimes manifests itself in the assessment of both academic and nonacademic dimensions.

What most distinguishes the celebrations of a master from those of a novice is the emphasis on the administrative skills of the former; this art, in the long run, might be useful in augmenting a department's visibility:

> He has been importantly responsible for pulling together the Department at ———— which is no mean feat. That Department started with nothing . . . it has managed to assemble a very respectable faculty, and I do believe that in years to come it will be recognized as one of our better Departments.

If this gift is not at first clearly perceptible, one need only look more carefully: "he has, I suspect, latent administrative ability."

Against this, young people need only be zestful and supple in handling committee assignments: "And he would be a useful man to appoint to committees working on such problems [e.g., building departmental library holdings]. He gets along well with a wide variety of types, and he would be a conscientious and imaginative committee member."

In an apparent belief that evidence about extra-academic facets of those with low status is essential, writers sometimes comment on this dimension even when there is little on which to base their judgment: "I have become acquainted with ———— during this academic year through a number of consultations. . . . I feel that [she] would be a stimula ing and cooperative colleague and a 'good citizen' in departmental affairs." In fairness, however, it should be said that even for matters more germane to traditional academic concerns, evaluations of a man beginning his career are just as often based on little concrete information. "I cannot be more specific about [him] since he had only one graduate course with me. However, I look for him to develop into a first-rate sociologist, and I recommend him strongly for your consideration." All in all, because the young sociologist has few concrete accomplishments, and because many who write letters for him do not know him well, his recommendations are often marked by vagueness and ambivalence. This is not the case for those with more renown, who are often given blanket endorsements. Not only are they vividly described as "splendid" and "delightful," but often the communicant will express a reluctance to poetize in such glowing terms for fear of losing a valued colleague: "The ambivalence with which I write this letter must be painfully apparent to you. In all good conscience I must give ——— the highest of recommendations. As a department chairman I would see ——— leave with great reluctance." There was no way of determining why such letters were so strong; there is no evidence to support the twice-told academic drollery that their strength is related to someone's desire to rid himself of an annoying or otherwise unwanted colleague.[15]

From letters submitted by other behavioral scientists, there is evidence that extra-academic considerations are as important to these fields as they are to sociology. There might, however, be some essential differences among disciplines. For example, anthropologists appear more interested in purely academic factors, while political scientists do not. Psychologists seem to be more sensitive about psychological qualities (rigidness, optimism). But these are only impressions. Persons in no other field seem quite as preoccupied with interpersonal relationships as do sociologists. This might be because it is natural for sociologists to think incessantly about social relationships, which, after all, are central to their discipline.

In any case, while everything that is said and written about American universities is premised on the belief that they are guided by ubiquitous professional norms and meritocratic principles, there is a distressing suggestion from this sample of letters that this is mostly untrue. Even those who have irreverently probed the academic world and sensitized it to its own burlesque and fraud have not recognized the possibility that the ideal of cultivating and rewarding excellence might not even underlie academic values. Here is how Caplow and McGee describe "professional evaluation":

> The data leave us with a strong impression . . . that although the scholar's judgment of his colleagues is often blind and biased, and occasionally downright crazy, it *is* professional. Men are not judged by their tempers or their table manners, unless either of these is unspeakably bad. The judgment made is based on performance and is as equitable as conflicts of viewpoint permit. Although the judge may not be impartial, he does seem

to confine his judgment to what is relevant—and to succeed remarkably well in keeping nonprofessional factors out of his consideration.[16]

A more modest conclusion would seem to be indicated. Whether the conviction that a puritan ethic should be viable has roots anywhere but in the minds of a handful of men in a handful of universities is an open question.

Moreover, it is depressingly ironic that while extra-academic considerations play an extensive part in the recruitment of faculty and are the foundation for the virtues ascribed to most candidates, they may produce in the long run what they seek to prevent: departmental divisiveness. Most new faculty members cannot live up to the advance publicity given them, with the result that some departmental member may feel defrauded and disappointed. This, in itself, is fertile soil for resentment, estrangement, and bickering.

THE SCIENCES, THE HUMANITIES, AND THE SOCIAL ETHIC

Persuaded that these findings are not generalizable beyond sociologists, it was felt that an examination of letters written by and for academics in more traditional disciplines than sociology was in order. After nearly ten months of a continuous but mostly fruitless search, a usable sample of 110 letters of recommendation written by full and associate professors on behalf of men seeking appointments at the level of full or associate professor was obtained. Almost all of the letters originated from nationally prominent universities, although a few came from prestigious liberal arts colleges located in the East and the Midwest. Half were written for men seeking a position in a chemistry department, and half were for men seeking a position in a department of English literature. The department of English was one of the most distinguished in the country, while the chemistry department had less national standing. In both cases, the appointment under consideration was to a large, reputable university recognized as having sound and mature graduate programs. Beyond what has been said, it is not possible to make precise statements about the nature of the sample, since in the majority of cases, before the letters were made accessible, most identifying information—that is, each mention of the candidate's name, the letterhead, the salutation, and the signature— was blocked out. Nonetheless, from the texts of the letters, which were not at all altered, there is no indication that any document ultimately used did not meet the conditions explained to those who made them available for this research.

Generally, there is almost as much emphasis on the social ethic in testimonials for chemists as in those for sociologists. Just as the letters for sociologists placed considerable emphasis on how "congenial, co-operative, likeable, and/or effective in interaction" a candidate was, the letters for chemists emphasize that candidates "get on well," have "good relationships," are "considerate" and "cooperative," and are "liked," "respected," and "popular." Just as the letters for sociologists characterized candidates as "amiable, warm, personable, pleasant . . . patient, modest, quiet, easygoing, relaxed . . . stable, well-adjusted, balanced [and] even-tempered," the letters for chemists characterize candidates as "pleasant," "genial," "agreeable," "friendly," "mature," "good-humored," or, in a word, "delightful." Thus, in both sets of letters considerable space is given over to affirming that individuals are remarkably skilled in social intercourse and to outlining how closely their personalities conform to the American ideal—someone who offends no one: "[He] is a fine person. He is considerate of others and gets along well with associates and students. I have known him well as a fellow member of the English Lutheran Church."

There are as many references to a man's personality in the letters of the literary scholars as in those for chemists, and being "pleasant" is without question a quality held dear. That someone is a "nice guy" is always worth mentioning; it appears that, all things being equal, without exception the man who is affable is a more desirable candidate than the man who is not.

> He has a tough, resourceful, and at the same time sensitive literary mind. In addition, he is one of the nicest people I know; this is not just an empty compliment but a real testimony to a warm and congenial personality.

> Has he a "first-rate mind?" I don't know—first enough, I'll say. He's a decent fellow, too—reachable, warm and interested in unifying his experience.

Yet there are striking differences between the letters of literary scholars and those of chemists. A significantly smaller proportion of the letters written for the former raises the issue of how well a man relates to his colleagues. The literary scholars just do not seem to care about this as much as other academics do. When the topic is touched upon, some literary scholars, with no embarrassment and, in fact, with some relish, detail those qualities of a candidate that could well sour departmental relationships.

> Though his manner is pleasant and he is an interesting conversationalist [he] has proven at times to be unnecessarily tactless and aggressive in his dealings with his colleagues and with the administration.

> If [he] has a fault, it is that he strikes some as rather cocky; but then he has something to be cocky about. I suggest to those who interview him that they ought not to be put off by this manner, because [he] is in every respect personally as well as intellectually above reproach.

At times, the tone of the letters goes beyond simple casualness, in that some writers indicate a definite admiration and pride for the man who is careless in his interpersonal relations. The writers are not just making the best of a bad situation; they seem to see abrasiveness as something desirable in itself, perhaps as a mark of honesty, as a sign of what some would call creative individuality, as insurance that departmental affairs will not become too arid.

> He is not, to be sure, a man who tolerates fools gladly, and he strikes many as abrasive, but I find him a most appealing person, and a warm friend.

> In point of personality, [he] is a bit frenetic, not always tactful; he steps on toes, gets people angry. He is also sensitive, witty, capable of inspiring the deepest affection.

> [He] is younger than some of his own graduate students; he is brash, even impudent sometimes; no doubt he is in some respects immature, for instance in the fulminations he writes about departmental policies or habits. But for me there is in all his motions a saving intelligence, self-irony, and relevance that makes him a most engaging and effective gadfly. Maybe I wouldn't want a whole department like him, but I do wish we had a couple more.

Whatever their motivation, it is of particular interest that some literary scholars on the surface are not apprehensive about how a candidate handles encounters with colleagues. Although there is no way of telling how any department considering such a candidate would react to these kinds of remarks—whether, for instance, a clique of oligarchs would feel threatened enough to block the appointment—at least an attitude that one should either overlook the fact that a man might not get on "splendidly with his colleagues" or to be frank about this has been embraced as part of the subculture of literary scholars.

After reading well over three thousand letters of recommendation (for a variety of research projects carried out over a seven-year period) from a number of disciplines written on behalf of both faculty and students, it would not be overstating the case to say that, on the whole, academics are obsessed by the desire to be surrounded by individuals marked by charm, a conforming personality, and skills in interaction. Against this, the impression that among literary scholars there is toleration for men who are not wholly engaging is indeed striking. To express delight over manifestations of nonconformity, even if the concession is only verbal and ritual, is a radical departure from what one finds among other disciplines. It might well be that along strictly academic lines literary scholars are also more flexible in cultivating and permitting diversity; surely the nature of their research, which does not require the degree of collaboration or cooperation that is necessary in complex scientific experimentation, would be conducive to this.

THE EXUBERANT PERSONALITY

Literary scholars may not brood about Rotarian camaraderie, but they are plainly preoccupied with the business of associates who are live wires, specifically the type of individual who "displays verve," "shows spontaneity," is "quite lively and stimulating," has "dynamic attitudes," "is sprightly," has "a truly vital personality," is "boundless and exciting," is "a mover and shaker," "is buoyant and personable," or "is an animated conversationalist." In only one letter is a man described as something that does not effervesce, and here the matter is broached equivocally: "He is a quiet, somewhat sober and reserved young man . . . [yet he] proves to have unexpected intelligence, sensitiveness, and force." It is almost as if being luminous in spirit has somehow become equated with having a brilliant mind, and vivacity is but a reflection of hidden intellectual resources. Although bubbling over may be a sure sign of cerebral ferment, there is no indication from the letters that the obverse is a tenet of the literary scholar's culture; sobriety and stupidity are never equated. To be sure, this may be because essentially everyone is blessed with lavish vitality, and there are few clues as to what might be thought about an individual somewhat more normal. For the man referred to above, we are assured that "he is unusully perceptive [and] a most promising man," but actually there is no telling whether this comment is intended to offset a possibly unfavorable reaction to the information about his restrained manner or is nothing more than supplemental data offered simply to apprize an interested reader.[17]

On the face of it, it is not so much a question of literary scholars demeaning those who are of moderate temperament as it is one of their placing unusual value on those whose "style is breathtaking." The man with "zest" and "a special charm" can, if nothing else, be counted on to amuse. To anyone caught up in a tiresome academic regimen, this is clearly a pleasant prospect. And it may be only natural that those in a discipline primarily concerned with that born of the lively mind would find the idea of being surrounded by lively men attractive.

The possession of a sense of humor is the surest sign that a man can at once brighten a department socially and intellectually. Even if it turns out that his sense of irony and wit do not truly reflect a clever mind, he is still a refreshing diversion. Thus, a sense of humor in a candidate is a quality that cannot help but be looked upon favorably, and not unexpectedly reference was made to it in almost a quarter of the letters.

> I am very fond of [him] as an individual. He is frequently our guest and we always enjoy and are stimulated by his incisive and witty conversations. The acuteness of his mind and the originality of his wit combine to an analytic acumen which is tempered only by his kindness and charm. He is cordial, but open; sharp, but fair. . . .

> Personally he is attractively witty, by no means overbearing but quietly imposing, sometimes a little disconcerting in his blunt disagreement with unwisdom and usually right in thinking it is unwisdom.

The light touch may be especially attractive in those men who are not always tactful with others; laughter, as everyone knows, is effective in dissipating tension. The candidate with a sense of humor can be expected to wear better than the commonplace extrovert, who himself has considerable appeal.

Turning to the chemists, as far as dynamism is concerned, an individual need be neither an extrovert nor an introvert; it seems perfectly all right either to have a "personal flair" or "charisma" or to be "quiet" or "unassuming," that is, as long as neither is in the extreme. There is an unmistakable expectation that the course one holds should not be too different from that of others; the more closely one's personality approximates the mode, the more readily he will be deemed suitable. A person who is too animated or too retiring might not become "a compatible member of the team."

> [He] is an individualist and non-conformer, but his abilities as a thinker and planner are superb.

> Personally, [he] is pleasant and voluble. At times, when under pressure, he becomes somewhat volatile. . . . In spite of his unusual abilities, I do not recommend [him] for your staff opening.

It should be noted that it is never a question of a man being so withdrawn as to be unable to teach effectively or to discharge his other academic duties. That, of course, would be a serious problem. It is instead simply a matter of assuring an interested department that a candidate is not inhospitable. The possibility that a colleague might stand aloof haunts a number of chemists; for many academics, the need to be admired has ripened into a need to be loved, and one can never be sure about a man who lacks bonhomie. It is good to hear that the fact that a man is not by nature sociable will not necessarily affect how much he might cherish others.

A ROLAND, PH.D., FOR AN OLIVER, PH.D.

To take note of dissimilarities between letters written for chemists and those written for literary scholars is by no means to suggest that there is not a considerable amount in their contents which is identical. To the contrary. In the general description of the ideal colleague, the two sets resemble each other more than they differ. To begin with, when the matter of academic performance is taken up in the introductory paragraphs, most of the letters touch the same bases. Candidates are invariably described as "competent," "diligent," "responsible," "intelligent," "creative," "conscientious," or "enthusiastic." Moreover, the format of a small, but by no means insignificant, number of letters is so standard that with little change—such as the name of the candidate—an account could well apply to any man in any academic discipline. To demonstrate this point, letters written for a literary scholar and a chemist are reproduced in full:

Dear Professor ———:

I would be happy to write you about ——— if it were not for the fact that I would hate to think I ever had anything to do with his leaving us. (So I'll write you unhappily.)

This is a very hot property, as I gather you realize. [He] is an absolutely first-rate teacher and a most agreeable colleague. He has boundless energy, very wide but also deep interests, and an extraordinary ability to keep on learning and growing at a stage when most of us begin to narrow our horizons. I do not know many minds as good as his. It is high-powered and genuinely creative but—a rare thing—it operates with real esthetic sensitivity and perception. If I were to compile a list of people who I think are going to be big names in our profession, his would probably come to mind first. I hope you don't get him.

Otherwise, best wishes.

Yours sincerely,

Dear Professor ————:

———— is one of my favorite characters on the contemporary organic chemistry scene, and I have recommended him several times in past years for positions of responsibility and challenge. He is a careful and imaginative investigator who always unearths something unexpected and important when he investigates a field. His quiet enthusiasm is contagious, and I suspect him of being quite influential in the good quality and quantity of research which comes out of ———— I have not seen him in an undergraduate teaching capacity but have heard him lecture on a number of occasions and know that he is a fine speaker. He is also personally a most desirable colleague whom I should certainly be most happy to have in my own department.

I wish you success in attracting him.

> Sincerely yours,

Aside from the literary scholar's ability to enumerate clichés with greater elegance, there is little that distinguishes his letter from that of the chemist.

It is not only when academic qualifications are reviewed that this resemblance is evident; it is just as apparent with respect to less professional considerations. For example, in both sets of letters substantial space is given over to the discussion of patterns of behavior that are in keeping with what most Americans would call decent, respectable, and normal, and not only do both literary scholars and chemists focus on the same themes and take the same position with regard to them, but they even express themselves in the same manner. Two cases in point would be remarks bearing on the candidates' families and appearances. From the literary scholars:

[He] is always nicely dressed and easy in conversation.

He is of an attractive personality and appearance, inclined perhaps at times to be a little on the frivolous side but this may be due to his ever-present sense of humor.

His wife is yet more shy, but essentially pleasant; and she will become more obviously so. . . .

His wife is herself an active intellectual with a strong interest in Classics; she is also a charming person. They and their three children appear to be an uncommonly stable family group.

And from the chemists:

> Dr. —— is of excellent appearance, good health, and attractive personality.

> [He] is tall and well-built, has a gentle yet persuasive manner, is well-liked by his colleagues; he is cooperative and will assume responsibility.

> He plays the clarinet with a proficiency bordering on . . . [not Caplow and McGee's recorder player].[18] [He] has three small children and a variety of interests.

> [He] is an individual capable of working long hours at his chemistry, with the aid and encouragement of his splendid wife.

Even on these topics, of course, the letters are not indistinguishable. Chemists and literary scholars both may place ample and equal value on a candidate's enjoying a conventional family life and appearance, but the prevalent ethos of each subculture sets the tone of other commentary. Given the literary scholar's penchant for permissiveness with regard to personal conduct, one would be making an obvious and correct assumption in guessing that the two observations cited below refer to chemists.

> But I believe he has dissipated a good deal of his energy in non-scientific endeavors—including two unsuccessful and disruptive marriages and substantial business ventures.

> [He] has a good personality and the only objectionable feature that I have noted is that this last semester he has raised a beard. I thought his appearance without the beard was very nice. I do not know how permanent the beard is. Otherwise I am sure you would be well pleased with him in this position.

Moreover, it should be pointed out that some themes were peculiar to only one set of letters and not the other. The most evident illustration of this is the recurring emphasis by literary scholars on the male candidates' manliness.

> He is vigorous (though not at all flamboyant) in manner and appearance.

> He is, that is to say, a fine person—hard-working, tough, demanding of others no more than he demands of himself, generous, witty, modestly imperious.

> [He] is a man of exceptional moral fibre, a masculine, clean-living person.

Chemists rarely remark on this subject.

By this time there should be little question that there is a great deal in these letters from which to conclude that, in evaluating a man, chemists and literary scholars are concerned with more than professional performance. Although additional constructions could be put on the evidence, the purpose here has been simply to demonstrate this basic point; not enough is known about what letters signify both to their writers and to their readers to suggest anything more.

PROFESSIONAL ASSESSMENT

To be sure, the majority of writers of letters of recommendation are primarily occupied with recounting a candidate's professional qualifications. It is an unhappy fact, however, that more often than not they lack specific information and consequently do not always have much to say about these matters. To hold forth on a topic from a position of ignorance, of course, presents its own special problems. As a case in point, given the tenet of academic freedom that it is somehow a gross violation of academic norms and etiquette to impinge upon a professor's autonomy while he performs in the classroom, the evaluation of teaching is largely based on hearsay, extrapolation, and conjecture.

I have never heard him present a lecture.

Except for the one lecture to my seminar (which was conducted with great verve and enthusiasm) I have no information on [his] abilities as a teacher. I should expect him to be good.

I have no direct experience, of course, on which to judge his teaching abilities, but I have heard him present an interesting seminar at Penn State.

Finally, and perhaps most important, he has an infectious enthusiasm for chemistry which made him a very stimulating member of the group here, and which should make him a stimulating teacher as well.

He is very poised and self-confident and very personable. . . . He is probably a very effective teacher.

Given the chimera surrounding declarations about a man's capacity to teach, it is not difficult to understand how extraneous considerations come to infect professional assessment, and, ultimately, professional life. To fill a void in discharging the normal professional responsibility of reviewing and measuring the professional quality of a fellow professional, seemingly irrelevant criteria are embraced. But, under the circumstances, on what else might an opinion be based than, say, the social ethic? After all, it is not entirely unnatural for a writer who is attracted to a candidate to be persuaded that students would be of the same mind and would be inclined to soak up his learning. An account had been made; the intercession is offered according to form.

Needless to say, when a writer has something more substantial to relate, this is rendered with enthusiasm.

> I have been teaching a course jointly with him for several years, and can say with confidence that he is an excellent and devoted teacher who establishes unusual rapport with students and is most stimulating for them.

> He taught organic chemistry, both graduate and undergraduate . . . for four years. He also taught general chemistry and a course in chemical literature. He was an extremely good and effective teacher, an excellent lecturer, and very well versed in all phases of organic chemistry, both classical and modern. His courses were very well organized and up-to-date. His courses were also rigorous and demanding, not unreasonably so, but he assumed his students were in college to learn. . . .

But given the tenuousness of what is known, such extensive comments are indeed unusual.

It should not be concluded that the reason teaching is handled so superficially and casually in the letters is that no one much cares about this question, that at bottom a department is really only interested in a man's research capabilities. This judgment is probably incorrect, since a detailed study of the letters also reveals that a number of writers, particularly literary scholars, are just as completely in the dark about the scholarship of the men they recommend.

> I gather that his research was first-class, but you'll have to rely on ———— for details.

> I cannot give you a detailed evaluation since he has been with me for five weeks. However, in this period I have been impressed by him.

> My knowledge of him is really quite limited. A year or two ago I visited the University of Illinois and was favorably impressed by [him] as a person. He showed a real enthusiasm. . . .

> I don't know his Dickens book. . . .

> I haven't seen his new book, now in press, but I will be very surprised if it is not a first-rate and important piece of work. In general, I don't see how you can make a stronger appointment. . . .

Comments reflecting unfamiliarity with a candidate's scholarly activities are less common than those reflecting unfamiliarity with his teaching.

Naturally, when the writer is at all knowledgeable about a candidate's research, a lengthy and informative account is offered:

> I am aware that he is currently involved in some fundamental work concerned with structural alternatives to the α helix, which is beginning to be recognized as having minor importance as an element of secondary structure in many proteins. He is also in the process of developing some absolute methods for determination of the sense of polypeptide helices which do occur in the α helical conformation. It is noteworthy that [he], while sticking to a general and important problem, has not limited himself to a particular experimental approach, but rather has turned to many different physical and chemical methods to provide the answers he seeks. He has not been unmindful of the organic chemical techniques which may be of use, and I believe that he has a sufficient feeling for biochemistry so that he would employ enzymatic and other biological approaches as well if they seem desirable.

> While his efforts in the polynucleotide field have not been so extensive as in the polypeptide field, and are restricted to theoretical work, this facet of his research is of very high quality. His theoretical critique of the DNA degradation and molecular weight problem is an excellent indication of the exacting and analytical approach he takes. Such attitudes have all too often not characterized the work of others studying biomacromolecules. Thus his work has had the salutary effect of demanding rigor from the work of others. His recent theoretical treatment of the helix-coil transition of oligonucleotides of varying chain length promises to be a milestone in this field, and may equal in importance some of the very fine work of Zimm.

Such full but rare accounts are more prevalent among chemists than among literary scholars. Alternately, it is most likely that among the latter nothing will be known about either the teaching or the research of a candidate.

> I have not read anything that he has written; but if he can write as well as he speaks, he may have ahead of him a distinguished career as a scholar and critic.

> I have not been able to obtain a clearly defined impression of his ability as a teacher. He seldom discusses his work in the classroom with others in the department. . . .

I have not read his manuscript on the French and English novel, but his talk makes it sound exciting; in any case, it looks as if he is ready to convert his prodigious learning into productive writing. . . .

I've not heard him teach, but he gave a first rate talk here, and impressed everyone he met through a day of consultations. I can't imagine his *not* being a good teacher.

DISPARITY AND ADDITIONAL UNCERTAINTY

And there is the additional wrinkle that even when relatively detailed information about an individual is implied, this may not be at all factual but instead may be only a reflection of some very unique perceptions. Put another way, two referees may give quite contradictory accounts of a candidate and his work, as in the examples below, taken from a sample of thirteen novice instructors or assistant professors of English literature. After reading a candidate's dossier, what is one to believe, for example, about his personality, teaching, or scholarly potential from the antithetical comments by his academic advisor, dissertation supervisor and committee members, or the chairman and/or director of graduate studies from the department where he is completing his degree? Is one to believe that "he is cheerful and well-adjusted" or that "[he is] hard-driving and humorless"? That "[he is] thoroughly mature, entirely modest, and altogether winning" or that "[he] at times affects a jaunty manner and generally gives the impression he would rather do anything than be dull"? That "he proved to be an exceedingly able teacher, sensitive to the needs of his students and stimulating in his handling of the literary and compositional materials of the course" or that "at times as a teacher, he lacks a little ease, a little grace . . ."? That he shows "articulate verve" or that he has "a rather muddling style in the delivery of his lectures . . ."? That his work was "thorough and imaginative, well organized and forcefully presented" or that "his work was somewhat marred in presentation by organizational problems"? Only in those instances when the remarks of two or more writers correspond is there more reason to believe that what is being said is valid, even if, when the observations are not positive, something is discreetly masked by a euphemism "He is potentially a fine scholar and a brilliant teacher" and "I should say that he is not yet widely read nor are his tastes fully developed . . ."; "[She has] a quiet, pleasant manner" and "She is not the boldest person in the world"). Such is the state of professional evaluation.

THE FUNCTION OF THE PRETENSE

Little needs to be said to summarize this chapter. In universities, there would appear to be less emphasis on technical competence, a keystone of the professional role, than we are sometimes led to believe. In assessing their colleagues, academics are clearly concerned with questions beyond professional performance; moreover, the somewhat murky process becomes complicated and more hit-and-miss by the fact that those who write letters do not always know a great deal about the professional activities of those about whom they write.

It might be worthwhile to speculate why, sometimes even in the same paragraph, academic men both affirm that university life is basically professional ("we realize that you would only want someone who cares about doing good work") and concede that more than simple accomplishments are necessary if one is to gain one's ends ("his age, good humor, and connections lead us all to predict that he will succeed and bring success to his Department and University"). And why is it that the same man may steadfastly defend both positions ("one book for tenure, and a second one to become a full professor" but "of course, you have to consider the personal factors which keep every department from unraveling")? Professional criteria are objective criteria, and objectivity is ostensibly what the academic enterprise is all about. At one time or another every scholar and scientist is taught that in the pursuit of knowledge and perhaps, ultimately, in the preservation of civilization objectivity is imperative. To be convinced that objective standards, clear and unequivocal as they are, prevail is understandably reassuring. Not only might this minimize the anxiety that always surrounds uncertainty, but it deceives many into supposing that the potency of other values, motives, and procedures that are generally dismissed as being alien to academic culture, such as paternalism, chauvinism, meanness, and myopia, are negligible. Since it is an article of faith that academics are limited by the rules of objectivity in their work, it is not puzzling why it is presumed that this is extended to their other activities.

Being persuaded that objective criteria are primarily utilized in making a hard decision, such as hiring a man or conferring tenure, is, if nothing else, comforting. A judgment based on something concrete speaks with authority; certainly it sounds more convincing than to concede that procedures happen as a result of chance, whim, personal predilection, hanky-panky, and the like. For the secure as well as for the insecure, the search for a colleague involves considerable risk—it is not easy to predict how a new man will behave after he gets caught up in departmental affairs. Based on his own experience, first-, second-, or third-hand, every academic can recite some horror story of high hopes, a truncated honeymoon, intramural strife, the exodus of innocent victims as well as of the least effective partisans, and the subsequent struggle to rebuild a department. And it would be reassuring to believe that impersonal, institutionalized practices operate to certify or disqualify any prospective colleague. It would be especially comforting for persons as obsessed about their social milieu as academics appear to be to have no doubts about the viability of these objective standards.

After reviewing and sorting out much of what it is said we know about the social life of man, Berelson and Steiner concluded:

> In his quest for satisfaction, man is not just a seeker of truth, but of deceptions, of himself as well as others. (As La Rochefoucauld said, "Social life would not last long if men were not taken in by each other.") When man can come to grips with his needs by actually changing the environment, he does so. But when he cannot achieve such "realistic" satisfaction, he tends to take the other path: to modify what he sees to be the case, what he thinks he wants, what he thinks others want.[19]

Thus, we can interject a happy thought: Both the conditions of university life, such as the need to work together to assure the success of activity that is social in nature, and the cultivation of so much cant to conceal this fact affirm the basic humanity of academic men. That academics are so much like other people is worth reiterating—at least on occasion.

4

The Genesis of the Puritan and Social Ethics

In this chapter attention is directed to the question of how the particular academic cultural life encompassing both a puritan ethic, which holds that self-discipline, austerity, and hard work are the keystones of success, and a social ethic, which turns upon the belief that charm, a conforming personality, or skill in interaction is essential for those who would effectively advance the work of the world, is perpetuated. The inquiry touches three basic themes: (1) the underscoring of certain traits in commending academic recruits, (2) work conditions of the professoriate that accent these qualities, and (3) the nature of the value system of men of learning in two countries whose educational institutions have direct and indirect historical and contemporary links with American universities.

COMMENDING THE NOVITIATE: THE FOUNDATION OF ACADEMIC CULTURE

First, through an analysis of additional letters of recommendation written in behalf of both sociology students seeking admission to graduate school and chemists seeking conventional academic appointments, an attempt will be made to shed fresh light on how and why the academic culture has taken the shape that it has and on how the pursuit of the routine tasks of research and teaching enforce both a social and a puritan ethic upon individuals and groups. It is a commonplace to observe that those qualities requisite for membership in any subculture are the source of some of its distinguishing features. At the same time, those qualities that are a hindrance in gaining membership also obliquely shape a subculture; when an organization changes prerequisites for membership, it essentially changes its character. Therefore, a review of what those engaged in the academic subculture deem to be the pertinent qualities for those who must undergo training to become academics should reveal something about the kinds of persons eventually admitted to the profession. In reality, these qualities may not be necessary for admission to or success in graduate school, and they may not be the same as those necessary for later professional success. Nonetheless, to the degree that they mark either some persons who become academics or some of those academics who specify them as being relevant, they surely figure among the ingredients that go into making up the academic subculture. The fact remains that the observations and evaluations of established academics play some part in determining whether a candidate is to get by the initial hurdles on the road to becoming an academic.

This line of reasoning first led to the examination of 160 letters of recommendation written by as many American sociologists for students seeking admission to graduate school in 1967 and 1968. All of the letters were directed to one institution, which merely requested that students applying for the M.A./Ph.D. program submit "two letters of recommendation from former professors or persons with knowledge of the applicant's academic ability." The writers held appointments in a wide variety of colleges and universities, public and private, denominational and nonsectarian, and a substantial number of the letters originated from nationally prominent sociology departments. Through their scholarly accomplishments or other activities, many writers would be readily recognizable to other American sociologists.

As far as could be determined, most of the students had academic records that would qualify them for graduate school; some had done admirably as undergraduates, most had done well, and some were only average students. At the time the letters were written most were college seniors; only a handful had ever been enrolled in graduate school. At least half of those from large institutions were not known well by their sponsors, and some letters are ceremoniously general and sketchy. Even in those instances when a letter is little more than a mechanical endorsement, its contents are meaningful, in that of many possible forms, they take but one particular form.[1]

The letters were selected randomly from the departmental files, so that any letter written for an applicant to the graduate school, regardless of whether the application had been completed or acted upon favorably, had an even chance of being included in the sample. Attention was given to those qualities that writers felt should be weighed in making a decision about the acceptance of a student to the program of graduate studies.

Each letter specified many functional characteristics that presumably affect one's performance in graduate school: qualities of the mind, qualification and promise, and determination. As far as various qualities of the mind are concerned, intellectual ability is referred to in 40 percent of the letters, although not always positively. Other related aspects mentioned in at least one-sixth of the letters are creativity, breadth of education, and thoughtfulness.

With regard to performance, the overworked concept "competence," usually found without definition in the lead sentence of the opening paragraph, is the trait most frequently used to describe candidates. In many cases it is obvious that this judgment is based on academic record or conspicuous oral or written work. Reference is less often made to research or teaching skills, interest, or potential; such evaluations apparently must wait until the academic experiences of these students disclose more about these dimensions.

Determination, the nucleus of the puritan ethic, is very highly esteemed; conscientiousness and dedication, in particular, are seen by some as essential for success in graduate school:

> He is a very serious and determined student of sociology. In most assignments he goes beyond the call of duty. . . . No matter what the objective . . . [he] usually produces more than is expected.

> The combination of his academic capabilities [unspecified] and apparent motivation makes him one of the most productive students I have known.

Determination, in fact, may be as significant as academic ability:

> I have been more than pleased by his work as my assistant. He has displayed considerable initiative yet works carefully. Of several research assistants I have had in the past, none has pleased me more than ———. He is also an excellent student.

It is a quality richly praised ("[she] throws herself wholeheartedly into her studies"), and no handicap is permanent: "Although she is rather short, she compensates by drive and perseverance and usually attains her goal." The stronger the determination, the more virtuous the student. A distinct Dickensian tone is evident in many portrayals, but none is as striking as one dated 26 December:

He is the oldest son in a family wherein the mother is widowed and has contributed substantially to his own education through outside work. Yet, he manages to budget his time in such a way that, if it interferes with his other assignments, no excuses are offered and his assignments are handed in on time.

It is as if this chimera were inspired by a seasonal reacquaintance with Tiny Tim and the Cratchits.

From this simple enumeration of qualities, there is no question that those reflecting an unswerving commitment to the puritan ethic are accorded liberal attention. Yet nonacademic qualities are also readily catalogued, and they are more than just adjunct remarks to add breadth or color. Academic and nonacademic qualities often are not clearly delineated; in many assessments they are blended in people's minds and seem to be of equal relevance.

He is very good in interpersonal relations and very articulate. He is not as strong in quantitative aspects but competent enough.

If there is any room left, I would certainly recommend this young, attractive, intelligent girl for the vacancy.

He combines a warm heart with a very cold intellect. . . .

Moreover, a generous endowment of nonacademic qualities might even offset intellectual deficiencies:

At this time, he does not rank in the very top group of comparable students, but . . . on the grounds of ability, motivation [he works hard and . . . has strong motivation], and personal qualities [he is invariably pleasant in manner and cooperative in all matters] . . . [he] has my strong recommendation for admission. . . .

The most direct challenge to any conclusion that the puritan ethic is predominant in evaluating students is the bounteous and constant reference to nonacademic qualities. An enumeration and examples of some of the most recurrent and typical comments are given in table 4.1. It can be seen from this table that considerable emphasis is placed on characteristics that would guarantee smooth surface relationships. The individual who is mature, personable, and/or skillful in social encounters is highly esteemed. Much satisfaction is expressed about the student who is "a presentable looking, nice young fellow with no apparent personality or nerve problem," who "has a wonderful presence . . . sparkle, wit, and pleasant manner," or who "has vim, vitality, personality, commitment, etc.—and all these mixed in with hoopla."

Table 4.1. Reference to Nonacademic Qualities in Evaluating Sociology Students

Quality	Mentions	
	Number	Percentage
Maturity[a]	33	21
Personality[b]	31	19
Interpersonal skills and relations[c]	28	18
Humanitarian concerns[d]	16	10
Appearance[e]	14	9
Involvement in student activities[f]	14	9
Character	11	7
Soundness of mind[g]	6	4
Self-confidence	5	3
Sense of humor	4	3

Examples:

[a] "He has a fine maturity and yet does not have a boring lack of youth."

[b] [He] is a very pleasant, friendly, likeable young man. He is very easy to get along with and held an excellent position in his peer group."

[c] "As far as I know, he is a person well dressed, pleasant to associate with and deeply interested in graduate work."

[d] "His experience in the Peace Corps . . . has served to convince [him] that for social change to be effective it must be predicated upon a firm understanding of the determinants of human behavior. It is through his graduate work in sociology that [he] hopes to acquire the knowledge requisite to effective social change."

[e] "He is a very handsome young man and has a most likeable personality. He dresses neatly and remains aloof from irritating 'mod' behavior."

[f] "[He] is dedicated to students' welfare on our campus, as indicated by his position as President of the Student Union Activities Organization . . . and his recent election to 'Who's Who Among American College and University Students.' "

[g] "It is important to know that his leaving was not the result of emotional disturbance or inability."

Upon becoming an academic, such an individual is likely to value these same characteristics in students and colleagues. If this path were set upon in earnest, it would not take long for a distinct academic type to emerge.

Notice should also be taken of the attention given to a wide assortment of other nonacademic qualities not classified in table 4.1. These range from remarks about family and friendship ("he is married to a capable and charming young woman"; "his wife is a skillful public school teacher and ready to support him in his academic goals") to assurances that the Negro candidate can be depended upon neither to sow the seeds of revolution on campus nor to carry on like Stepin Fetchit:

As a black man he is determined to equip himself for responsible leadership in the racial revolution of our time. His militancy is not the emotional type which handicaps his best academic performance, but which supports such performance.

> Apparently this applicant is a responsible person in the manner to which we are accustomed. . . . we have had a number of colored students who have simply washed out even if their undergraduate record was good.

They even extend to noting that a young man's life and experiences were comprehensive ("[he has] worked as a junior forest ranger and as a maintenance man in factories and schools").

It is also apparent that the more inoffensive the student, the more likely that a description will be enthusiastic, while the more mediocre the inoffensive student, the greater the dependence on nonacademic qualities. The applicant who is "a good boy" and who "promises to be winning although his record leaves something to be desired" is invariably portrayed as being "one of those special individuals" or someone with "a great knack for bringing out the best in others." There were hardly enough letters for persons both academically weak and "thorny" (that is, disagreeable) to determine what, if any, stylistic pattern would emerge in such cases.

Generally speaking, the writers place an equal emphasis on assertiveness ("independent," "inquiring," "enthusiastic") and compliance ("cooperative," "shy," "serving," "responsive"). Perhaps contrary to the expectations of a now despairing reader, autonomy is not always seen as inauspicious:

> There is no basis for asserting with confidence that [she] is now ready to settle down, jump through the hoops and become a pedestrian scholar.
> Let me say that I think he may well become discontented with conventional sociology, may demand of it more relevance than it appears to have.

These certainly are not sketches of the obsequious assistant professor (that is, the successful graduate student) who some contend flourishes on campus. Of course, the number of candidates of this type who are admitted to, neutralized in, or succeed in graduate school is unknown. Bernice Eiduson, however, does provide one clue of how one graduate school screens students:

> In the United States, the students who are bright and well-rounded are often singled out as the promising talents in the profession. In one institution, which draws many brilliant and erratic youngsters and where there is a great deal of concern about how to motivate and bring their creative abilities to fruition, there is no question that a creative *and* adaptable youngster is more highly regarded than a creative but odd one.[2]

It should be mentioned that initiative is particularly valued if it is translated into the reliable performance of tasks, specifically those required of a research assistant. Yet, being a tractable employee is also prized: "During one year as a research assistant to me, he was a cooperative addition to the team, taking special interest in a variety of IBM operations." It is altogether possible for one to be too aggressive, but it is highly unlikely that one could be too submissive. Of course, perfection is marked by a touch of both: "He is industrious, follows directions well and works independently with minimal guidance." Although there is perhaps more tolerance for contentious individuals in universities than in other American institutions, there is probably less than what some people who have spent many years on campus may believe.[3]

THE SOCIAL ETHIC AS A MEANS TO AN END

The next question which needs to be asked is, Why for both faculty and students are those dimensions of the social ethic such as being pleasant and likeable considered significant in qualifying one to pursue an academic career, while other qualities, such as, say, candidness, participation in hobbies, dietary habits, or even, as was already commented upon, character (decency, honesty, courage), are seldom or never mentioned? It was felt that if attention were directed to the structure of the university or to the patterns of academic life which obtain for all the professoriate, a more basic understanding of the problem might be possible. Thus, a somewhat larger sample than originally utilized of 142 letters written for chemists by chemists was examined with the intention of specifying some of the conditions of academic life that give rise to the persuasion that the application of the social ethic is as important for the attainment of scholarly ends as the application of the puritan ethic. As was the case for the first set of letters for and by chemists, the university to which they were sent was not one of the leading dozen graduate centers in the United States but would unquestionably qualify as one of the top thirty to fifty.

In initiating this phase of the research, it was hoped that if some illustrations of how or why individuals conceptualized the practice of a social ethic as furthering academic ends could be delimited then it would be possible to understand better its influence in university affairs. As a first step, it was necessary to find a discipline where there would be no suspicion that use of the social ethic had lapsed to an end in itself, where instead to some extent it was seen as the means to the end of successfully furthering academic functions. This was solved by using letters from a traditional, scientific discipline, where, we are told, people know what they are about.

Again, before these letters were obtained, most identifying information was blocked out, and it is not possible to make any precise statements about the nature of the sample. From the body of the letters it was surmised that there were approximately fifty candidates, all but one being male, who were being considered for faculty appointments at all levels. Most candidates do not appear to be recent entrants into the discipline; in two dozen letters there was an indication that the candidate already held a tenured full professorship. It appeared that all writers were located in large graduate departments—some acknowledged associates and associations at institutions such as Cal Tech, Chicago, Berkeley, Harvard, Minnesota, and Stanford—and all letters from which the date had not been obliterated were written in the late 1960s.

Generally, as would be expected, these letters emphasize that candidates "get on well," have "good relationships," are "considerate" and "cooperative," and have all the other positive attributes of personality —and more—discussed on page 64. In sum, considerable space is again given over to testifying that individuals are remarkably adroit in social intercourse: "It is my impression that he got along well with everyone and was respected by his associates and the staff. I cannot contribute any firsthand information concerning his originality and creativity."

More than with other samples, the platitudes are stunning; surely many correspondents find their indiscriminate use an intellectual affront. Most letters could well have been written by computer, since genuine meaning is seldom conveyed: composing a letter would seem to be the functional equivalent to playing solitaire.

THE IMPORTANCE OF COMMUNICATION

Whereas it was not always possible to determine why sociologists attached such great importance to a candidate's companionability, it is perfectly clear why chemists are preoccupied with this matter. Chemists view human communications as the nucleus of the academic enterprise. Someone who is unable to make himself understood would be seriously handicapped in transmitting his skills to students. A man who does not or cannot reciprocate in swapping ideas ("I would rate [him] as outstanding in . . . originality, . . . research ability, . . . ability to exchange and share ideas, perseverance . . .") is neither pulling his weight nor maximizing the likelihood that his research will be productive:

He has a hard time selling his own work (i.e., his grantsmanship has not been unusually successful), and at times he manages to be obscure in his scientific writing. Sometimes the obscurity is deliberate, for he is scientifically somewhat selfish. He wants to milk a field dry before releasing enough details for others to get into the business.[4]

It is my understanding that [he] is quite isolated there, that there are no biochemically oriented people in the chemistry department or on the same campus with whom he could interact.

Chemists, without doubt, give more attention to the basic problem of communication than do sociologists or literary scholars. Roughly one-third of the letters make some reference to how the candidate expresses himself in his relationships with both students and colleagues and in the classroom; but most often the question of the ability to communicate is touched upon in only the vaguest terms. Commonly a catchword like "clear," "clearly," or "clarity" is used, without much elaboration. Chemists are rarely described as articulate, which could leave an impression that someone is smooth-tongued or a mountebank. Also, there is but one extended reference to the quality of written communication: "he writes well—a consequence of thinking clearly plus an inherent ability to set ideas down in a way intelligible to others." Sometimes the idea of lucidity is coupled with the knack of being cogent or concise. And when reference is made to lecturing, organization is mentioned.

Chemists hold to what is indeed an odd syllogism, namely, that when there is harmony among men, the work of the university can proceed untroubled. Men who can readily make themselves understood can help the work of the university proceed untroubled. There will be harmony among men who can readily make themselves understood (except, a few letters suggest, now and then when someone speaks the truth).

THE ACADEMIC ROLE AND THE SOCIAL ETHIC

University faculty generally divide their time among teaching, research, and administrative chores. A great deal of the recent criticism of university life has centered on how much attention is given to each, but few, on or off campus, have challenged the basic formula. These are the primary responsibilities of most faculty in most institutions, and it is presumed that academics spend their days preparing lectures, giving instruction, or meeting with students; working in the library or laboratory (and of late the computing center); or sitting in on some committee or cleaning up paper work. If this is taken as axiomatic, then in a large number of letters it is obvious why the social ethic is touched upon: the writers see a relationship between a candidate's personality, skill in interaction, or the like and his performance. The practice of the social ethic is nothing more than an instrumental activity, in that it serves to further academic ends. In approximately one-third of the letters there is at least one example of how being faithful to the social ethic is regarded as being germane to a variety of day-to-day duties of chemists (several illustrations of this are presented in table 4.2).

The examples in table 4.2 speak for themselves: there are countless expressions of the social ethic that are looked upon as directly advancing academic ends. What goes on in a university is defined as social in nature, and it is appropriate that what passes in American society as natural social behavior be deemed an essential aspect in ascertaining the value of a man. Since it is widely believed that scientific advances are in large part the result of collaboration, the scientist in a university is not expected to pursue his research in isolation.

> The single or lone experimental investigator is rare today; though many scientists rebel against team research or interdisciplinary research, not too many actually do any investigation exclusively by themselves or with one assistant. . . . This undoubtedly has an effect on the selection of desirable workers for the group. . . . The large laboratory has to be a smoothly running operation in order to run at all, which means that it has to be an organization that is relatively free from conflict. . . . Most of these men, therefore, feel that the scientist with unusual work habits, quirks, or emotional disturbance not only involves his associates in stressful and painful situations but also diverts the psychological energies of the group —energies that should be going into research.[5]

For every reference in the letters where an explicit connection is made between embracing the social ethic and promoting academic work, there are about five in which an observation about the social ethic stands alone. In a majority of cases there is no way, of course, of knowing why the writer chose to comment on this aspect of a candidate. Surely, in many instances the social ethic is seen as bolstering scholarly ends, but in what way is not always specified.[6] At other times writers seem to regard the social ethic as an end in itself— something that, apart from university matters, has its own value. Patterns of behavior, for example, that are in keeping with what Americans would generally call not only natural or normal but also

Table 4.2. Reference to Nonacademic Qualities—Social
Ethic Related to Academic Functions (Chemists)

Quality	Number	Percentage
Personality		
Teaching[a]	8	6
Research[b]	6	4
Consultation	2	1
Administrative/service	1	1
Interpersonal skills		
Teaching	4	3
Research[c]	6	4
Consultation	3	2
Administrative/service[d]	3	2
Character		
Teaching/research[e]	3	2
Consultation/administrative/service	1	1
Personality, interpersonal skills, character	9	6
Leadership	8	6
Teaching[f]		
Research[g]		
Reference or relationship obscure[h]	9	6

a "He is a very pleasant person and is very enthusiastic about his work. . . . When he was at ——— both the students and faculty found him helpful and friendly. . . . I think that he can direct graduate students in a wide variety of problems and that his undergraduate teaching would be quite stimulating."

b "From a personality standpoint I have found him to be an extremely cooperative and valuable person. He is the kind that . . . does . . . much more than his share with regard to the group activities necessary for maintaining an efficient graduate laboratory."

c "The group of which he is a member at Los Alamos has a wonderful spirit of cooperation, and they devote a good deal of their time to discussion of the problems which are under investigation in the laboratory. From these discussions, many fine research ideas are generated. [He] has not only taken part in these discussions, but has played an important role in building up this cooperation and inspiring attitude."

d "As a co-faculty member, I have found [him] to be completely reliable, considerate of others, and competent in the handling of his share of departmental administrative duties."

e "His character traits have always reflected a combination of patience, understanding, and friendly attitude with the high ethical and moral standards required of the professionally competent teacher."

f "I very much liked [him] and valued my personal relations with him. He is completely forthright, very energetic, and as my administrative officer ran my large course with clockwork precision. I am aware that to many (both students and staff) he seems a rather chilly and remote personality, and not much given to flexibility in negotiation. Yet my dealings with him were always amiable, and I found him entirely open to reason and fully cooperative. I conclude that he needs careful—but not inordinately careful—handling."

g "[He] is a highly respected man in our group, and since he displayed qualities of leadership, I asked him to serve as my lieutenant during the present year."

h "He is well-known on campus, takes part in many activities and entertains a great deal. His contributions to the University as a whole have been diverse and include membership on the committee which selects artists for our Lecture-Concert series."

decent and respectable catch the eye of some writers and are remarked upon in sizing up a man. Again, one theme that occurs with
some regularity is that of personal appearance:

> He is normally extroverted and prefers to form close friendships with a
> few rather than casual friendships with many. As a graduate student he
> gave little attention to personal grooming, whereas on social occasions his
> appearance was prepossessing. He has a good sense of humor which is
> often masked by his usually serious manner.

In addition, allusions are made to domestic affairs, most often in the
form of passing remarks about a person's marriage:

> I would say that [he] has an acceptable personality and gets along well
> with his superiors. In addition, he has a very charming wife.

> [He] has an excellent personality and would be a wonderful colleague in
> any department. He is very cooperative and pleasant. He is married to a
> fine girl and they have an adopted child.

> [He] has three . . . children and a variety of interests.

The fact that home life is mentioned in one-seventh of the letters
suggests that a number of chemists view what goes on there as having
some bearing on a man's work. Very few writers, however, speculate
about how a man's family will actually affect his work. Will Aphrodite
inspire him or entice him out of the laboratory at 3:30 in the afternoon? Will three children absorb all of a man's energy or keep him in
the laboratory past midnight? Only a handful of letters offer even a
hint: "[He] is an individual capable of working long hours at his
chemistry, with the aid and encouragement of his splendid wife. . . ."
Nevertheless, taken together, there are enough examples that elucidate
the genesis of the social ethic in academic life. And it is clear that both
the puritan ethic and the social ethic play a significant part in academic assessment. This of course, is not surprising, and it has been
pointed out by others:

> The attributes that make for success anywhere are equally effective in
> science: personal charm, capacity for fluent relating to others, tact for
> oiling the machinery of interpersonal relationships, all operate in the
> achievement of scientific success.[7]

Yet a mythology persists which maintains that the former dominates
campus life. What student or junior faculty member has not been told
that he need only work hard and do well in order to get ahead? Who
on the other hand, is ever told that being "prudent, conventional in the

best way, always affable" will significantly alter his career? To the contrary, as Jencks and Riesman assert: "The dedicated professional scholar would be appalled by the idea of giving a student credit for spending his 'leisure' on campus rather than at home, just as he would be appalled by a proposal to give tenure for hanging around the faculty club and making good conversation."[8] Perhaps.

THE DIFFUSENESS OF NONACADEMIC CONCERNS AND THE CONSEQUENCES

In any case, a great deal of the foolishness brought to pass by academics has customarily been interpreted as deriving basically from the graduate experience. Tales of tasteless course work, trivial dissertations, and imperious professors who stifle the pluck of the still undeveloped scholar lend weight to the impression that graduate schools do much to erode any seriousness of purpose in young men of letters and science. And, to the extent that this is true, how can men so destroyed by graduate education, it has been asked, live by a puritan ethic?

Viewing the failings of graduate schools from his administrative vantage point, Jacques Barzun attributes yet another academic evil to their still not fully understood training process:

> The young mandarins accordingly pawn their intellects at the institution for a number of years and expect on retrieving them a passport to the available affluencies.
>
> Nobody should feel surprised at this outcome, for an institution necessarily reproduces its kind, and the young qualifiers reflect in their persons the scholars in orbit. . . .[9]

Those more troubled by academic fatuousness contend that the graduate schools are even more derelict, in that they cast aside the student deemed unmanageable. For example, Lewis Coser has written that "the weeding-out process which begins in the first year of graduate school operates with such efficiency that few rebels survive Ph.D. training. . . ."[10] Indeed, the infrequency of remarks about annoying behavior in the letters lends support to the contention that the less winsome are not encouraged to pursue an academic career or may have difficulty finding sponsors to support their applications in the first place.

These points may be relevant and true. Yet, our concern here has been with still another aspect, namely, recruitment, which may help explain how men who especially value the social ethic could gain the ascendancy in universities. It is evident from letters of recommendation written in behalf of applicants to graduate school that distinct qualities are valued by the gatekeepers of the academic profession. Intelligence is important but by itself does not guarantee admission. Determination is also prized. At the same time, one should know his place, fit into a subordinate position easily, and have no irritating habits. In Jencks and Riesman's words, "the novice is supposed to display a certain amount of diligence and the right mixture of assertiveness and docility. . . ."[11] Academics may thus look askance at excesses that could eventually produce truly unique and significant scholarship. The student letters testify to this:

> Sometimes she may get too involved in her courses and studies. . . .

> A fine student with just enough anxiety about her work to do an excellent job.

> While a consistently good student, he is not a "grind."

However, becoming a good club member, exuding charm, and developing superficial relationships may be a diversion from activities germane to higher learning; both the time and inclination to undertake serious work may be attenuated. Why resort to the puritan ethic? Why, to return to Tawney, be a "practical ascetic"? Why be "tempered by self-examination, self-discipline, self-control,"[12] some may ask, when there could be easier, more profitable, and even more acceptable avenues to success?

On the other hand, the perpetuation of the academic subculture requires, among other things, effective training and socialization of students and, given complex technology and instrument-centered laboratories, collaboration or cooperation in research. In light of these requisites, it is not surprising that the puritan ethic itself is sometimes thought to be insufficient to insure an effective academic performance. But this alone does not explain why the social ethic, although it is sometimes valued solely as a means to an end, most of the time degenerates into an end in itself. Regardless of why this is the case, the dynamics cannot be fully understood until some attention is given to those societal values which academics bring with them to their profession. And since the core American value of "success" has left its mark on many professors, just as it has on most of the citizenry over three years of age, it might be worthwhile to consider briefly one of its manifestations in academic life.

The need to succeed is obvious in universities, not only from the standard pose of frenzied scholarly activity but also from the overpowering proclivity of faculty to become involved in building "a successful department" and from believing that this can come about only if each man lends support to all others. It would seem that the obsession with collective success, together with the desire of most Americans, academic or otherwise, to be liked and popular, has led to an almost peculiar preoccupation with the social ethic. (It is noteworthy how attention is often diverted from individual success by concentrating on the success of the group, thereby reducing interpersonal conflict as well as individual pressures.) As a consequence, the social ethic has become recognized as something good in itself. The task of keeping the distinction between the social ethic as a means to an end and the social ethic as an end clearly in mind has lost its significance; it is evident from reading these evaluations of former students and colleagues that in the eyes of many the distinction is not even viable. Those qualities which originally might have been appropriate means to an end but with changing conditions may seem out of place are also invoked from time to time. In any case, we can expect everything and anything that might please others to be mentioned in the letters.

In the last analysis, the assumption that all aspects of an academic, from top to toe, bear upon his performance is potentially an insidious encroachment upon academic freedom. If the puritan ethic were the primary criterion in academic assessment, as it is purported to be, an individual would need to be judged only on the way he relates to his work and not on the basis of his whole being. But the meaning of academic freedom is attenuated for the academic who by definition has no private life; and this would be doubly so for the man compelled to modify his behavior to conform to expectations largely irrelevant to academic performance or to what may be mostly illusory: the image of an Admirable Crichton, Ph.D., several articles (published or in press or in progress), and glowing references.

THE EUROPEAN HERITAGE: A REINTRODUCTION

Not so much with the purpose of showing that the centrality of the social dimension to the culture of American academics is something more than a unique aberration, and with the specific intention of exploring the effects of its European heritage on faculty values, we will now turn to an examination of letters of recommendation written for British academics by British academics and, beginning on page 102, for French academics by French academics.[13]

Several attempts were made to secure letters from a number of departments in several British institutions. The reaction to the request for letters ranged from disbelief through shock, outrage, incomprehension, and anxiety to sympathy: as a consequence it was only possible to collect them from one department. This part of the analysis is therefore based on a scant fifty-seven letters, written for thirty-three candidates seeking positions in a department of English language and literature. Most of the candidates were young; about half were seeking their initial academic appointments; and slightly fewer than half (42 per cent) were female. All the writers had supervised the candidates as postgraduate (graduate) students. Generalizations of greater substance and reliability, of course, could be made with a larger sample of letters. But, given the secrecy and solicitude surrounding them, this limited number from which only the most tenuous conclusions may be drawn can be considered a definite find.

THE SOCIAL ETHIC IN GREAT BRITAIN

A number of these fifty-seven letters promise that an applicant will be "pleasant," "friendly," and/or "agreeable," for this is essentially the way in which individuals manifest "substantial and satisfying qualities." A useful supplement to someone's "great sense of congeniality" may be "a sense of humour" or "a rather quiet personality." It is important to note, however, that although being reticent or modest is proper, being withdrawn is not.

> Although she has still got a quiet and unassertive manner, the shyness and diffidence that I once remarked in her seems to have almost entirely disappeared.

> [He is] somewhat reserved in his manner, but agreeable and friendly on further acquaintance.

Having a "well-balanced personality" and being "outgoing" are indeed highly valued but not over and above "not [being] provocative." One, of course, can be straightforward as long as one is "decent": "He is a man of strong and attractive personality, modest about his attainments as he is very much aware of how much there is to know." An individual must never celebrate himself. Although magniloquence is not rare in university circles and consumes as many scholars as does humility, it is never welcome; it is a part of nature considered quite objectionable.

Some men also believe that being perennially cheerful is consistent with effective teaching: "She has a pleasant manner . . . and I think she has the right kind of personality to make a very competent teacher." Not everyone, however, would wholly agree that someone need be passive; there is also the antipodal expectation that candidates show genuine fervor.

> [She] has a lively, attractive personality, and this quality in combination with a strong character makes her an eminently suitable person for the teaching profession. She is bound to be a stimulating teacher and I am sure she will get on well with colleagues.

In the event that there is a question whether someone with a wholesome personality who also incidentally would invariably be "sensible" or "mature" would really be "easy to get on with" or be "a lively and pleasant companion" or be able to "elicit one's respect and warm liking" or be "generally very well liked in the Department" or have "a courteous manner" or be "interesting to talk to" or be "a great joy to work with" or take "a fair share in the general life of the college" or be "agreeable to talk to (he has great charm and communicates easily)" or, in sum, be "on good relations with all of us," a letter will go to great lengths to make short work of such a conjecture. It appears that the model man of learning is expected to be sort of a virtuoso in social interaction. In being unclubbable, one risks offending others: they may suspect that they have not won your affection.

Again, with regard to social interaction, care is taken to testify that whatever the candidate's virtues, he is able to steer a middle course:

> His treatment of me as his tutor has always been extremely friendly but also extremely punctilious and courteous.

> His manners are excellent even if by the most advanced standards of the day a little old-fashioned—he bears the marks, I think, of his Rhodesian upbringing.

Only seldom is it clear whether the talent of getting on well with nearly everyone is seen as an end in itself or only as a means to an end: "He has a very pleasant personality, and gets on well with those with whom he is in contact. He would do well as a teacher of English, or in a secretarial or administrative capacity. . . ."

To many writers the social ethic is but a rough indicator of an individual's enthusiasm for both academic and nonacademic matters, and it is for this reason they draw attention to it. At bottom, the concern is that a candidate is not precociously senile, that he will not find a sinecure and precipitously turn up his toes. Consequently, in these letters, more so, in fact, than in others, a great deal of space is given over to creating an image of lavish vitality. It is not only a matter of how "alive" a candidate is; it goes much beyond this: from simply being "full of ideas, and always interesting," having "an interesting academic record," or being "stimulating" through being "widely read [reads voraciously]," having the breadth to "carry out a large-scale study," being "capable [knowledgeable, interested] in both the linguistic side and the literary side [a recurrent declaration]," having "a wide range of interest," or "know[ing] many subjects" to being "a man of wide culture and considerable charm," having "sure and sensitive literary judgment," having "fluency and grace of style," having "always written with some distinction," or doing work which makes "amusing reading."

> [Her] main literary interests lie in the nineteenth century, but are by no means confined to this period. I am confident that she would have no difficulty in communicating to others her own understanding and enjoyment of a wide range of literature.

> He is certainly a man who should be in University teaching. He is not in any sense a go-getter, but he is the kind of man who would have a really civilizing influence on your students—not, I am sure, that they need to be civilized at ———.

> [She is] greatly concerned with the connection between literature and society. . . . She has wide social and political interests, and she has some experience in journalism.

> All three are genuine swans, not geese.

Basically no one is presented as being simply a bareboned academic, and there is some latitude as to what one might bring to a department to help make it effervesce. Yet, in line with the widespread belief among academics that unpredictable behavior will convulse a department, there is no indication that eccentricity, no matter how harmless, is valued.[14] Life in a department can be made savory and cozy with divertissement from sober and temperate colleagues. Over and above the unmistakable attractiveness that an out-sized candidate might hold, there is still some uneasiness about those who do not tread on well-worn paths:

> In short, I think [he] is well worth seeing, provided you are prepared to consider a candidate a little outside the conventional mold.

> My main uncertainty about [him] is whether he is, in a narrow sense, academic.

In any case, whatever may happen, those who bubble can always be depended on to perform well in the classroom.

Males and Females

There was some expectation that if there were differences between letters written for males and those written for the almost equal number of females, this would be most evident in those comments describing social skills. Thus, it was of interest that unlike the case in the United States, as will be seen in the next chapter, the pictures that one gets of male and female candidates essentially do not differ, and this holds for every aspect of individuals treated in the letters. Yet, some of the phrasing for females might be inappropriate if applied to males: "[she] is a young lady with outstanding qualities and qualifications"; or "she is certainly ripe for university appointment." Sexual imagery aside, there is a striking similarity in what is said about all candidates: "[she is an] attractive young woman"; "he is an attractive person and would certainly be a very pleasant colleague." Or compare the remarks made about a female scholar who completed a study of a female literary figure with those made about a male who, even if lacking innate intuition, is still obviously qualified: ". . . a sympathetic and judicious understanding of her subject, both as a woman and as a writer"; and "The subject of his thesis was 'Catholic Fiction . . . ,' and though I did not examine it I understand it was a very good piece of work. ([He], by the way, is a Catholic.)" The issue, then, is not one of sex (or religion) per se, but one of trusting an insider to find and recognize the truth.

THE PURITAN ETHIC IN GREAT BRITAIN

In the majority of British letters the principal method of demonstrating aptitude is to direct attention to the variety of ways in which individuals abide by the puritan ethic. When it is possible, of course, substantive testimony is provided about a candidate's competence.

A good speaker, excellent in discussion and likely to stimulate interest and maintain high standards as a teacher.

[He wrote] a stimulating and very reliable book.

He has real power of mind, a natural literary sense, and plenty of reading.

Yet, this sort of information is often disposed of quickly, as if it were too prosaic a means of making a convincing case. It is not enough to excel; one must demonstrate that a good performance is the result of effort. After all, amateurs do well, but the professional scholar must manifest a special durability if he is to vigorously grapple with and work through a research problem. In addition, even teaching itself seldom offers immediate rewards, and here zeal and persistence are also necessary resources. In the academic world, where so much, but by no means all, achievement depends on passionless toil, the knowledge that a man—drudge, hack, artisan, technician, celebrity, genius— is a relentless doer immeasurably enhances his worth. Likewise, the dabbler is always held cheap and must be markedly superior to others before being taken seriously. In Eiduson's words, effort has

> become so mechanically affiliated with scientific work, that [it seems] to have become merged with the values of scholarship, rigor and discipline, and represent[s] the only "proper" ways they can be seriously pursued. . . . Thus, persistence, patience, and tolerance for monotony become virtues in morality patterns. There seems to be no place for the dilettante in science, the man who as one subject put it, "sticks one toe into the water of research."[15]

Thus, the manifestations of the puritan ethic are irrepressibly protean and kaleidoscopic. Entire sections of a thesaurus could be reconstructed with the vast array of expressions used to describe candidates; the three dozen terms indexed here, taken from the same number of letters, are but a partial list:

accurate
careful
conscientious (thoroughly)
dedication
dependable
determination (solid)
diligent
(well-) directed
drive
effective
efficient (extremely)
effort (sustained)
energetic
exact (ing)
hard-working
herculean
independent
industry (formidable, great)

initiative
interested (deeply, genuinely, keenly)
methodical
(well-) organized
patient
pertinacity
perseverance
practical
rapid
reliable (thoroughly)
resolve
resourceful
responsible
serious (-minded)
steady
systematic
thorough (admirably)
vigour

The greater the number of words strung together, the more persuasive it all becomes ("She is extremely efficient, clear-headed, practical, determined, and hard-working,"); and it is even better when the description is confined to specifics: 'She showed great industry, patience, conscientiousness and exemplary devotion to scholarship, despite two illnesses, one of them caused by the unaccustomed severity of the English winter."

Again, as in the United States, many letters sound very Dickensian: "never one to be deterred by difficulty." To earnestly embrace the puritan ethic is to possess an unparalleled virtue; however, one should not display too much autonomy: "He is independent but co-operative, and is willing to accept advice. Indeed, I think he has the makings of a good scholar." And because singleness of purpose is of paramount importance in achieving academic success ("it was, in fact, his failure to get down to honest work in Language that proved his undoing"), general inability or other deficiencies melt away or become trivial when and as long as that holds a candidate to his course.

STRANGERS AND FRIENDS

The most interesting finding about these particular letters is that the relationship between writer and candidate pretty well dictated the method by which the former attempted to assure the reader that the candidate was truly qualified for a position. It was thus possible to classify the letters roughly into three groups: (a) those written for an only dimly remembered student, (b) those written for someone with whom a strictly professional association had been established, and (c) those written for someone with whom a personal friendship had developed.

In the first type of letter the smallest bit of information, real or imagined, about any aspect of that candidate is introduced, seemingly in the hope that someone can find in the account (not so much brief as sketchy and vacuous) sufficient rationale for hiring him. Sometimes the connection between specific abilities and academic performance is explicit: "Although I have never heard him teach, I understand he is willing to work hard at it. . . . Undoubtedly, he will succeed in the classroom." Mostly, though clues might be supplied, one has to guess at why a particular comment is included at all: "He was called up for national service (in the Intelligence Corps) at the end of his first term." At other times, there is more room for interpretation: "His wife is Swedish, but I have not met her."

These disconnected, random, and miscellaneous glimpses into the personal life of the candidate are generally perplexing and unsettling. There is no way of determining what to make of them. It is possible that what is being said will raise some telling questions. (For instance:

What kind of man marries a foreigner? What emotions could a Nordic Venus arouse in the rest of the staff and their wives? More to the point, will the morale, minds, and morals of the lecturers be favorably or adversely affected?) But it is more probable that it is all introduced for lack of anything else to say. All in all, there is little of substance in these letters. Whether by design or unwittingly, this sleight-of-hand approach strains rational communication.

The most peculiar aspect of this fraction of the letters is that though they do not seem to be based on any detailed or even concrete information, they have a great deal to say, little of which is tentatively cast. Somewhere towards the beginning, there is a disclaimer that ordinarily is followed by substantial analysis or flamboyant praise or both, as if almost total ignorance, rather than setting limits on what one might say, gave one profound insights. At times, writers felt that they could generalize from one dimension of a candidate about which they knew something to one about which they knew nothing: "I have no personal knowledge of his powers as a teacher, but he is incapable of slovenly work, and I should think he would carry conviction and put the duties and responsibilities of the teacher as high as those of the scholar." This intuitive extrapolation is not altogether unreasonable. In fact, alongside conclusions based on hearsay, empty guesses, hopes, and bald assertions, it sounds almost scientific:

> I have, of course, no experience of her as a lecturer, but I feel sure that she will hold the attention of those whom she teaches, and impart to them her own interest in literature.

> I have not [seen] any written work . . . not that I have any doubts as to its possible quality; on the contrary, I have complete confidence in [his] capacity to produce a scholarly and interesting piece of work.

These assessments would seem to be more closely related to the writers' fantasies than to the candidates' talents or skills. It is as if acknowledging ignorance and unburdening oneself left the brainpan entirely empty and divination floated into the mind to fill the void. Yet, even if these conclusions have a hollow ring, the optimism is stupefying. In effusiveness, these British academics were not unlike the proverbial Jewish mother.

The apparent strategy of the second group of letters—those written for candidates with whom the writer had only a strictly professional link—is to overwhelm the reader with an endless assortment of examples of a candidate's concrete accomplishments, as if the sheer weight of this enumeration would guarantee acceptance:

And within weeks of my meeting him, he had produced a long and extremely thorough and clear description of the state of scholarship on ———— Within the next few months, he completed the first really accurate analysis ever made of the complex ———— manuscript in the British Museum, bringing to light many inadequacies in the ———— University Press edition of the ———— He also located and began work on the ———— in the ———— collection in America. . . . [Further] the university thought well enough of him to put him up from the MPhil with which he began, to the PhD status. . . . [In addition he was] awarded a full studentship after his first year of research.

All things considered, the candidate, writer, and reader should be collectively exhausted.

Somewhere in the second half of these letters an effort is generally made to dispel the natural conclusion that a candidate is really a sort of zombie, mechanically powered by a work ethic; and a remark or two indicating humanity can be found. For the man referred to above, there is the explicit assertion: "I have never found him a scholarly bore." In most instances, the question is not confronted so directly, and one may find only a cursory "interesting" or "refreshing." But most often, evidence is given that the candidate is not actually moribund: "infectiously alive," "liveliest and most interesting student," "a lively teacher," "was able to treat her theme in a fresh and lively way," "a lively and pleasant companion," "very much alive and creative." In spite of the variety of such comments, a resolutely sober tone dominates this second category of letters. Compared with the other two categories, there is little hocus-pocus.

Needless to say, letters written for friends—the third category— show considerably more imagination and improvisation. The range of evidence offered in praise of the candidate is so wide that it almost defies categorization. Each letter is almost a unique work of art (or artlessness). Yet one common theme is that a candidate is not merely superior or exceptional but approaches the majestic. It may not be enough that a man's "marks for his work [were in the] distinguished class," that someone "is altogether out of the common run and should have a distinguished career," or that a candidate completed a "substantial and distinguished study," for within the scope of these letters such descriptions are not at all exceptional. You need something like this:

A keen intelligence of fine range and strength, his written work at first very good, with flashes of brilliance, showed steadily increasing power, and by the time he took his final degree he had attained a level of consistent brilliance which . . . will endure.

It appears that the greater the intimacy, the more eloquent the evaluation. Even if nonprofessional, it is all very human—very academic.

A special bond between writer and candidate need not exist for the candidate to be portrayed as extraordinary, since everyone, after all, has something that sets him off from others and can be counted as exceptional. It can be said, in fact, that the purpose of a letter of recommendation may be really nothing more than to discover what this something is and to make sure that it is neither too bizarre nor pathological and holds no other kind of potential threat to a smooth-running department. It should be something that one's colleagues can point to with pride.

Much of what is extraordinary about candidates is typical of a large number of academics: "in some ways I would say that he is the best student I have had since I returned"; "he is, among my former students, one of the most interesting and intelligent that I have had at ————." The letters are also studded with accounts of awards, prizes, and studentships won; of how university rules were altered to accommodate an unusual student ("he was granted permission to change his course of studies"); and of distinctive work ("was top of the list in the final honours examination"; "will be the first scholar to deal with this [topic] properly").

Most letters specify one or at most two qualities that could presumably set a candidate apart from others and let it go at that. The pattern varies, however, when a writer has a special interest in a candidate. When this is so, not only are there more examples—splendidly embellished—but aptitudes in addition to the truly academic may be touched on: "I have come to have a firm respect for his gifts of personality."

The most striking feature of letters founded on affection is the amount of space given over to placing a candidate in a better light than objective evidence would suggest: "For he is a much better man than he may appear to be on paper." On the other hand: "the first class honours degree in English, which she obtained, was a fair measure of her ability." And often, if not always, there is an explanation for the most mediocre performance: "Unfortunately, illness in the months preceding her final examination in ———— prevented her from doing herself justice and she was placed in the third class, a result which by no means represents her." A poor academic record is too sensitive an issue to let pass without comment. Dons give considerable attention to this subject, and it cannot be too easily glossed over. These somewhat laborious explanations are thus almost inevitable. On all accounts matters must be set right. The justifications are bountiful, and nothing is above or below mitigation. The form all of this takes is fairly standard—a compound sentence beginning with a candid disclosure of the deficiency immediately followed by an outright dismissal of the whole question. The conjunction "but" is almost always used, so that the dispensable confessional and purification might well be called "buttressing the candidate." The dazzling array and monotonous frequency of this formula cannot help but draw uncommon notice:

> She had done less teaching than ———— but she has had some experience this year in tutorial work with us, and I have every reason to believe that she would have no difficulty in lecturing.

> [His post at the British Council] is not the usual job, lunching with visiting oriental professors and introducing them to various people, but is mainly concerned with teaching.

> If he had managed his choices as a postgraduate student more cannily, he would have completed his initial research and found the opportunities he deserves more quickly, but on the other hand his getting off on the wrong foot was as much our fault as his.

The excuses are inexhaustible, and since the gamut is run from teaching experience through academic capacity to more personal concerns, it would seem that with a little adroitness any failing could be discounted. It is paradoxical that traditionally, in the face of depreciation by the hoi polloi, the professoriate has vigorously maintained that only a special breed can be, should be, and is admitted to its ranks. Yet, there is evidence here that many academics are willing to overlook a great deal, at least if they are partisans of someone seeking a position in a department other than their own.

One can only guess why these generally rhapsodic letters are engorged with this avowal-disavowal pattern. By anticipating that a candidate's qualifications might be contended and giving his own absolution in advance, the writer is neutralizing in part the criticism of any detractor. In any case, generally the key is to specify a variety of virtues; the more bases touched, the greater the probability that every reader will find something appealing about a candidate. As long as nothing that could evoke a negative response is mentioned—and it seldom is—a letter is, at bottom, a compilation of neutral and positive stimuli from which no harm can come. Each reader can study it and, while ignoring that which to him is not apropos, can spot something which he values. The letters, then, have evolved into a kind of Rorschachian projective test, eliciting not bats or moths but only an array of butterflies, all gaily decorated. On reading them, notwithstanding experiences to the contrary, one cannot help but marvel at the quality of academic men.

THE SOCIAL ETHIC IN FRANCE

The 129 letters of recommendation written by French academics were on behalf of applicants for fellowships to pursue academic work in the United States. Fifty letters were written for persons in sciences, forty for persons in social sciences, and thirty-nine for persons in humanities; all were written in the late 1960s. The letters were randomly selected from the files of an agency charged with overseeing the international exchange of academics, scientists, and scholars.

As in the letters collected in America and Britain, the social ethic emerges as a central concern of French academics. Regardless of discipline, there are generally observations about the candidates' manners and morals. In actuality, considerably more attention is given to the former than to the latter. For every remark pertaining to trust, character, probity, ethics, or decency there are six or seven pertaining to appearance, modesty, pleasantness, maturity, sense of humor, joviality, congeniality, balance, temperament, equanimity, adaptability, warmth, modesty, disposition, liveliness, spontaneity, cheerfulness, or mental health.

The most pervasively expressed aspect of the social ethic is "how pleasing" and "accommodating" an individual appears. The person who is "quiet, good mannered, even-tempered and very pleasant" or who "has a nice personality [and who] adapts easily" is viewed as "exceptionally gifted," someone who "will be an asset." And it seems that all candidates meet these qualifications. Rarely is someone described as "slightly immature," "too shy," or "méditerranéen." Everyone is "level-headed," "modest," and "equable." Of course, from time to time other qualities central to the social ethic are touched upon. These range from "[having] a dynamic personality" through "[having] a real interest in social activities (the student club in our Department owes much to her enthusiasm)" to "never [being] resentful of authority." It is evident that, insofar as the social ethic is concerned, manifold qualities persuade sponsors that candidates will be successful in their academic work. As long as an individual is someone who will offend no one—sort of a silken everyman—it is taken on faith that he has satisfied necessary conditions for successfully undertaking academic work.

When the matter of an individual's skills in social interaction is considered, as it invariably is, the thematic element is cooperation:

that a man "is a born moderator with a gift for personal relations" or has *"l'espirit de club"* or is "eager to cultivate various human contacts" or "intuitively adopts behavior in order to obtain the adhesion of others." The contrary of this notion is never found, suggesting that writers do not even want to raise the specter that a candidate might be something less than "polite in a discreet fashion."

Scientists and social scientists seem to regard having "a sense of human relations" as more significant than do humanists. As has already been shown, in a large number of instances it is evident why scientists are so preoccupied with this skill: complex technology makes it imperative that scientists share equipment and collaborate on research projects, and interpersonal competence could facilitate this. It is simply the means to the end of efficiently and successfully carrying on with the research enterprise.

In letters written by social scientists and humanists, how well a candidate gets along with others is regarded as something good in itself, and one must really guess at what is in the mind of the correspondent who communicates this information; a fuller development of how this serves to further some instrumental task is found only in letters written by scientists:

> He is a collaborator with whom it is very pleasant to work in a team. He is always ready to share with the entire group his knowledge and his results.

> [She] adapts well in team work and she has good and easy relations with the other members of the laboratory.

Humanists seem to believe that academic life in the United States is primarily social in nature, sort of an endless round of entertainment in which people, particularly females, must only be outgoing to succeed.

> I would not say that she is brilliant, and that she may be expected to carry out research at a high level, but her human qualities will stand her in good stead in an American academic community, where a special premium is put on sociability and willingness to cooperate.

> [She] is open minded and young which already makes her a person adapted in the New World.

Even if this not completely absurd image is somewhat of a distortion, it might have led some writers to place more emphasis on the social ethic than they might otherwise have done.

Still, why the capacity to interact is so engrossing to these French social scientists is somewhat of a mystery. This is their subject matter, and perhaps it is not easy for them to discard their professional roles and those precepts with which they have been taught to comprehend the world. In addition, it is possible that social scientists have adopted the value for durable relationships articulated by scientists. But by overconforming to a criterion that has evolved in response to needs not necessarily their own, they seem to caricature scientists. Lastly, the letters reveal that many social scientists are more anxious than humanists and scientists to impress others with the worth of those about whom they write. It is possible that their candidates are, in fact, more meritorious than other applicants; or that they are less meritorious, which promotes compensatory rhetoric; or that social scientists have doubts about their discipline, are unsure what they have to contribute to human knowledge, and as a result overcompensate by being grandiose in their descriptions of colleagues and former students.

At any rate, French social scientists are extravagant in their praise, and their use of adjectives and adverbs is almost unseemly. Where a scientist or humanist might describe an individual as "intelligent," the social scientist will describe him as "very bright" or "most brilliant" or "possess[ing] a lively and shrewd intelligence." Where a scientist or humanist might observe that an individual is "sufficiently motivated," the social scientist will observe that he is "extremely interested," has a "thirst for learning," has "an earnest, deep-rooted interest," is "extremely enthusiastic" or "is highly motivated," or "has the greatest interest" or "a love for work." Where a scientist or humanist might note that an individual or his career is "successful," the social scientist will note that it is "a brilliant career in sociological research," that "she is one of the most capable of students of her generation," that "his accomplishments are highly remarkable" or "his success exceptional," that "he [has demonstrated] eloquent academic achievements," or that "he is one of the leaders of his generation." Where a scientist or humanist might offer the assurance that an individual is "likeable" or "pleasant," the social scientist will offer assurance that he "is capable of dynamic participation," "has a dynamic personality," "is very exceptional as a person," "is very popular," or "is exceptionally gifted in human relations [and] leadership." The letters by social scientists are turgid with hyperbole; it is not uncommon to find the adverb "very" three or four times in a description of 150 words. One becomes almost giddy on learning about the "remarkable concentration," "great deal of self-control," "good deal of wisdom," "great originality," and "outstanding qualities of rigor and finesse" of social scientists. The five most common terms in order of frequency after "very," are "most," "extremely," "highly," "remarkably," and "exceedingly." Such expressions appear between two and three times as often in letters for social scientists as in letters for scientists or humanists.

THE PURITAN ETHIC IN FRANCE

From even this relatively small number of letters, one can confidently infer that the puritan ethic has permeated French academic culture. At bottom, scholarly achievement in France is seen as a natural outgrowth of "systematic, rational, and empirical study."[16] The individual who is able to "earnestly pursue his research in a well organized and efficient manner" is thought to have a good deal of what it takes to "make a scientific contribution."

For scientists, work method is particularly important. We are told that every beginning student is taught to be thorough and careful in his laboratory experiments. Not only will being an "excellent technician" help one achieve the best results and also create fewer inconveniences for those who must share space and equipment, but there seems to be an assumption that an ordered work bench reflects an ordered mind. In fact, most of the time the observation that someone is "meticulous" or "scrupulous" or "painstaking" is left unqualified, and it is not at all clear whether such references are to work habits or intellect.

Although social scientists and humanists place less emphasis on this detailed style than do scientists, they are as likely to celebrate those qualities that seemingly confirm that someone is constantly faithful to the puritan ethic. There is hardly a letter among the 129 in which a person is not portrayed as "serious" (easily the most common adjective here), "hard-working," "enthusiastic," "responsible," "conscientious," "eager," "diligent," "tenacious," "reliable," or "dependable" or as having "initiative." If scientists or humanists outdo themselves in the letters, it is in their attempts to demonstrate that a candidate is completely committed to his craft. Some accounts are lengthy, consisting of whole strings of graphic phrases. One cannot have too much of a "capacity" or too much of a "love" [for work], and too much cannot be said about this:

> The patient and intelligent labor which enabled him to become *agrégé d'anglais*, his success first as a *lycée* teacher, then as *assistant de Faculté*, the great conscientiousness and care with which he has always discharged his various professional duties, the quiet energy and courage with which he has added to those, on his own initiative, a large-scale research project, all testify to his ability and seriousness.

Still, social scientists are again more likely than humanists or scientists to elaborate ad infinitum.

Although the social ethic and the puritan ethic bear upon discrete facets of behavior, some writers see both as necessary complements for professional success. The manner in which remarks about personality and work habits are intermixed makes it obvious that in France, too, some not only see both as equally valuable for completing academic work but have blurred the distinction, at least as far as it applies to day-to-day events ("I recommend [him] for his qualities as a scientist and his sense of civic responsibilities"). Humanists are less likely than others to infuse a single sentence with such disjointed ideas.

AN INSTRUCTIVE DIGRESSION INTO THE TWO-CULTURE DEBATE

A good deal of academic culture in France is shared by scientists, humanists, and social scientists. Not only have the social ethic and the puritan ethic permeated the whole of academic life, but the professoriate shows the same interest in other matters, and this is indicated by almost identical expression by individuals in dissimilar disciplines. It is always noted when an individual is "brilliant" or does "brilliant work." Even when someone is merely intelligent, a writer is likely to enrich this with indistinguishable adverbs ("highly," "keenly," "solidly," "remarkably," "deeply"). Sometimes there are two adverbs. Everyone esteems the individual who is "imaginative," "curious," "creative," "inquisitive," "original," "clever," or "ingenious." When someone has a "clear mind" or a "logical mind," this point will be stressed. And it is highly probable that any letter, regardless of discipline, may make any one of these points not once but twice.

The letters also testify that both scientists and humanists are taken with individuals who have a knack for administration. Given what has already been said about the cooperative nature of scientific work, it is not surprising that scientists are more likely to refer to these qualities of leadership than are humanists.

All of this is not to imply that academic culture is of one piece, that the obsession with petty concerns is the only reality that has meaning in the daily life of men in universities. Not only would it be invalid to draw such far-reaching conclusions from this limited number of letters, but, obviously, social reality is more complex than this. We know that some matters bring scientists together, that others bring humanists together, and that still others bring all academics together. Not only do all academics find themselves in essentially the same social environment, but they are confronted with a number of complicated and serious issues, all somewhat similar: the more similar the disciplines, the more similar the issues.

Added to these general truisms, it is demonstrable that some of the letters reflect values that are exclusive to one subculture or the other. For example, as one might conclude from commonplace observation, as well as from reading C. P. Snow's essays on the two-culture problem,[17] humanists place a great deal of emphasis on how closely persons are tied to traditional culture ("he is well-bred and well-brought up"; "her family is very well known and highly esteemed and has a large circle of acquaintances"), while scientists seem more interested in what one has accomplished ("he was granted an internship at the French Government National Institute of Health and Medical Research"; "he is the author of 13 publications"). Aside from this telling and marked difference in the attention given to ascription and achievement, humanists and scientists also diverge on the question of altruism —self-service. Here is how the awarding of a fellowship is typically justified by humanists:

> He will benefit from the experience . . . of learning about the anglo-saxon world.

> It will give him an opportunity to participate in the "community" life [of Americans].

And by scientists:

> He will be of great help to the team with whom he would work.

> To complete his formation.

These findings are consistent with Snow's observations, and the charge against humanists that they are unconcerned with larger social issues may not be unfounded,[18] and may, in part, explain the intemperate response of some humanists following his original essay.[19]

In 1959 Snow was convinced that the two cultures represented by humanists and scientists were steadily drifting further apart, and in more than a dozen years that have passed nothing he has written indicates that he is now more sanguine.[20] However, it would seem that Snow has not given the equalizing effect of the human condition sufficient weight. Humanists may be characterized by one world view and scientists by another, but the fact that both are tethered to the values of their society and of human society would arrest a process whereby they would drift continually out of hearing. As long as the intellectual world is made up of individuals who are not spared a share of success and frustration, friendship and discord, boredom and exhilaration, then the two cultures may have enough in common to communicate and understand one another.

Snow believes that the gap between cultures can be narrowed with programs of general—as opposed to specialized—education, a task to which sundry educators throughout the world pay lip service but to which too little serious attention is given. The introduction of a standard curriculum for undergraduates so that scientists can get a taste of the humanities, and humanists of science, might go a long way in reducing the "mutual incomprehension" which concerns Snow and many other thoughtful persons. To expose as many young people as will benefit to as broad an education as possible would undoubtedly help—and such a program has the advantage of expeditious implementation.

There is yet another approach to reducing the distance between the two cultures: social scientists, "a third culture," can serve to bridge the chasm in communications. Snow does not believe that such a body has quite come into its own. But when it does, "some of the difficulties of communication will at last be softened: for such a culture has, just to do its job, to be on speaking terms with the scientific one."[21] Whether or not they are entitled to the full status of a discrete and mature culture, many social scientists apparently will be prepared should they be called upon to perform this task. Yet, whether very many people would want them to act in such a capacity just now is an open question.

This lengthy analysis should have demonstrated by now that some of the contours of academic culture have been etched by the process of recruitment, by the nature of teaching and research, and perhaps by the heritage in which the American university is rooted. In any event, it seems fairly clear, at least as indicated by letters of recommendation, that the principle of merit does not seem to be a potent force in molding academic culture—in the United States, nor in Great Britain, France, or probably any other place.

5

The Appointment Process: on Achievement and Ascription

An elementary distinction made by students of society, social stratification, institutions, and organizations is one between achievement and ascription, between a status acquired through effort, ability, knowledge, and skill and one acquired because of other statuses already held. There is a general assumption that placement in the academic world is determined more by achievement than by ascription.

Common sense tells us that in order to attain recognition as a scholar or scientist one has to have done something that others would be able to recognize; that is, one would have to have achieved something. To hear most people in major institutions tell it, the relationship between achievement and a desirable university appointment is pretty close. Indeed, the coupling of advancement and merit is a recurrent theme in many descriptions of the American university. Caplow and McGee reflect this consensus in their contention that "unlike other employers, who may legitimately base the preferment of their employees on seniority or the hazards of office politics, the university is committed to the ideal of advancement by merit. In a community of scholars, scholarly performance is the only legitimate claim to recognition."[1] However, accomplishing something in one's discipline does not necessarily lead to a desirable university appointment. Although the two are related, there is clearly a less than perfect relationship; this flaw has bred some differences of opinion about, and has stimulated limited inquiry into, their degree of correspondence.

109

If scholarly performance is to be equitably rewarded, it must first be identified. However, it defies precise definition, for there is disagreement regarding the elements it embraces and the meaning of each of these. As a consequence, what some hold to be ascriptive criteria are inevitably introduced in the evaluation of academic careers. In addition, as Parsons suggests, competitive strains and the insecurity which flows from them in a structure marked by the primacy of the universalistic-achievement pattern could weaken individual motivation.[2] An enduring concern with producing some tangible accomplishment could well lessen the drive of many. As a result there must be shelters where any set of individuals can expect to be welcome, where possessing one or another characteristic (youth, age, white skin, black skin, and so on) is enough to guarantee success or avert failure; with enough havens, almost everyone could expect a reduction of pressure at one time or another.

One consequence of this condition that in the end increases the effects of ascriptive criteria and moderates achievement is that in the academic world, as perhaps everywhere else, there is very little of what Ralph Turner has called contest mobility ("a system in which elite status is the prize in an open contest"), whereby "all the players compete on an equal footing." Victory "is taken by the aspirants' own efforts." The situation more closely approximates sponsored mobility ("a controlled selection process"), whereby "elite recruits are chosen by the established elite or their agents, and elite status is *given* on the basis of some criterion of supposed merit." As a consequence, "individuals do not win or seize elite status; mobility is rather a process of sponsored induction into the elite."[3]

One pivotal difference between these two ideal-type processes outlined by Turner is that in a system in which contest mobility is stressed, placement in an elite position is gained only after one proves himself in that province for which he is to be given a superior position—final selection to elite status is delayed as long as practicable in order to minimize premature judgments and to insure "a fair race." Where sponsored mobility holds, assessment is based on "aptitudes" or "inherent capacities" rather than on performance, and selection to an elite status occurs in enough time to enable incumbents to control effectively the training of aspirants.[4]

In this chapter, considerable evidence is presented to substantiate the thesis that ascription and sponsored mobility are at least as potent in affecting the careers of university professors as are achievement and contest mobility. Focusing first on the dissimilarity between the two examples of mobility highlighted just above, that is, whether movement is anticipatory or delayed, the findings and reflections of almost two dozen other researchers in higher education are reviewed. Particular attention is given to the matters of how departments fill vacancies and of what qualities increase or lessen the chances of individuals for obtaining these positions. Because their experiences most patently belie the contention that what you do is more important than who you are, the focus in the last half of the chapter is on academic women.

OPEN RECRUITMENT: SOME EXCEPTIONS

Looking initially at the degree of inbreeding among faculty, an examination by A. B. Hollingshead of all appointments at Indiana University between 1885–1937 revealed that 43 percent were alumni, and 20 percent had family members on the staff. His striking conclusion that "these three factors (alumni, friendship, family) account for at least four-fifths of all appointments, and that only a small minority may be attributed to professional competition"[5] would certainly no longer characterize many, if any, American universities since higher education became a mass commodity and the number of faculty began mushrooming after 1945. Nonetheless, as will become evident, institutions, especially the more prestigious, are still in the habit, more often than most believe, of hiring their own graduates. Although this practice mitigates the uncertainty that waits on those who must recruit new colleagues, by significantly reducing the pool of potential candidates and enhancing the opportunities of some who may not be qualified, its overall effect is to make the academic enterprise somewhat anemic. For example, on the basis of his painstaking analysis of the relationship between academic structure and scholarship, Peter Blau, who himself is employed at the institution where he earned his doctorate, concludes that inbreeding has "adverse effects on faculty quality" in all academic settings.[6] Regardless of what the true amount of inbreeding is in various types of institutions, Hollingshead's figures are still important because they were the first to substantiate the fact that considerations other than purely professional ones play more than only a minor role in recruitment.

Looking at the whole of the academic profession at the time Hollingshead was reporting his limited findings, Logan Wilson observed that "between eligible individuals [candidates] of apparently equal ability and training, preferment is always shown for 'connections.' "[7]

In the first careful examination of mobility within the wider academic marketplace, Caplow and McGee delineated "the two kinds of recruitment in general use—'open,' or competitive, hiring and 'closed,' or preferential, hiring."[8] Amplifying on this dichotomy, they added: "In theory, academic recruitment is mostly open. In practice, it is mostly closed."[9]

The recruitment ritual Caplow and McGee anatomized turned out to be insanely elaborate and complex, but after one cuts through the shell of pretense, it is evident that most of it is noncompetitive. First,

> the initial choice of a graduate school sets an indelible mark on the student's career. In many disciplines, men trained in minor universities have virtually no chance of achieving eminence. . . . [T]he handicap of initial identification with a department of low prestige is hardly ever completely overcome. Every discipline can show examples of brilliant men with the wrong credentials whose work somehow fails to obtain normal recognition.[10]

Second, Caplow and McGee's data indicate that departments with high prestige consider fewer candidates for each vacancy and replacement and are more likely to hire those with whom they have had "prior contact" or with whom they are familiar than are departments with lower prestige.[11] For example, to recruit at Harvard, an ad hoc committee is named to select the new incumbent. It proceeds by surveying the entire discipline to determine the best possible candidate— that is, it seeks the best man in the country. As a remarkable coincidence, however, in a four-year study, "the best possible candidates" for 79 percent of the appointments to associate professors and 88 percent to full professors were found to be located already at Harvard.[12]

As would be expected, Caplow and McGee's respondents generally insisted that "prior contact" made no difference in the ultimate selection of candidates, but such protestations were not entirely convincing.

> He had had some [contact] with me. His father and I had both been on the faculty at another university together, so I had known him when he was small. But this had absolutely no influence on the appointment. His father is dead now and wasn't in this discipline anyway.[13]

It is true that an individual's job history is a function of his disciplinary prestige, but Caplow and McGee are conscious that this, itself,

> is a feature of a social system, not a scientific measurement. It is correlated with professional achievement but not identical with it. A man may, for example, publish what would be, in other circumstances, a brilliant contribution to his field, but if he is too old, or too young, or located in the minor league, it will not be recognized as brilliant and will not bring him the professional advancement which he could claim if he were of the proper age and located at the proper university.[14]

In light of this, Caplow and McGee contend that there is little point in trying to determine how good someone really is; what matters is what others think of him, since this, in effect, is how good he is.[15] This evaluation is often a function of a man's specialty. When a label (a Lewinian or Boasian or Freudian) is pinned on someone, it not only denotes his point of view but implies a set of personal relationships and rights and obligations. All of this "serves the function for its adherents of automatically identifying alignments of friends, enemies, and possible allies in any academic situation."[16] Not the least of these, it should be added, would be assistance in finding the best possible position—anywhere between the Bay Bridge and the Back Bay. In outlining their tentative recommendations, Caplow and McGee sum all of this up with this melancholy aside: "Nothing at all is lost by open advertisement, except the opportunity to practice nepotism and the coyness which has become part of the employer's approach to the academic marketplace."[17]

Inferences similar to those of Caplow and McGee are reported in two separate research monographs on the academic labor market by David G. Brown. To some extent, what Brown unearthed indicates that sponsored mobility is even more widely diffused than is indicated by the interviews conducted by Caplow and McGee. One point that Brown underscores is that once someone has a position, it is unlikely that he will be dismissed unless he is grossly unfit (or, as we will see in the next chapter, too much of a bother to have around).

> Only in instances when the incompetence is excessive or where the damage that could be wrought by a slightly less than competent person is great is firing worth the trouble.
>
> The amount of forced movement among teachers is relatively small and concentrated at the lower ranks in the better schools.[18]

Or as Jessie Bernard puts it: "It has, in fact, been found to be practically impossible to remove academic personnel on the grounds of incompetence because there is always someone—student or colleague—who will swear that so-and-so is a wonderful teacher."[19] This reluctance to fire people means, as Logan Wilson noted many years previously,[20] that almost all hiring in universities is at the lower ranks; openings at the level of associate or full professor are filled by promoting individuals already on the faculty.

Although "the publication habits of movers differ little from their more stable colleagues,"[21] it must be noted that for those who change positions, publishers—"persons who have published more than ten articles"—"have between a 25 percent and 30 percent greater chance

Table 5.1. Methods Used in Seeking Jobs

Source	Percent of candidates using source in search	Mean number of jobs found per candidate using source	Percent of candidates who found current job through source
Informal			
Graduate professor	40	1.41	12
Graduate department office	32	1.72	6
Undergraduate professor	16	0.82	3
Graduate school classmate	17	0.61	3
Faculty colleague	20	1.07	7
Other professional friend	25	1.01	8
Publisher's representative	2	0.86	—
Recruited	23	1.82	26
		Total	65
Formal			
Blind letters	46	2.14	19
College placement office	36	2.75	6
Church-related placement service	5	1.30	1
Professional association	14	1.96	2
Advertisement—candidate available	3	2.56	—
Advertisement—position available	9	1.73	2
Convention placement service	14	2.42	2
Public employment service	3	1.65	—
Commercial teacher's agency	7	3.05	3
		Total	35

SOURCE: David G. Brown, *The Mobile Professors* (Washington, D.C.: American Council on Education, 1967), p. 119.

of increasing in each of the factors (rank, quality [of school], salary) than nonpublishers"[22]—"persons who have published nothing."

Table 5.1 shows the various sources utilized in Brown's diverse sample of mobile professors in searching for and finding a new position. In brief, it would appear that although formal liaisons for seeking a new appointment are more effective than informal ones, they are used significantly less often; only half as many faculty actually placed themselves through these sources. The blind letter is the only method that compares favorably with the assistance of former professors, graduate department contacts, and simply doing nothing as a means of successfully locating a position. These figures from Brown's over 7,200 respondents also suggest that the numerous opportunities located but not obtained through formal channels are less attractive and therefore do not culminate in a final match between candidate and position.

The use of friends, acquaintances, friends of friends and acquaintances, and acquaintances of friends and acquaintances is clearly the best way to get a job. One's future is greatly influenced by one's past. From his interviews with 103 social scientists who had recently been on the labor market, Brown concluded:

> Friends were the most frequent source of promising leads. By letter, by phone, and in person, friends and acquaintances were the ones who had made nearly 50 per cent of our respondents aware of the jobs they now hold and this figure does not include the respondents' graduate school professors, many of whom are more friends than teachers.[23]

Here is a sample of what some of the individuals he talked to reported:[24]

> The person who was leaving here wrote to me. We had worked together in 1951–52.

> The former department chairman had taught me when I was an undergraduate at another school.

> The dean's wife was a patient of my father who is a physician. One summer the dean visited my parents at their summer home. The job was mentioned.

> I first learned about the job while attending a meeting sponsored by the AFL-CIO, from the current dean who is a personal friend.

> While teaching botany at ——— I got to know the younger generation in the economics department through Newcomers' Club. At an August picnic I learned that economics needed another professor for September. Since my appointment in botany had not been renewed, I needed a job and got the one in economics.

> While I was teaching undergraduates at Duke on a one-year appointment, a Duke graduate student told me of the opening at ———.

> [I learned about my job] at a Russian Institute through a friend who had taught at ——— in the past and had kept up his contacts.

> A fellow graduate student of mine at Harvard had been given a letter from ——— telling of a vacancy. Since he wasn't interested, he referred the letter to me.

A mutual friend of the department chairman and me, who was working at the Federal Reserve Bank, brought us together.

[I found out about the job] through a friend who had a friend here.

Not only are formal channels not very helpful, but it is widely believed that only the ingenuous or desperate depend on them. On the departmental level, reverting to any type of clearinghouse for recruiting "is to admit defeat publicly,"[25] which, in turn, results in a loss of face. "To use the bureaus is to sacrifice prestige."[26]

All of the previous studies with which this author is familiar tend to confirm that the smaller, less prestigious departments are the ones that turn to formal candidate-locating facilities in time of need.

Further confirmation is offered by the present study. When the fifty Southeastern department chairmen were asked "How did you go about locating names of persons who might be qualified to fill your vacant position?" eleven of them indicated that they had used some type of formal service such as a university placement office, a commercial teachers' agency, or the want ads in professional journals. . . . [A]lmost all of these chairmen were from small departments located in the less prestigious schools. None of the chairmen from the larger departments (eleven or more full-time staff members) had found it necessary to use formal methods to locate personnel whereas nearly half of the chairmen from the smaller departments (ten or fewer full-time staff members) had felt such a need.[27]

It would appear that entrée into any but the most marginal departments is indeed restricted for those who would hope to find a position solely on the basis of their teaching ability or research accomplishments.

If . . . a candidate's availability has been advertised by formal means, many schools will investigate no farther. Reasoning that formal means of advertising are used only by the relatively poor candidates, the candidate will be cut immediately. Similarly, it is reasoned that the most prominent referrers suggest the most qualified candidates and cuts are made accordingly.[28]

If more support is necessary to uphold the theme that the wider academic labor market is a good deal less than fully open, there is added evidence from Brown's national survey that the most prestigious institutions fill their vacancies with graduates from the most prestigious institutions. Students from elite schools had a 16 percent chance of finding employment at another elite school, while there was only a 2 percent chance of this happening for those whose graduate training was in a school outside the top decile.[29]

Yet, the picture Brown paints is not all dark; he is convinced that individuals can publish themselves out of the academic hinterlands, though he acknowledges that it is easier to start at the top and resist downward mobility.[30] Invoking the Horatio Alger idol (or icon) he affirms: "Apparently there is no barrier to interquality movement except a lack of ability or desire."[31] On the other hand, he does recognize that promotions from within and nepotistic hiring practices create an academic labor market which is a "curious hodgepodge" of informal channels of communication where many positions and candidates "never reach the open market." All of this makes the academic scene not unlike the black market, where contacts, connections, and friendships become crucial factors for getting what one wants.[32]

Studies limited to comparing a narrower range of disciplines or to profiling a single one basically corroborate the findings of Caplow and McGee and of Brown. Howard Marshall, in his investigation of 970 departments of chemistry, economics, and English, found that between one-fourth and one-third followed no other policy but that of promotion from within, and of the 574 departments responding, only 14 indicated that they always looked outside to fill a senior position.[33] He also reported that of a sample of 420 economists, 25 percent (105) secured their last position through a friend, while only 18 found theirs through an advertisement in the *American Economic Review*, a private employment bureau, or a university placement bureau.[34]

A Prestige Degree as an Accessory: More Evidence

In their survey of political scientists, Albert Somit and Joseph Tanenhaus classified the attributes contributing to outside job offers for those with the Ph.D. After amount of publication, those factors contributing to outside job offers are school at which doctorate was taken, ability to get research support, and "having the right connections." Quality of publication was fifth, and teaching ability was tenth or last.[35] But when it came to actually getting an appointment in a ranking graduate department, the possessors of a prestige doctorate had a nearly 10:1 advantage over someone holding a lesser degree.[36] Somit and Tanenhaus charge that "these figures, however elementary, leave little doubt that the leading departments pursue a discriminatory policy, insofar as doctoral origins are concerned, in selecting their staff."[37] Borrowing from Bernard Berelson, whose research is considered shortly, they reason: "In our profession, too, the evidence suggests, 'where a person gets the doctorate has a determining effect on where he winds up.' "[38]

As far as those attributes which political scientists are convinced are the principal contributors to their career success are concerned, school at which the doctorate was taken and "having the right connections" were listed right behind number of publications. Quality of publication was fifth, luck or chance was seventh, and teaching ability was again tenth or last.[39] Since over half of the doctorates in political science are granted by less well regarded institutions, Somit and Tanenhaus astutely note that the discipline as a whole is in the anomalous position of discriminating against the majority.[40]

In his inquiry into the education of sociologists, Elbridge Sibley reported that holders of doctoral degrees from the eleven most prestigious departments "are, as would be expected, relatively likely to be appointed to the staffs of leading universities; scarcely any of them are found teaching in junior colleges or lower schools. Conversely, the universities belonging to the American Association of Universities seldom appoint Ph.D.'s from universities outside that group."[41]

A comprehensive analysis of graduate education in the United States in the late 1950s by Berelson revealed that the academic position of over eighteen hundred graduate faculty from ninety-two institutions depended on the standing of the institution where an individual took his doctorate:[42] "Leaving aside anything else . . . the institution where a person gets the doctorate has a determining effect on where he ends up. The higher the institutional level of the doctorate, the higher the subsequent post in academic life. . . ."[43] The best universities attract the best undergraduate students and help them locate the best positions irrespective of how effective their graduate training programs actually are, either in general or in particular cases.[44]

Berelson also found that the most prestigious institutions have a higher rate of inbreeding than the less prestigious: in the top twelve universities (Chicago, Columbia, Cornell, Harvard, Yale, and so on) 47 percent of the faculty earned their highest degrees from the institution where they were teaching. The comparable figures for the ten universities ranked next (Minnesota, Pennsylvania, Stanford, U.C.L.A., and so on), other universities which were members of the association of graduate schools (Brown, Duke, Iowa, Kansas, North Carolina, Texas, and so on), and other universities with established graduate programs (Boston, Buffalo, Connecticut, Maryland, Oregon, Pittsburgh, Rutgers, and so on) were 27 percent, 20 percent, and 15 percent, respectively. Further, 85 percent of the faculty in the top twelve universities received their highest degrees from one of these institutions.[45] Those who teach in prestigious institutions are trained in prestigious institutions.

The Effects of Social Class

Diana Crane's secondary analysis of Berelson's data—for both graduate faculty and recent Ph.D. recipients—suggests that the prestige of the institution from which a person receives his Ph.D. and his social-class origin are as important as publications for placement in leading universities. Her examination of this national sample representing a number of disciplines reveals that social-class background affects the quality of both the undergraduate and graduate degree of academics and consequently the likelihood of finding a position in a major university. Needless to say, those whose family of orientation (the family into which an individual was born and in which he was socialized) was lower class were more likely to have received their degree from lower-ranking institutions.[46] In addition, when the quality of the institution where the graduate degree was obtained was statistically controlled by Crane, she was able to demonstrate that the higher the social class, the better the chances for younger academics—those who have yet to prove themselves—of finding their first position in a major university.[47] Lower-class individuals from high-ranking universities are simply less likely than their middle-class counterparts to obtain positions in prestigious universities.[48] Since not all institutions of higher learning offer the same resources and opportunities for research, and since resources and opportunities help determine research output, social-class origin affects productivity and the eventual course of the academic career.

Young academics with a disadvantaged social-class background apparently do not receive encouragement and help and are not sponsored by men from the departments in which they complete their graduate studies. It may well be that because of different experiences and values, lower-class students are unable to form close relationships with their middle-class instructors and advisers. The attitudes and behavior of lower-class students may appear inappropriate in a middle-class milieu, and this, in turn, would limit the amount of encouragement and help they receive from those who would be expected to sponsor them.

Various researchers, among them Stewart West and Jessie Bernard, have addressed themselves to the issue of how the careers of some individuals are given an extra boost, and there is general agreement that some sort of sponsorship can be decisive:

The attitudes of professor toward student determine not only his granting or denial of financial help in the form of fellowships or assistantships, but also whether he brings opportunities to the attention of the student or otherwise encourages him.[49]

The association of the graduate student with his mentor may make all the difference between success or the lack of it in his subsequent career. If a top man takes him under his wing, doors will open for him and he will be in the club. If no one takes him on, or if a lesser faculty takes him on, he may never arrive professionally. He will not be recommended for the best jobs; he will not be in.[50]

The picture sketched by Blau from an array of statistical correlations bearing on the social origins of faculty suggests "that academic institutions with superior reputations exhibit some class bias in faculty recruitment."[51] A larger percentage of persons with modest social-class origins from the 115 four-year institutions with liberal arts curriculums in Blau's sample were located at schools where heavy teaching loads and large class enrollments leave one little time for research. Consequently the possibility of moving into a spot where productivity can be maximized becomes even more remote.[52] Blau explains this more fully:

The scholarly research of individual faculty members depends to a considerable extent on the colleague climate in their institution. To be sure, by the time a person joins a faculty, his ability to make contributions to knowledge has been largely formed. But whether his or her scholarly potentials are stimulated and realized or stultified and dissipated hinges in large part on the colleague climate at the institution.[53]

The salaries of those in Blau's study who started only a few steps from the bottom of the class structure were inferior to those not so handicapped, who were located in institutions where compensation is never niggardly—always reaching at least a middle-class standard. This is true in part because they are better prepared academically but also, as Blau puts it, "probably . . . owing to discrimination."[54]

The Cumulative Effects of Ascriptive Qualities

Ascriptive qualities such as the social class into which one is born and where one takes his doctorate are not only as potent as those which are achievable in setting, in Caplow and McGee's words, "an indelible mark" on an academic career, but their additive, cumulative, and lasting effects—in the sense of bearing on the quality as well as on the quantity of one's scholarship—make it nearly impossible ever to escape their influence. This point becomes particularly evident from a review of the work of Lowell Hargens and Warren Hagstrom, Diana Crane, and Jonathan Cole.

Focusing on the 576 natural scientists from the Berelson study, Hargens and Hagstrom assessed the relative influence of both the school from which one took his doctorate and "scholarly merit" on the distribution of rewards in the academic community.[55] Their most basic finding is that the institution where one received his doctorate was related to the prestige of the institution where he was teaching, even when productivity was controlled. This relationship was particularly strong among younger scientists.[56] The prestige of a scientist's doctoral institution was almost as important as his productivity in recruitment into the top graduate institutions but had less effect in preventing placement in less well regarded institutions.[57] Impressive credentials apparently can help one to find a good job, but by themselves they are not protection against downward mobility.

As has been suggested, a large university provides a very different environment for scholarly and scientific research from that of a small college where undergraduate teaching is supposed to be the foremost and almost singular concern of the faculty. Light teaching loads, access to research funds, opportunities for counsel and collaboration, and other supportive elements that are common in a university setting help the individual placed there to increase his productivity. Quite simply, where one is employed is a matter of great importance, which makes one's social class of origin, where one went to graduate school, and the like of great importance.

Logan Wilson has observed that papers submitted from major universities look better to the editors because of the institutional prestige and authority behind them.[58] This assertion was probably as true in 1972 as it was in 1942, when it was made. Although not a great deal of evidence pertaining to this matter has been gathered, Crane has found that the academic characteristics of authors of articles selected for publication by scientific journals are similar to the academic characteristics of the journal's editors. The diversity in the academic affiliation of editors is related to the diversity in the academic affiliation of contributors, and the diversity in the doctoral origins of editors is related to the diversity in the doctoral origins of contributors.[59] On the basis of this, she concluded, as was stated in chapter 3, that "the evaluation of scientific articles [by scholarly journals] is affected to some degree by non-scientific factors."[60]

Moving on to what happens to work after it is published, Cole, who studied the citing practices of physicists, found that persons from the most prestigious departments made reference more to the research of others from the same types of departments than to the work of those from departments of lesser rank. The more eminent the physicist, the greater the probability that in his scientific papers he found the work of physicists at the most prestigious departments useful and ignored the work of physicists removed from centers of research.[61]

When the quality of the work was controlled, the rank of the department where a physicist was located made a substantial difference in citation patterns.[62] Research produced at undistinguished universities "is universally invisible,"[63] but when someone from these institutions is cited, it is at about the same rate by persons at both high- and low-ranked departments:

> If an obscure person has done something and then publishes it in an obscure journal, fewer people will look at it than if an outstanding person had done the same thing, because when people pick up a journal they scan the titles and look at the names of the authors . . . the work of certain authors will always be looked at. . . . It is also true that well-established people will have their work accepted quite readily, without too much refereeing.[64]

In addition to having a not insignificant influence on whether someone will become professionally productive and have his papers accepted for publication by leading journals, ascribed attributes also have some influence on whether someone will receive scientific recognition and honors. Where one teaches is closely related, not only to productivity but also to recognition.[65] In fact, Crane reports that "productivity did not make the scientist as visible to his colleagues in his discipline as did a position at a major university."[66] Academic affiliation with a major university is of such importance in obtaining recognition because "contacts with scientists outside his own university [which this provides] have the most effect on a scientist's chances for recognition."[67]

Such support might be necessary even to initiate a research program. The editor of *Science*, the official journal of the American Association for the Advancement of Science, writes:

> The system [of choosing men for review panels from eminent institutions] leads . . . almost inevitably to concentration of research support in a few institutions. A man of proved research productivity in a small school in the Middle West may submit an excellent proposal, but almost invariably his proposal will receive a rating below that of a comparable application originating at Harvard. . . . One group rated grants on the basis of a scale from one to five. The quality of applications originating from Harvard varied considerably, yet few if any were turned down, and

most received a rating between one and two. Proposals from less well-known schools received severe scrutiny, were often rejected, and seldom were given a rating better than two.[68]

Needless to say, the successful completion of one's research, particularly in the sciences, depends on adequate funding. All of this suggests an inescapable maze: who one is determines where one is, which determines how one's work is received, which determines where one is. It also suggests countless opportunities for some and dead-end careers for others.

Not unlike the case in chapters 3 and 4, the thrust of this chapter so far has been to suggest that the more closely one approximates what is held to be the model academic, the greater the probability of receiving more than one's fair share of amenities. Thus, those to whom the middle-class aptitude for articulateness and ready conviviality comes easily, those with the most estimable pedigree, those whose attitudes and behavior are moderate rather than in the extreme—in other words, those who are not disreputably distinguishable from others—can expect to be more readily accepted in academic circles than are others.

Perhaps the largest category of academics who stand out—whose ascribed status makes them different—are females.

ACADEMIC WOMEN

Females are not an insignificant minority in the academic world; though their proportion is only two-thirds of what it was at its peak in the 1930s, they are about one-fifth of those in university and college teaching,[69] being primarily situated in the latter. Although in the late 1960s and early 1970s considerable attention has been given to increasing this proportion, one study conducted by the American Council on Education revealed that between 1968 and 1972 their representation rose from 19.1 percent to only 20.0 percent.[70]

A great deal of evidence indicates that females are not evaluated in terms of merit, that something more than their competence is taken into account when they are candidates for a vacancy in a university. In Caplow and McGee's words:

Women scholars are not taken seriously and cannot look forward to a normal professional career.[71]

Women tend to be discriminated against in the academic profession, not because they have low prestige but because they are outside the prestige system entirely and for this reason are of no use to a department in future recruitment.[72]

This matter of the place of women in the academic world is now to be considered.

Females played essentially no part in the early history of higher learning in America. It was not until Georgia Female College was chartered in 1836, exactly two hundred years after the founding of Harvard, and Oberlin College became coeducational four years after its 1833 founding that it was possible for young women in the United States even to go beyond their somewhat spotty secondary education.[73] After the Civil War, the number of institutions of higher learning admitting women began to grow at a slow but appreciable rate.

Impediments to Becoming "Academic Men"

By World War I, the number of females enrolled in graduate school had begun to grow substantially, though their total enrollment was still half of that for males. For some years after World War II, the ratio of females to males earning master's and doctor's degrees began to decline; by the end of the decade of the 1950s it was two-thirds of what it had been in its peak years, and by the end of the 1960s it was still lower than it had been between 1920 and 1940.[74] By 1967, although only 30 percent of graduate and professional students were female, they received 36 percent of all master's and first professional degrees awarded in 1968.[75] This is no mean achievement if the following comments made by female graduate students about a range of problems they encountered at the University of California at Berkeley are at all typical.[76]

A reported interview from a social science department:

"I suppose you went to another college?"
    "I attended U.C., Berkeley."
"But you didn't finish?"
    "I was graduated with a B.A."
"Your grades weren't very good?"
    "I was named to Phi Beta Kappa in my junior
    year and was graduated *Summa cum laude*."
"You have to have 16 to 18 units of X. You don't have that, do you?"
    "As my transcript shows, I had 18 units of
    X, mostly A's, one or two B's."
"I'm going to disallow all 18, because they were so long ago. You understand that, don't you? There's no point in your trying to replace the undergraduate courses in order to qualify. You could not do it part-time; you would have to take 18 units in one year. Then you would probably

not get into graduate school. If you did you would meet so much hostility that I doubt if you could stay in. Most women do not finish their work, and we couldn't take a chance on you. We don't want women in the department anyway, and certainly not older women. This may be unfair to you in the light of your record, but we just are not going to chance it."

On being discouraged from entering:

My faculty adviser was, and said he was, very much prejudiced against women, and often advised me against graduate work. Besides the discouraging advice . . . my parents were told not to *allow* me to follow a science major! They were contacted privately and told they were very foolish to allow me to continue a major in physics or nuclear engineering because a woman would "never" be hired in these fields.

I was told "I'd never accept a woman graduate student unless she was unmarriageable," etc.

On being told scholarship is unfeminine:

I entered UC as a freshman and upon my first interview with an adviser, was advised that it was silly for a woman to be serious about a career, that the most satisfying job for a woman is that of wife and mother, etc. . . . The advice was repeated upon several later occasions. . . . Now that I'm in graduate school, I am reminded that I am a risk, that I shall probably get married and forget my training, this coming from faculty and advisers. . . ."

I was asked . . . in a formal interview, with two other professors present, whether I felt that my husband and I were competing intellectually. I'm sure he would not have asked such a personal question of a male student.

A professor in the life sciences informed a student that women don't belong in graduate school because they didn't use their education; another in the same department suggested that women are intellectually inferior to men. "Women have trouble with science" said another. An adviser in the physical sciences steered women away from a course that only men take, and another spent part of the first class period explaining why women shouldn't get Ph.D.'s.

A woman in the biological sciences was told that for the fieldwork for her dissertation she should do something in the LSB courtyard "because women can't go out in the field and do a study." He also suggested that women aren't capable of mental work on a par with men.

On being excluded from informal training:

> I received no help from faculty, other than that associated with courses, in securing a career. One faculty member even refused to review two manuscripts in his field when I asked where they should be sent for publication. I know that this was to the contrary regarding several males. Another told me that "women do not contribute," another that "women seeking Ph.D.'s must be personally disturbed."

On being denied support:

> In our department at least one professor cut off funds to a married student when she became pregnant, thus forcing her to TA and increasing the time it took her to finish. He said the reason for cutting off funds was that "you should be home caring for your family."

The quotations below, gathered "from various institutions" by Ann Sutherland Harris for her inquiry into the status of women in the academic world, would lead one to believe that the University of California at Berkeley is not at all atypical.[77]

> The admissions committee didn't do their job. There is not one good-looking girl in the entering class.

> No pretty girls ever come to talk to me.

> A pretty girl like you will certainly get married; why don't you stop with an M.A.?

> You're so cute. I can't see you as a professor of anything.

> Any woman who has got this far has got to be a kook. There are already too many women in this Department.

> How old are you anyway? Do you think that a girl like you could handle a job like this? You don't look like the academic type.

> Why don't you find a rich husband and give all this up?

> Our general admissions policy has been, if the body is warm and male, take it; if it's female, make sure it's an A from Bryn Mawr.

> Somehow I can never take women in this field seriously.

Jo Freeman collected other inimical remarks from the University of Chicago.[78]

They've been sending me too many women advisees. I've got to do something about that.

You have no business looking for work with a child that age.

I'm sorry you lost your fellowship. You're getting married aren't you?

I see the number of women entering this year has increased. I hope the quality has increased as well.

All of these statements may not only help explain why a higher percentage of women than men leave graduate school before completing their studies,[79] but they are also testimony that a large number of the mostly male faculty have different expectations—based on status and not ability—about the performance of male and female graduate students. Ann Heiss, who interviewed top administrators and faculty from ten prominent graduate universities, concluded:

> Not excluding academic qualifications, sex is probably the most discriminatory factor applied in the decision whether to admit an applicant to graduate school. It is almost a foregone conclusion that among American institutions women have greater difficulty being admitted to doctoral study and, if admitted, will have greater difficulty being accepted than will men. Department chairmen and faculty members frankly state that their main reason for ruling against women is "the probability that they will marry." Some continue to use this possibility as the rationale for withholding fellowships, awards, placement, and other recognition from women who are allowed to register for graduate work. . . .
>
>   In the interviews for this study several department chairmen volunteered the information that women are purposely screened out as Ph.D. prospects and as faculty members. For example, the chairman of a department of biochemistry mentioned that the men on his faculty had a pact in which they agreed "not even to look at applications from women. . . ." In another interview the chairman of a psychology department worried about "what would happen to the department next year" as a result of admitting seven female students in a class of twenty-five. The imponderable effect of the military draft on male students had impelled the department to cover the available slots.[80]

The Durable: A Pool of Talent

Gaining admission to graduate school is actually not the first point where females encounter prejudice in institutions of higher learning. It would seem that they are dissuaded from becoming students even earlier, although as the figures below indicate, to the degree that there is prejudice against women, it is probably greater at the graduate level than at the undergraduate level.[81]

Student category	Percentage of males	Percentage of females
High-school graduates who enter college	65–70	50–55
Entering freshmen with high-school grades of B+ or better	29	44
Bachelor degree recipients who go on to graduate school	44	29
College seniors with a grade average of B or better	35–40	43–48

There is also an obvious implication here that from the beginning the hurdles females face on the way to the doctorate are more arduous than those for males, and as a consequence, they may well be better qualified after completing their graduate training. There is, in fact, some evidence that this is the case.[82]

When Lindsey Harmon compared the high-school records of a sample of men and women who were awarded their Ph.D.'s between 1959 and 1962, he found that the women had had higher intelligence test scores as youngsters and had achieved better academic records in high school.[83] The differences between test scores of males and those of females were largest in physical science, which suggests that women with the motivation and persistence to become scientists would be exceptionally able. It is such facts that have led Bernard to observe that: "as a whole, the women who receive the doctor's degree are, no doubt because of the greater selectivity involved, superior insofar as test-intelligence is concerned to men who receive the doctor's degree."[84]

Discrimination in the Recruitment of Women

A great deal of evidence indicates that females, regardless of their capacity, have a more difficult time than males in finding an academic position: they are less likely than males to be hired by universities and are instead placed in the less desirable four- or two-year colleges, where teaching as opposed to research is emphasized. Even when all of their qualifications, such as degrees, experience, publications, and other accomplishments, are on a par with those of males, in the end they are less likely than males to be offered a position.[85]

According to Brown, in recruiting, the better universities ("the top decile schools") "draw 29.1 percent big publishers, 40.1 percent small publishers, and 30.8 percent non-publishers."[86] On the basis of these figures, given the publication rate of women, 12.7 percent of the faculty at these institutions would be expected to be female. Actually, however, Brown found that only 8.8 percent were female.[87] Not only do these select universities discriminate against women, but so also did the top 60 percent of the institutions in Brown's study; they hire "too few of them [women], even after accounting for their differential research productivity."[88]

At the University of California at Berkeley, where between 1966 and 1969 women made up 42.1 percent of undergraduates, 26.2 percent of the graduate students, and 12.4 percent of those who received doctoral degrees, they accounted for only 3.8 percent of the faculty.[89] This is a marked decrease from 6.0 percent in 1948–49, 9.3 percent in 1938–39, and 8.3 percent in 1928–29.[90]

Arie Lewin and Linda Duchan did a survey of the potential for discrimination that could affect hiring decisions of all 179 graduate departments of a physical science discipline.[91] They developed four versions of a standardized résumé in which the applicant was married with two children and had been an assistant professor for four years. The vitae were varied according to sex and professional accomplishments. The chairmen were asked to evaluate and to provide their overall impressions of and inclination to hire each applicant.

The results from the 111 departments which cooperated "showed a definite tendency for the chairmen to prefer the average male over the average female, but to recognize a superior woman."[92] Males were rated higher on educational background and were more often considered prospective candidates than females with identical résumés.[93] "The bias seems to hold especially for higher-quality schools, in departments with younger and newer chairmen, and for chairmen from schools located in the eastern and western parts of the country."[94]

On the basis of these results and of an analysis of the unsolicited comments that led to the hypothesis that different criteria "based on personal values and attitudes reflecting widely held socially accepted beliefs regarding the role of a woman in the family and the perceived difficulties regarding her compatibility with male colleagues"[95] are utilized in evaluating women competing for academic posts, Lewin and Duchan concluded that "when two equally qualified applicants are being considered for an academic position, a male would be chosen over a female."[96]

Career Advancement: Blocked Passage

When a female is employed in a university, it is generally in the lower ranks. She is seldom part of the tenured, senior faculty. In the academic year 1959-60, women totaled 9.9 percent of the professors, 17.5 percent of the associate professors, 21.7 percent of the assistant professors, and 29.3 percent of the instructors in four-year colleges and universities. And the efforts to fill out the vertex of this pyramid that began in the last years of the decade had not taken hold by the 1971–72 academic year, when the figures were 8.6, 14.6, 20.7, and 39.4, respectively.[97] In 1972, of the 4,470 tenured professors in seven Ivy League institutions plus the Massachusetts Institute of Technology only 151 were women.[98] The ratio of women to men is even more unfavorable at the level of full professor. For example, for the 1969–70 academic year no full professor at Harvard was a woman (except the holder of one chair endowed for a female).[99] It was reported in *Science* in 1972 that in major universities one in fifty full professors was a woman.[100] Over a period of close to seventy years, no woman junior appointee in six social science departments at the University of Chicago was advanced to the rank of full professor.[101] In the spring of 1969, 11 out of 475 full professors at the University of Chicago were women (and only 16 out of 217 associate professors were women).[102]

All of this is consistent with Helen Astin and Alan Bayer's conclusion, arrived at through complex and thorough statistical procedures that controlled "for a large number of variables that account for rank differences among academic personnel," that much of the differential between men and women with respect to academic rank

> could still be attributed solely to sex. Indeed . . . sex is a better predictor of rank than such factors as number of years since completion of education, number of years employed at present institution, or number of books published.[103]

> When a woman attains the doctorate from a prestigious institution and demonstrates great scholarly productivity, she still cannot expect promotion to a high rank as quickly as her male counterpart.[104]

When they are employed alongside males, female academics are discriminated against in assignments to key university committees, in appointments to administrative positions, in the speed at which they are promoted, and in the rate of remuneration.[105] Considering the question of their compensation in some detail, every study in which the salaries of males and females are compared has substantiated that females with the same rank and experience in the same or a comparable institution are paid less than males.

Unequal Pay for Equal Work

In the late 1960s, Bayer and Astin showed that female scientists earned less than male scientists, independent of field of specialization, employment setting, and academic rank.[106] At that time their median salary as a percentage of men's had decreased over the previous thir-

Table 5.2. Median Salary Differentials (in dollars)

Rank	Year				
	1967–68	1965–66	1963–64	1962–63	1959–60
Professor	1,400	1,125	1,450	1,900	1,275
Associate professor	500	750	775	1,050	700
Assistant professor	500	575	550	350	450
Instructor	500	400	400	525	300
Aggregate	1,200	1,550	1,400	1,275	1,050

SOURCE: Michael A. La Sorte, "Academic Women's Salaries: Equal Pay for Equal Work?" *Journal of Higher Education* 42 (April 1971): 269.

teen years by almost six percent, from 63.9 percent to 58.2 percent.[107] In 1971, Michael La Sorte summarized the overall situation:

the salary studies of the past two decades have shown discernible aggregate median and mean salary differentials between women and men academics. That this difference has persisted over a number of years is no longer debatable. What remains an issue, however, is whether the differential is a result of blatant sex discrimination against women academics or can be explained, in part or wholly, in terms of other factors.[108]

To shed light on this question, La Sorte undertook a comprehensive comparison of salary differentials of academic men and women from 1959 to 1968. He, of course, verified that very few females, regardless of professional status, make as much as their male counterparts.[109] Table 5.2 gives the figures by year and rank. Amplifying on these general disparities, La Sorte adduces two fine points. First, "men are rewarded above women regardless of whether they do research in addition to teaching or teaching only."[110] Second,

women teachers upon entering academia initially encounter a small salary inequity which then increases in size with the acquisition of high rank, tenure, and professional experience. Accordingly, the most academically qualified women, those of greatest value to the institution, over time fall progressively behind in salary.[111]

All of this admits to "no other interpretation than that women are being treated unfairly."[112] Or as another highly statistical analysis concluded:

To award women the same salary as men of similar rank, background, achievements, and work settings would require a compensatory *average raise* of more than $1,000 (1968–1969 standards). This is the amount of salary discrimination which is *not* attributable to discrimination in rank.

The amount of actual salary discrimination, attributable to discrimination in the types of institutions that employ women, the opportunities they are given for administration or research, and advancement patterns, would substantially increase this figure of $1,000.[113]

An analysis conducted for the Carnegie Commission on Higher Education which controlled for a number of variables (such as highest degree, number of years employed, professional activities, prestige of institutions with which one had been associated, number of publications)[114] shows that "residual salary differences were largest" in the most prestigious institutions (See table 5.3). It appears that the Women's Movement in the late 1960s to eliminate sex descrimination in institutions of higher learning had little impact in reducing the extent of this disparity. According to the Office of Education of the Department of Health, Education, and Welfare, females employed full-time in universities in 1972–73 earned on the average $3,500 less than their male counterparts, averaging $12,325, as compared with $15,829 a year. At the smaller two-year colleges the differential was smaller: $11,862, as compared with $12,889.[115]

Setting Aside Some Common Fictions and Half-Truths

The usual explanation for the relatively small proportion of females employed by universities is one or any combination of the following: females are less ambitious; females are less productive; females earn their advanced degrees later in life than males and can expect a more modest career; females are trained at less prestigious institutions than males; females are more casual about their careers, which is evident by the way they frequently interrupt them to have and raise families or move with their husbands. Yet, regardless of which way they are per-

Table 5. 3. Differences between Actual Salaries of Male and Female Faculty Members and Predicted Average Salaries, 1969

	Number of men (25% random sample)	Average differences for men (in dollars)	Number of women	Average differences for women (in dollars)
Research universities I	3,760	+ 2,729	2,649	− 2,009
Research universities II and other doctoral-granting universities I and II	3,151	+ 2,303	2,551	− 1,015
Comprehensive universities and colleges	985	+ 1,066	1,066	− 385

SOURCE: Carnegie Commission on Higher Education, *Opportunities for Women in Higher Education* (New York: McGraw-Hill, 1973), p. 116. Used with permission of McGraw-Hill Book Company.

muted, there is as much evidence to refute many of these propositions as there is to support them.

For example, Helen Astin's study of two thousand female doctorates almost ten years after completing their graduate training showed that 91 percent were employed; of these, 81 percent were working full-time, and 79 percent had worked continuously since beginning their careers. Those who took time out to raise children did so for a relatively short period—about fourteen months.[116] A second survey of almost the same number of females (1,764) three to nine years after receiving their doctorates found that 96 percent of the unmarried women were working full-time; 59 percent of the married women with children were working full-time, and almost 25 percent were working part-time. These figures are not as impressive as the 99 percent of the almost five hundred men also surveyed who were employed full-time,[117] but they should temper the exaggeration that "graduate training is wasted on women, most of them never find jobs, anyhow." Statistics gathered by the American Council on Education indicate that a higher percentage of men than women interrupt their careers.[118] To be sure, these data would not substantiate the contention that females are less professionally committed than males. We can better predict the turnover rate of a job by knowing its status than by knowing the gender of its holder: a part-time instructor will move from one position to another more frequently than will a full professor, regardless of sex.

On the matter of productivity the picture is somewhat mixed. Bernard believes that academic women

> tend to be less productive, as measured by published work, than academic men. When the major variables associated with productivity are held constant, however, the differential is reduced and academic position (college, university, or, in the case of scientists, laboratory) turns out to be a better predictor of productivity than sex.[119]

One national study of academics did show that 63 percent of the females in the sample had no publications, as compared with only 39 percent of the males, and that 11 percent of the males and only 2 percent of the females had twenty-one or more articles.[120]

In their examination of the research productivity of about fourteen hundred female Ph.D.'s employed full-time, Simon, Clark, and Galway found that "married women publish as much or more than men, and unmarried women publish slightly less than men. The differences on the whole are not great."[121] This, in spite of the fact that the research of women is not supported to the same extent as that of men:

Men are more likely to receive research grants than women (married and unmarried) in the social sciences and the humanities. In education there is no difference among any of the categories and in the natural sciences the proportions are about the same for unmarried women and men. Married women are less likely to receive grants.[122]

That the productivity of females, particularly those who are unmarried, is not what it might be could be a function, as is suggested by some of the remarks collected from the University of California at Berkeley and elsewhere, of the milieu in which female academics must work and their placement outside of normal networks of communication. As was pointed out in one report at which the publication rate of females was found to be somewhat less than expected:

> The relatively low productivity of Radcliffe Ph.D.'s can hardly be ascribed to their training as such. It is more likely to result from the environment in which they find themselves, the tradition of scholarship, the amount of time and facilities available for research and writing, the attitude of their colleagues and the college administration, and the material inducements to publish. . . . In many smaller colleges atmosphere and opportunity are much less conducive to research and publication. Relatively few Radcliffe women hold professorial status in large institutions where scholarly pursuits are inspired by faculty and demanded by competition.[123]

Obviously, it is the institution where one teaches and not one's sex that is most directly related to productivity. Since females primarily teach in colleges, their overall productivity would not be expected to be high. That it is as high as it is, is remarkable. As Bernard has noted, females in universities are more productive than males in colleges.[124]

It is almost a truism to state that those who do not have a number of students, colleagues, or mentors to call new ideas to their attention, those who are not consulted by others for advice and information, those who are not in correspondence with those on the frontiers of research, those who do not have friends in high and important places who might help them advance their careers, are not in the best position to know what is going on in their field. And as far as such factors are concerned, women are in a more disadvantaged position than men. Bernard reports that women are less likely to be invited to participate in situations—visiting appointments, editorial boards, professional panels, committees, and research teams—leading to opportunities for informal communications than were men.[125] To be sure, most academics can recall one or more examples of a scholar or scientist who thrived in his isolation. But for most, productivity is a function of one's position in the communication system in a discipline.[126] In any case, it would appear that if enough variables were controlled, differential productivity between males and females would be reduced to insignificance.

The Benign and Tractable Invisible Hand

Brown's explanation of why females are underrepresented on the faculties of universities and why they generally make out so poorly in all types of institutions of higher learning reflects much of the conventional wisdom that has only hindered the cause of academic women. In discussing his finding that "women's colleges, on the average, pay men $1,200 more than women . . . paying men 16.8 percent more than women," Brown contends:

> Evidently, women prefer to work in women's colleges, even at some sacrifice in salary.
> . . . Only part of the discrimination is employer-initiated. Just as the woman's preference for women's colleges means that she will receive less remuneration, so also does her preference for emphasis upon teaching. Much of the apparent discrimination against women appears to be self-imposed.[127]

Brown is in effect arguing that females are discriminated against partly out of choice. They wish to be concentrated in women's colleges and other low-prestige institutions where they have heavier teaching loads but are paid less than men.[128] This is also the consequence of what he calls "differentiation"—

> treating two persons who are equal "in the eyes of God" as unequals— because they are not equally productive. It is allowing the best player, regardless of religion or race, to represent the U.S. in Davis Cup competition. . . . It is paying more to the better qualified and more productive professor. It is justifiable inequality.[129]

Thus, it is understandable why

> women *are* treated unequally. They are paid lower salaries (at least to start) and given lower academic rank but are assigned heavier teaching loads. They fill disproportionately high percentages of the positions at the least prestigious schools and are underrepresented in the most prestigious ones. As a rule they have fewer alternative job options from which to choose.[130]

It is simply a case of people getting what they deserve. His data, after all, do show that the percentage of women in academic positions who have earned their Ph.D.'s is only half of the percentage for men.[131] Moreover, they appear to have considerably less interest in research, and the proportion of those with extensive bibliographies is one-third of that of men. Women also have less experience and are less often educated at the most prestigious schools.[132] Thus:

> To some degree the lower salaries paid to women professors, the lesser academic appointments in terms of both academic rank and institutional prestige, and the higher teaching loads reflect the fact that, on the average, women are not as qualified and as committed to an academic career as are men.[133]

As Brown sees it, because

> 88 percent of the women spend more time teaching than researching, women want to teach. Women are not subject to the same prestige motivations as men. . . . Women actually prefer to accept jobs in institutions that emphasize teaching and do not expect research.[134]

Not only are women paid less because their employers know that they are less professionally committed to their work, but "even when women are equally qualified the nature of the products they produce are not as prestige-giving to their employer."

> Women, with their emphasis upon teaching, are of more economic value to the poorer schools. The types of products that they would be asked to produce at the top-rated schools are not ones they desire, whereas the lower echelon schools which emphasize teaching are willing to pay more for their services.
> All of these arguments simply show that women should earn less because they are less productive. They do not indicate how much less.[135]

This reasoning might not be as pernicious as alleging that the poor are poor because they are lazy and shiftless; but it is as fatuous as holding that they are poor because they want to be poor—that after weighing alternatives such as the heavy tax burdens of the rich, this is the choice that each has made.

Finally, citing a study which showed that female teachers had more success with less able students than with brighter ones and that male teachers did better with superior students, Brown concludes that "since the poorer students tend to be located at the poorer schools, it may be desirable that women are there also."[136] The world is indeed very rationally ordered.

These interpretations of Brown have for the most part remained unchallenged,[137] and it would seem that too few academics are as perceptive as Nobel laureate James D. Watson, who in the final paragraph of his "personal account of the discovery of the structure of

DNA" has this to say about the most difficult individual with whom he had to deal during his tenure at Cambridge University:

> We both came to appreciate greatly her personal honesty and generosity, realizing years too late the struggles that the intelligent woman faces to be accepted by a scientific world which often regards women as mere diversions from serious thinking.[138]

However, the attribution of the unequal distribution of women between universities and colleges to preference is not a strictly masculine thesis. It is one of the four factors on which Jessie Bernard focuses in her consideration of the matter. Bernard believes that because universities "demand the man-of-knowledge" and women are not likely to fill this role (after all, how can a woman be a man?), they gravitate to college teaching.[139] "They may actually have preferred college positions, as some people apparently do. . . . many may even have a vocation for college teaching";[140] "they prefer teaching to research."[141] It would appear that such decisions are well-taken: "There is some evidence that both men and women who teach in the less productive institutions do, in fact, like their positions."[142]

It is difficult to determine whether it is bad will or bad science that compels someone to hold women themselves accountable for what are, compared with those of men, generally modest academic attainments. To be sure, blaming the victim is not an unusual phenomenon, nor is it uncommon for those who must endure suffering to agree with those who inflict it about its indispensability and utility. It is as pointless to impute motivation to those whose questionable conjectures are more harmful than beneficial to academic women as it was for them to conjecture. The cause of understanding why female academics do not reach the same eminence that male academics do is perhaps best served, not by invention, but by a more positivistic thrust. Thus, we will turn our attention once again to letters of recommendation to consider the type of endorsements female academics seeking their first appointment receive from the graduate faculty who have trained them. The sources of this material are a document published in the official newsletter of the Modern Language Association and the completed dossiers containing sixty-one letters for nine females completing their graduate studies at five universities (three of which are Ivy League).

Mistresses, Wives, Mothers

The Modern Language Association's Commission on the Status of Women examined an unspecified number of recommendations looking for depreciative remarks touching on the (1) physical attributes and personality, (2) marital status, and (3) activities in women's studies and the contemporary feminist movement of young female literary scholars. Here is the body of their report:[143]

> One young woman, for example, after completing numerous interviews and being offered no jobs was finally told by a frank department chairman that phrases in her dossier like feminine timidity and sweet, retiring nature suggested that she would be unable to survive in the competitive world of the university. Another young woman finally learned that being labeled intellectually assertive, aggressive—qualities appropriate to a male job applicant—had kept her from being granted interviews; male dominated hiring committees are prejudiced against hard-headed women. And still another discovered that a benevolent, protective adviser had simply indicated that this mother's place was in the home, or perhaps a high school, a conclusion that prospective employers readily accepted. . . .

> Physical appearance. Personality. Male dossiers do sometimes include phrases such as dresses well, poised, charming, but such language does not represent a tacit comment that what the male professor lacks in brains, he makes up in beauty. Our experience of women's dossiers confirms that a letter writer, often unselfconsciously, diminishes a female candidate's intellectual power by stereotyping her as too feminine, too pretty. These comments, a composite from a typical candidate's dossier, make a damning package: sweet, but not saccharine, quiet, unaggressive, shy, but very pretty, a decoration to the classroom. Another letter of recommendation from a prestige graduate school confirms the formula that males see social grace as a substitute for intellectual brilliance: "While ——— probably doesn't have the stamina for independent scholarly work, she loves big parties and mixes well."

> Women candidates, to win entire approval, have to be both chic and brilliant, and so the woman who is plain-looking, a spinster-scholar type, evokes a negative response for she is not a complete woman; she lacks sociability, and will not flatter the egos of male department members. Dossier after dossier divulges irrelevant, negative commentary: "——— is a large broad-boned somewhat awkward young woman who must be close to six feet in height"; her mousiness belies a sharp mind; "——— is . . . tall and proportioned like an Olympic swimmer"; she is a steady woman who will never marry. And within a single paragraph from a male at an elite graduate school, she has a "comfortably upholstered" person and personality, she performed "athletically" in a particular course, she would be the "wheel-horse" of any committee on which she served. And of an older woman, "if she has any faults, they are those that usually accompany the ambitious woman of her age." In other words, the rare comment on a male's appearance is simply a footnote, the frequent comment on a female's, a thesis statement.

> Dossiers betray a range of responses to the character of women candi-

dates from the outright misogyny exemplified above to subtle doubt of intellectual equality. The subtle doubts would appear to any good critic of texts. For example, figurative language praising men shows that the writer conceptualizes the candidate's course as active, linear, progressing through time—from lowly instructor to full professor, from fledgling writer to serious scholar, from small reputation to appropriate renown. The young male candidate has "talent," "drive," is "at the start of a long career," "will be on the move," will continue "to surpass himself," to advance; he is "a live wire," "dedicated, industrious, dynamic"; in the classroom his posture is "commanding"; his prose style is "energetic, vigorous." The young woman candidate is praised for being "cooperative, sensitive"; she has "warmth," "good manners," humor, and particularly "rapport with students." She may even be endowed with a "lively intellectual curiosity," and her writing style, if mentioned, is "lucid," "witty," "elegant," or "graceful"—"truly readable," one writer said. (Does that mean "light?") If *her* future career is under consideration, it is most often to be a "good" one. Letter writers rarely create the expectation of remarkable success so common in recommendations of men. While one would not judge the vocabulary used to praise men as connoting higher moral or ethical value than that praising women, given the values of the university world, the concern for professionalism, the emphasis on publication, the shape of a scholarly career, the qualities ascribed to the woman candidate have a seriously limiting psychological impact. Universities as well as many colleges desire candidates with the traditional commitment to career and profession. Until these values change, the stereotype of the woman candidate that emerges here has the effect of damning her with faint and delicate praise. Though the letter writer himself may clearly admire the personal, private virtues, the gentleness and the modesty he considers appropriately womanly, he himself would never designate these qualities as befitting the public, dignified role of college professor. Men writing recommendations see women as objects of regard, pleasing or otherwise, I mean objects to be regarded, looked at, as mistresses, as wives, as mothers; women are already tracked in their minds, and they simply track them for employers, reinforcing the vision of woman as helpmeet or playmate, not as intellectual equal and full human being.

Marital Status. Dossiers on women show two distinct patterns—overt discrimination against older women—married divorced, or single—especially those just entering the job market; second, an almost humorous, but revealing tendency of male letter writers to praise, contrast, describe the work of a female candidate's husband rather than her own, while in men's dossiers wives are rarely mentioned, except as social adornments. . . .

Thesis directors and graduate advisers often speak sensitively of their older female students—"Mrs. ——— though a woman and older should be as well received as a younger man," "Mrs. ——— has an adolescent son, knows how to treat teenagers"—virulent prejudice is revealed in the notes hiring and review committees append to dossiers under their scrutiny. Said one reviewer's note on an older woman "Woman named ———— . . . . Should direct mixed choral groups in Pinole." Let her run her household, not our department, said another. By contrast, the dossier of a forty-year-old man asserted that one should hire this man; his distinguished career record (army, public relations) "has been a better preparation for the university than uninterrupted schooling could have been. . . ."

The invisibility of the female job candidate emerges nowhere more unselfconsciously than in the dossiers of young, married graduate students. The dossiers of undeniably brilliant, serious, promising women, filled with letters of eminent advisers, very frequently compare the woman with her husband, stereotype her as the teacher not the scholar-thinker, and so the less valuable member of the couple. Indeed, one often wonders for whom the letter was written. One woman's letter contains this sentence: "Mrs. ————'s husband . . . is an excellent scholar, rather more disciplined and professional in his scholarship. Mrs. ———— compliments him with her more imaginative and enthusiastic . . . literary rather than historical perspective. . . . As in the case of her husband, I can recommend ———— without reservation. . . ." Or another begins: "———— and her very able husband ————" and continues, "like her husband, she. . . ." Such letters affect the reader by reinforcing his notion that a woman is an appendage, her career second to her husband's; her talents shine in the light of his. . . .

Antifeminism. Some dossiers provide a commentary on the extent to which the women's liberation movement and its academic component, women's studies, present a threat to the university. One recommender praises his candidate by saying: "If you want a woman who can compete with men on absolutely equal terms—but does not take kindly to letters from the Women's Liberation Front addressed 'Dear Woman'—then I recommend ————." Another, enjoying his wit, says she is "feminine indeed, but no feminist. . . ." Another, apologizing for his candidate's decision to write a thesis on nineteenth-century women novelists, claims she is "no fem lib type," but "a real gentlewoman"; that is, her feminism is safely confined to the scholarly. But even with these disclaimers, two prospective employers who read dossiers of women writing dissertations on women were disposed to ask, "Do we need all this feminism that she so militantly carries with her?" and to jeer, "Let's interview her and Ms. ———— [already in the department] can protect the working males." The message, confirmed by this year's reports from the job market, is "we must hire women, but no feminist *activists* need apply."

Very, Very Bright . . . But Quite Feminine

A reading of the supplementary and heretofore unanalyzed sixty-one letters of recommendation also written for and by scholars of English language and literature bears out the theme that sexism is pervasive among faculty but that much of it is surely unconscious. Otherwise, why would so many of these letters ostensibly written in support of candidates be studded with remarks that many of the same would find empty and perhaps insulting ("In person [she] is very attractive, managing to appear both mod and chic")? For a female nearly fifty years old: "I should add that she is a very good-looking and very charming woman." This for an honors graduate, Woodrow Wilson Fellow, and Fulbright Scholar who passed her oral examinations with distinction:

> [She] is the kind of person for whom one writes letters of recommendation with pleasure, satisfaction and extreme confidence. She is outstanding in almost every way. She is charming, pretty, considerate, modest, thoughtful, versatile, and intellectually acute.

> [A]nd in the less formal atmosphere of the coffee lounge she mixes easily and gracefully, making friends without effort and earning the respect of all.

These are not meant to be unfriendly observations. In fact, it might be that the zealously sexist male would probably not be inclined to sponsor a female and/or be less apt to make his true sentiments part of the not strictly confidential record.

What seemed to the Commission on the Status of Women to be more or less irrational animosity on the part of those who would be expected to be the benefactors of individuals beginning their careers makes a great deal of sense if it is considered in the larger context of the thesis advanced at the beginning of this chapter—and throughout the book: there are relatively clear standards among academics regarding what is acceptable or socially normal behavior, and those who in one way or another are not prototypal are less welcome as colleagues than are those who conform. Females who by virtue of their sex-related physical and behavioral characteristics are initially stigmatized as different are, regardless of competence, attractiveness, or commitment to the Women's Movement, not expected to trade aggressively on their strengths. This would serve only to make them anomalous, but not in a way that would bring credit to them or a department.

> She is a thoroughly professional grown-up young lady who knows what she can do and what she wants to do. She is self-confident and assured without the slightest touch of arrogance. . . .

> [W]ithout being aggressive she is inquiring and searching in the sort of questions she asks.

Very, very bright . . . but quite feminine. . . .

The most immediately striking thing about ———— is her physical beauty; she looks more like a Swedish starlet than a graduate student or what she is soon to be, a professor. It therefore took me some time to realize that behind [her] fair face is a keen, tough mind genuinely committed to the serious study of literature.

She is active without being an activist; she is concerned over the profession without being a blithering blatherskate boiling over with bile and boreal blight. . . . As one talks with her, however, her mind and personality are the things that loom large in one's consciousness not her physical generosity of construction. . . .
   No petulant or peevish peregrinator, she.

(It is worth mentioning that this alliteration is from a professor and the dean of the college at one of the leading universities on the West Coast.)
   By contrast, females are not supposed to be so passive that they would not be professorial.

[She] is a very attractive young lady, charming in a rather quiet and reserved way, and yet outgoing.

With the possible exception of her very soft speaking voice, I believe she has all the qualifications of being a good teacher.

As a teacher she will, I dare say, give an early impression of meekness, but her authority shows through very soon after first acquaintance.

The ideal female is somewhere between the hag and the narcissist, between a Gorgon and the Graces—always engaging, never mousy. The message here is not really outrageous: in academia, the focus of the conquest is nature and the unknown, not other people. What is remarkable and reprehensible is that this message is almost always conveyed when the individual under consideration is a female, less often when it is a male.

CONFORMING TO THE IDEAL

However, for the most part, the prejudice is against, not females per se, but the fact that they are unusual as academics; and, unless they greatly increase their representation on university faculties, by definition they will remain so. At present, they simply do not conform to very many people's conception of the typical university professor.

We have seen that any individual or category of individuals who deviates from the norm receives special attention, sometimes with a show of tolerance, sometimes with rigidity. As the final examples below from a matching set of twenty dossiers for young male literary scholars make clear, academics are expected to conform to an idealized image that the professoriate apparently hold of themselves or hope or believe is widespread throughout society—of someone who acts and looks as if he has what it takes to be on the side of truth, someone committed to tested and true ideas, not ideology.

In person and character [he] is friendly, big and bearlike, bearded and talkative, honest and frank without being edged.

Personally, [he] is tall, broad shouldered and somewhat rugged, though slender. He gives the impression of dignity and confidence. His voice is quiet but clear. He seemed to me steady and dependable in every way.

I was quickly attracted by his personality—a gentle and very perceptive spirit within a big bulk of a man, relaxed and alert like a handsome shepherd dog.

Personally he is an attractive man, tall athletic-looking and in fact (so I hear) a good basketball player.

[He is] a very short man . . . immature [and] precocious. . . . He is an energetic and ambitious personality, who expects to do well, and is ready to work at it.

If he has any handicap as a teacher, it is his small stature. He is slight in build and only five feet in height. Remembering the late John Livingston Lowes, who was I think even shorter . . . but, who was an enormously effective teacher, I think [he] can overcome this handicap. He has not Lowes' great force, but his own quick mind, confidence [etc.]. . . .

He has a rather high, unique voice range, which can be distracting until one gets used to it.

Personally, despite his beard, he is a thorough gentleman, without any signs of eccentricity or the rebellious spirit presently fashionable in certain academic quarters.

He is a very conventional man—and I *don't* mean stodgy. It's just that he really is profoundly interested in the rather old fashioned academic issues of renaissance scholarship and criticism, cuts his hair and wears neckies [sic], and worked systematically through his graduate requirements and exams on schedule and with very high marks.

Perhaps at this time when qualified Ph.D.'s are somewhat plentiful and calm campuses are not, personal qualities become more important than they have been in the past. His performance . . . is very much a part of his personal strength, and my description so far must convey some impression of his surprisingly well-balanced attitudes. . . . I believe that he is a whole and healthy person. . . .

During the T.A. [teaching assistant] strike he met and attended all his classes with the sense of loyalty and commitment which I expect of those who have a true sense of the meaning and importance of the intellectual life. As a mature member of a class containing younger students, he gave them an exemplary view of what it is like to be civilized though under thirty. I should emphasize, however, that he is not a reactionary; just decent middle-of-the-road. He has obviously been brought up to value and to use good manners and general civility.

He is a serious and competent young man, and I am confident he will never be seen leading any student demonstrations.

At present he leans towards a liberalism that sometimes seems extreme, but he is a thoroughly responsible person. . . .

These letters were written at the culmination of a half-dozen years of frenzied political activity on campuses across the nation. At that time, and perhaps at all times, there was something more plausible, professorial, and professional about a Gargantuan and almost noble specimen (presumptive evidence of a large brain?) than about a dwarf, barely able to reach the blackboard, spewing forth quasi-Marxian rhetoric in a falsetto voice. If nothing else, the former could work to reverse the influence of the countless freaks trading in mischief on soap boxes, swarming the halls of the student union so that it looks like a scene from a Fellini movie, pilfering the dean's office, operating the vegetarian co-op in collegetown, or teaching in the free university (without even a Master's degree!).

Beyond Calumny: Get Thee to a College

By now it is fairly evident that those within the academic mainstream are ambivalent about the individual with one or more qualities that cast him outside of it. The question seems to be one of determining how serious the latter are. Even when there are assurances that the puritan ethic has been well internalized, some uneasiness is evident.

Still, since the letter writer has an investment of emotion and time in and responsibility for the candidate, he must help him or her to secure an appointment. One way out of this paradox is to assist the applicant in finding a second-rate position. Apparently, this solution suggests itself to many writers. In slightly over half of the letters written for females, the candidate is commended to a teaching position, that is, to a college as opposed to a university.

[For a female with all A's in her 22 regular graduate courses (almost 90 hours) who had graduated Phi Beta Kappa from Radcliffe College] Altogether I recommend her quite strongly as a teacher.

[For a *magna cum laude*, Woodrow Wilson Fellow] Her work here has fulfilled and excelled every promise they made. . . . She will make an admirable and exciting teacher.

[For an honors graduate who was awarded a Danforth Fellowship] It is, especially, her qualities as teacher I am most sure of: she is lively, adventurous intellectually, warm. . . . [She] will certainly prove competent in the field and well-informed on the level of undergraduate teaching.

She should be an especially attractive candidate to any department emphasizing vital and effective teaching. . . . I expect the dissertation to be . . . the basis of a solid book.

She was clearly to be ranked with the best two or three students in the seminar. . . .
    I have not had an opportunity to observe her in the classroom. Some of my colleagues . . . will be able to speak to that topic. My guess is that . . . she would make a good teacher for lower-division students. . . .

Some comparative observations for males:

He has the temperament and qualifications for becoming a first-rate scholar-teacher.

I think that he will be an effective teacher, especially at the advanced undergraduate and graduate level, where his sophisticated knowledge and penchant for discussion will be most useful.

The implication of all of this is that, indeed, "women scholars are not taken seriously" and therefore are not matched with positions in the top universities. It is not so much a case of actual discrimination, although some persons contend that this occurs with some regularity:

In one interview I had, about 8 women and one man were interviewed for the job. The man got it. And I know positively that nearly all the

women, including myself, were better qualified for the job, better teachers, more conscientious, more interested in teaching, etc.[144]

Instead, what appears to be happening is that even before their professional debut females are tracked into colleges whence, as it should
now be abundantly clear, it is very difficult to commence a research
program that would make it possible to ascend to a university. Since
one's first position essentially sets the course for one's career, frequently the point is not reached where males in universities even have
an opportunity to discriminate against their female colleagues in promotions, the distribution of salary, and the granting of tenure.

ACHIEVEMENT AND ASCRIPTION: CONCLUDING REMARKS

If the principle of merit were as potent as it is alleged to be, then
there would have been considerably less evidence in the studies reviewed in this chapter signifying the influence of ascription on academic careers. For example, the fact cannot be overlooked that social
class affects the appointment process in prestigious universities both
indirectly and directly: the more modest one's class background, the
less the likelihood that one will attend one of the better institutions
from which similar institutions recruit. Leaving aside where someone
takes his degree, the more modest one's class background, the less the
likelihood that one will be recruited by one of the better institutions.
Since most senior positions are filled by promotions from within, initial
placement takes on added significance. And since the elite institutions
are also more likely to hire their own graduates and to exclude females
from their faculties, it would appear that in those institutions where
we would expect the most marked emphasis on achievement we find—
with the rejection of those outside the middle class, those with the
wrong credentials, and females—the least.

The system is less open than is generally acknowledged, and as a
consequence the access of some individuals "to the means of scientific
[and scholarly] production" is severely limited. In the most simple
terms, what is operating here can be called the Matthew effect: "For
unto every one that hath shall be given, and he shall have abundance;
but from him that hath not shall be taken away even that which he
hath."[145] With differential opportunities, cumulative advantages, and
"a basic inequity in the reward system that affects the careers of individual scientists [and scholars],"[146] the principle of merit cannot help
but recede into the background.

6

The
Bearing of
Merit
on Academic
Freedom

In the last chapter we considered a number of factors affecting the recruitment of faculty; in this chapter we turn our attention to some common problems attendant to holding onto an appointment. If academics were guided by the principle of merit, then it would follow that those who lose their posts do so primarily because they have been judged incompetent. However, it would seem that this is seldom the case. There is enough deadwood in every department on every campus that one cannot help but conclude that academics are quite willing to live with their mistakes—if they would even call them that. More important and to the point, there is a great deal of evidence that factors peripheral to the central functions of teaching and research intrude themselves in instances where individuals are forced out of a position. The consequences of this on the personal level are irregular careers for those who do not fit into the conventional mold and incessant and bitter disputes over the matter of academic freedom. Institutionally, it could insure the total eclipse of the principle of merit.

ACADEMIC-FREEDOM CASES, 1916–70

In an attempt to get a comprehensive picture of what conditions are antecedent to individuals being discharged from institutions of higher learning, those dismissals which were investigated by the American Association of University Professors and reported in their official publication were examined, from the first account in 1916 through 1970. It is the practice of the AAUP to publish the accounts of ad hoc committees established to investigate those cases in which persons who were precipitously dismissed felt so strongly about being wronged that they requested an inquiry and assistance from an independent body. A total of 217 cases—sixty-seven between 1916 and 1932 (World War I, pre-depression); forty-eight between 1933 and 1944 (depression, World War II); fifty between 1945 and 1962 (post–World War II, cold war); and fifty-two between 1963 and 1970 (campaigns in Southeast Asia and on campus)—were included in the sample.

These cases surely do not comprise a random sample of the totality of incidents in institutions of higher learning in which the services of individuals were involuntarily terminated. Those individuals who have patently violated some tenet of academic behavior or who have reached some accord with the institution so that the dismissal would not result in a loss of prestige for either party or develop into a cause célèbre are surely underrepresented. This latter arrangement is doubtlessly not uncommon, and most individuals who were conspicuously incompetent would be hidden by it.

The sample consists only of openly contested cases in which the dismissed person was confident enough about both the rightness of his cause and the justness of the system to appeal to the AAUP to intercede in his behalf. Although the incidents utilized are clearly atypical, we will proceed informed by the adage that "the nature of things can well be understood by the examination of extreme cases."[1] These reports are, so to speak, only the tip of the iceberg. In discussing some of these very cases, Walter P. Metzger has written:

> In 1934, it was estimated that for every case written up in the *Bulletin* of the Association, three were settled informally and quietly through mediation. . . . [I]t was estimated that only half of the non-mediated cases received a full-dress investigation. . . . As a consequence, too, the accounts of cases published in the *Bulletin* do not give an accurate picture of the state of academic affairs. On the one hand, they soften the outlines by presenting only a fraction of the abuses that come to the attention of the Association (mediated and non-pressed cases are presented only in statistical form). On the other hand, they make the picture too harsh by detailing only those cases that are not amenable to compromise or conciliation.[2]

There is no way of determining the number of instances in which flagrant violations of academic norms against individuals are not reported to the AAUP. An attempt was made to obtain other sets of data, but to no avail. For example, in answer to a request for any information, the New University Conference, an organization that socially active, younger scholars who had been unceremoniously fired might contact for assistance, wrote: "since we are a political organization and have difficulty in terms of black lists and the like, it is impossible to give you our files on dismissals." It was decided to make do with what could be found.

All published materials of the ad hoc committees which provided any information about the conditions leading to dismissal were utilized. Any information which was presumed to be apropos of the professional backgrounds of the persons fired, of the institutions in which they were employed, and of the circumstances surrounding the decisions to dismiss them was abstracted and coded. Since the presentations of the published accounts were not uniform, relevant data, particularly factual material about the complainant, are sometimes lacking.

Who Is Dismissed and Why

The investigation was concerned first with the sort of individuals who had been dismissed. Many who have studied the academic community are convinced that those who are forced out of positions are generally abrasive individuals whose academic and/or interpersonal skills are below par. For example, Logan Wilson has argued

> that not only are there in the objective situation pressures brought to bear on whoever has to make decisions concerning individual employees, but also that persons about whom such issues arise rather generally tend to be deviant individuals in their personal characteristics as well as their institutional behavior. In other words, they are more commonly than not 'difficult' people. It usually takes a combination of such personality traits with academic unorthodoxy to make a problem case. If an academician has the combination, he usually undergoes considerable inter-institutional mobility during his professional career; perhaps the most important factor in publicized cases is inept handling by the university president or executive responsible for his dismissal.[3]

This remark cannot be discounted as the singular point of view of an administrator (or aspiring administrator); it corresponds with the opinions of many others. Riesman, for example, notes: "doubtless most victims in cases of academic freedom are tactless, or disingenuous, or too ingenuous. . . ."[4] Again, when this research was being described to him, an officer in a chapter of the AAUP commented "You'll find there are always a few bastards who will make trouble for themselves, and for everyone else. These are [the ones] who push everyone to exasperation by not making themselves wanted in a place, and then ask for help to stay there."

It might be expected, then, that those who are troublemakers, and unfit to boot, would comprise a significant number of those who are asked or forced to resign from their positions, However, the composite of evidence used to rate all persons in the sample from "very good" to "poor" as teachers, as scholars, and in interpersonal relations does not support this supposition. First of all, there is nothing to indicate that the academic performance of those dismissed from institutions of higher learning is substandard—the principle of merit is just not involved. If anything, the data suggest the opposite conclusion: for the years between 1916 and 1962, only nine of the ninety-eight individuals for whom information was available were regarded as poor teachers, and not one of the ninety-seven for whom information was available was found wanting as a scholar. If it were truly the case—which it surely is not—that not one of such a large number of individuals was below par academically, then we would have an exemplar that the faculties of the best American universities would do well to emulate. It is likely that there were some hidden instances of incompetence in the 40 percent of the sample coded "not indicated" for each of the two measures of job reputation. This can be inferred from the fact that of all the reasons given by college and university officials for dismissing a person, 12.6 percent specified "incompetence," although this may simply reflect an attempt to give their actions a guise of legitimacy. There is the added possibility that the professors writing these reports did not stress the problem of incompetence in an effort to protect the reputation of the individual who had been discharged so as not to put his career in further jeopardy.

As far as interpersonal relations are concerned, one-fifth of the entire sample, nearly one-third of those for whom information was available, were involved in some conflict with students, colleagues, or administrators. Yet, the significance of this finding is unclear. First, there are no comparative figures available regarding conflict among faculty not involved in cases of dismissal. There is some reason to believe, however, that a smaller proportion of academic relationships are acrimonious. Second, the reputation of people whom Wilson would call "difficult" could have developed subsequent to the incident that terminated in dismissal or subsequent to the dismissal, particularly if it were vigorously protested. As Upton Sinclair pointed out over fifty years ago:

> Some spoil their chances by bad manners or bad judgment; and, of course, many others are accused of doing this. You will seldom find a fight over a question of academic freedom where there are not other

factors present or alleged, personal weaknesses or eccentricities. It is always easy to find defects in the characters and temperaments of persons whose ideas are offensive to us.[5]

A review of the cases of the turbulent period beginning in 1963 bears out these interpretations. From the total of fifty-two faculty members dismissed, only two were said to be below average in teaching ability, and only two others were reported to be poor scholars. With regard to reputation in interpersonal relations, only nine, or roughly 17 percent, were involved in continual strife. It is indeed doubtful whether those who are dismissed are lacking in basic academic skills or are so disruptive that they prevent their colleagues from performing their duties.

For the three early periods, it was possible to classify the reasons given for dismissal into four categories: (1) incompetence in discharging academic responsibilities; (2) problems in interpersonal relations or behavior (from being quarrelsome to being sexually immoral); (3) administrative necessity—insufficient budget, overstaffing; and (4)

Table 6.1. Reasons for Dismissal Given by Institution, 1916–62

	Period		
	1916–32 (N = 75)	1933–44 (N = 69)	1945–62 (N = 54)
Incompetence	5.3 (4)	24.6 (17)	7.4 (4)
Problems in interpersonal relations or behavior	58.7 (44)	31.9 (22)	33.3 (18)
Administrative necessity	14.7 (11)	26.1 (18)	11.1 (6)
Ideological position	21.3 (16)	17.4 (12)	48.1 (26)

Table 6.2. Reasons for Dismissal Given by Complainant, 1916–62

	Period		
	1916–32 (N = 52)	1933–44 (N = 61)	1945–62 (N = 39)
Incompetence	– (0)	– (0)	– (0)
Problems in interpersonal relations or behavior	59.6 (31)	39.3 (24)	38.5 (15)
Administrative necessity	7.7 (4)	32.8 (20)	5.1 (2)
Ideological position	32.7 (17)	27.9 (17)	56.4 (22)

radical ideological position on political, economic, moral, racial, or religious matters.

The reasons given by the institution and by the complainant were not treated together because it was anticipated that there would be marked discrepancies in how each viewed the dismissal. The two distributions are presented in tables 6.1 and 6.2. It should be noted that in any column the total number of reasons, and not the total number of persons, is given; for some no reasons were offered, for others there are two or more reasons.

There is a somewhat closer correspondence in the distributions than was expected. It is of some interest that the institutions supplied more motives for the dismissals than did the complainant. The fact that incompetence is put forth as an apparent cause twenty-five times by the institution but not once by the complainant—which is not surprising—would account for a little more than half of the excess number of reasons.

An incompatible (mostly leftist) political ideology (31), insufficient budget (23), dissension with superiors (27), and incompetence (25) are the four most common justifications given by the institution. They account for 60 percent of the total. Two of these, budget and incompetence, which account for about half, could make the dismissal seem justified. On the other hand, of the four reasons most commonly given by the complainant—dissension with superiors (52), inconsistent political ideology (29), insufficient budget (18), and a progressive religious ideology (17)—only the third, which was given in only 12 percent of the cases, would indicate that the dismissal was not in violation of fundamental collegial rights.

What is most noteworthy about tables 6.1 and 6.2 is how the distribution of apparent causes varies in the three time periods. In the first period, problems in interpersonal relations or behavior are the overwhelming cause in dismissals (probably reflecting social pressures in small and intimate academic communities); in the second period, that of the depression and World War II, more credible and more acceptable reasons—incompetence and administrative necessity (retrenchment and the like)—become more prominent; and in the third period, most actions center on the ideological position of the complainant. This last set includes some of the casualties of the systematic attempt in the 1950s to rid American institutions of higher learning of suspected subversives through loyalty oaths, disclaimer affidavits, certificates of allegiance, and pledges of patriotism.

The data for the first three time periods show that the percentage of full professors in the sample who were dismissed for problems in

Table 6.3. Average Number of Cases of Contested Dismissals, 1916–70

Period	Cases per year
1916–32	3.9
1933–44	4.0
1945–62	2.8
1963–66	4.5
1967–70	8.5

interpersonal relations or behavior is over one and a half times that for assistant or associate professors. That a smaller percentage of full professors than of assistant or associate professors were discharged for the ideology they subscribed to may be illustrative of the tendency to grow increasingly conservative with age and consequently to conform to the prevalent ideology. These findings, as will become apparent in the following section, refute the argument that persons who have tenure in institutions of higher learning are free to be more irksome or deviant than those who do not.

A careful examination of the dismissals for the years 1963–70 reveals several additional factors. A significantly larger number of cases was reported between 1967 and 1970 than in any other years; only eighteen cases were recorded between 1963 and 1966, whereas there were thirty-four cases between 1967 and 1970. While it is possible that this increase is either the result of more faculty submitting cases to be adjudicated or simply an increased number of faculty, it is most likely that it is a manifestation of developing faculty aggressiveness and a corresponding administrative response. In this regard, it is important to note that prior to 1966 campus unrest was sporadic and not broadly based; after 1966, both the frequency and the intensity of faculty, as well as student, activism increased.

Table 6.3 compares the average number of contested dismissals per year for the various time periods. Note how constant the figures are until the sharp rise in the number of cases per year for the 1967–70 period. It would appear that the security of academics was greater during the right-wing vigilantism of the 1950s than in more recent times. If one accepts the premise, for which support is given below, that larger social issues led to a redefinition of the relationship between faculty and administrators, then this increase in the number of contested dismissals may be seen as nothing more than an administrative solution to a challenge to the existing distribution of power within the university. As will become clearer, in recent years administrators have not been egged on by those outside the college or university to root out subversive elements. Accordingly, it would seem that they had

Table 6.4. Reasons Given for Dismissal, 1963–70 (N = 52)

	Period	
	1963–66	1967-70
By institution		
Incompetence	6	3
Interpersonal relations	1	6
Behavior	2	9
Administrative necessity	1	4
University governance—insubordination	0	17
Ideological position	12	15
Bureaucratic conflict	2	11
Uncooperativeness	1	0
By complainant		
Incompetence	0	2
Interpersonal relations	0	4
Behavior	1	4
Administrative necessity	0	0
University governance—insubordination	0	24
Ideological position	16	16
Bureaucratic conflict	2	5
Uncooperativeness	0	0

other reasons for unburdening themselves of unwanted persons, with the specter of a vengeful citizenry being raised when there was a real or imagined violation of some academic norm. Some of the issues affecting the wider society were merely reflected on the campus: established authority was being questioned and, feeling threatened, was reacting. Additional evidence bearing on this argument can be found in table 6.4.

As was noted earlier, since the university is subject to the same influences and pressures as the larger society, it was not unexpected that, given the pervasive paranoia among Americans generated by the growing economic and political power of some non-western European countries, the ideological position of faculty would continue to be a prime factor in dismissals during the 1960s. During the early years of the decade, most disputes centered on questions of race (particularly integration), nuclear war, and sex; after 1965, the same issues were involved, with general opposition to war focusing on Vietnam. In addition, involvement in public demonstrations became a particular matter of contention.

America's moral and military failure in Southeast Asia, the growing concern over the ever expanding catalog of social problems, and, most particularly, the expanding bureaucracy on campus not only aroused the typically indifferent undergraduate; it was a prelude to a new type of conflict and dismissal. From 1963 to 1966 there were no dismissals prompted primarily by conflicts relating to university governance or insubordination because there was little overt opposition to administrative policies and programs. From 1967 to 1970 institutions charged faculty members with insubordination (as it related to university governance) in nearly one-fifth of the cases, while faculty reported insubordination as the reason for their dismissal almost one-third of the time.

Thus, while holding an ideology somewhere off dead center has been a prominent factor in faculty dismissals since the end of World War II, after 1966 it often became linked to the question of university governance. In other words, in the early years of the cold war a faculty member might be dismissed for holding or expressing views counter to those prevailing in the larger society, but after 1966 what seemed to be a new phenomenon became conspicuous: the distinction between the purely philosophical radical and one who translates his philosophy into action and inevitably challenges the prepotency of administrators was informing more and more college and university officials.[6] When radical ideology was combined with active defiance of the administration's claim to power, dismissals resulted—a contingency practically nonexistent prior to 1967. It is important to note that in addition to the radical-activists who were done in, a handful of examples were found where practicing liberals, who unfortunately were persuaded that collegial norms mitigated relationships in the university, were dismissed for questioning what administrators had heretofore viewed as their prerogatives.

What is being reported for this period is not limited to a single geographic area or a particular type of institution. No specific region experienced either an appreciably greater number of contested cases or a notable increment after 1963. For example, the South and the Northeast each had fourteen cases. While the Northeast contains more institutions, the figures do not present a dramatic contrast when this is taken into account. However, as might be expected, faculty in the social sciences and the humanities had the highest dismissal rates; almost 80 percent of all faculty involved were from the soft disciplines. Finally, in contrast to the three earlier periods, junior faculty were slightly over-represented (and therefore slightly more vulnerable): of the fifty-two cases, 15 percent were instructors, 39 percent were assistant professors, 27 percent were associate professors (some with term contracts), and only 15 percent were full professors.

The Shield of Seniority

As far as the general question of academic rank is concerned, the data for the first three time periods show that for the 106 individuals whose rank could be ascertained only six full professors (11 percent) had any history of controversy with the administration, an indication that they were not particularly quarrelsome. Moreover, in only eleven (20 percent) of the cases involving full professors had the controversy which resulted in the dismissal extended six months or longer. The corresponding figures for assistant and associate professors were four (14 percent) and seven (32 percent), respectively.

As previously suggested, there is simply no evidence that full professors are allowed greater latitude than assistant or associate professors before being held accountable for their behavior. Intractableness in a full professor is, of course, more of a problem to an institution than intractableness in an associate or assistant professor. Since virtually all full professors have tenure, it is more difficult to fire them than those in lower ranks. The promise of promotion or the threat of withholding it may effectively control a recalcitrant assistant or associate professor, while the full professor need not concern himself with either question. Unruly professors can be dealt with only by isolation or removal. The former is perhaps most successfully applied to an individual who slowly drifts away from his colleagues and whose actions become even more enigmatic. Since the type of conflict in which the persons in this sample were involved typically was of short duration, apparently no procedures by which to handle it developed. Consequently, it is not surprising that there was a conspicuous use of the technique of dismissal.

Not only do these minimal differences among ranks, as far as the duration of the conflict is concerned, vitiate the notion that the full professor is freer to be contentious; they also invalidate the belief that full professors may become surly because of advancing age, a false feeling of security, or ennui. In only a few instances was there any evidence that a full professor's dismissal was the unforeseen and direct result of his chronic acerbity.

In fact, it is somewhat bewildering that under the alleged circumstances full professors were not more disagreeable than they appear to have been. Thirty-four (61 percent) reported that their superiors acted in an authoritarian manner (were arbitrary and capricious) and harassed them. Only seven (25 percent) assistant professors and six (27 percent) associate professors made the same charge. Although at first glance this finding seems surprising, it is an affirmation of the observation of Caplow and McGee that a senior "professor can . . . be seriously harassed . . . toward the end of his career. . . ."[7] Such a denouement often follows "the rapid loss of bargaining power, personal influence, and independence which occurs near the midpoint of the normal academic career, as the professor loses the potential mobility which gave him some defense against local pressures."[8] Perhaps some of the full professors in this sample were victims of this phenomenon.

Still, full professors are not as vulnerable to the vagaries of an antagonistic superior as assistant or associate professors are. First of all, they have tenure, which, although not a guarantee of job permanency—a reservation to which many in this sample would certainly attest—is an achieved right not casually violated by college and university administrators. To do so might create a reaction among others with tenure (and those allies which any professor routinely acquires after years of service at a college or university). Furthermore, the greater prestige of full professors, compared with that of assistant or associate professors, serves as a deterrent to high-handed administrative behavior. In addition, administrators may hesitate to take action against a full professor if they have reason to believe that, fearing the difficulty of finding another position, he will actively resist any attempt to discharge him. Hence in all likelihood it would take a greater impetus to compel an administrator to dismiss a full professor than it would to compel him to dismiss an assistant or associate professor.

A close examination of these 106 individuals of the first three periods whose rank was known was made to determine the percentage of persons in each academic rank on whom pressure to resign was brought to bear by the central administration, the regents or trustees, or others not officially connected with the university. Obviously, one would predict that there would be decreasing pressure from the first locus of power to the third. This holds true in the cases of assistant and associate professors. In the case of the full professor, however, the regents or trustees exert more pressure than the central administration; and although the number of cases involving community pressure is considerably smaller than the number involving pressure from the administration or the regents, it is high compared with the incidence for the two lower academic ranks.

It seems clear that the administrative superiors of full professors must draw on a number of resources in order to discharge them. This does not necessarily mean, however, that more of such dismissals originate outside the college or university than within it. A number of instances were found in which an officer in the college or university went to an alumnus or politician to initiate action leading to a professor's dismissal, thus removing the onus from the institution. It is only when an academic outrageously violates public morality that concerted forces outside the college or university act without a concomitant movement from within the institution.

It was found that a number of levels in the power hierarchy of a college or university—the department, the dean, the central administration, and the governing board—play more than a perfunctory part in effecting most dismissals. Of course, it takes less concerted action to remove an assistant professor than it does to remove a full professor. The sorts of people involved in finally removing both associate and full professors are quite similar, which merely reflects the fact that most individuals in these two ranks have tenure.

In sum, it would seem that full professors are safer than assistant or associate professors from the effects of the decisions of their superiors, although the needs of the institution as perceived by administrators may perhaps be more responsible for this than the needs of individual academics. Veblen noted over fifty years ago that "so far as popular esteem is a truthful index of scientific achievement, the proposition holds, that scientists [or scholars] who have done great things have a business value to the captain of erudition as a means of advancing the university's prestige. . . ."[9] And since it is probable that the full professor has achieved more renown as a scientist or scholar than the assistant or associate professor, "it is not an easy or a graceful matter for a businesslike executive to get rid of any undecorative or indecorous scientist [or scholar]. . . ."[10] This is perhaps because

> whatever expedients of decorative real-estate, spectacular pageantry, bureaucratic magnificence, elusive statistics, vocational training, genteel solemnities and sweat-shop instruction, may be imposed by the exigencies of a competitive business policy, the university is after all a seat of learning, devoted to the cult of idle curiosity,—otherwise called the scientific spirit. And stultification, broad and final, waits on any university directorate that shall dare to avow any other end as its objective.[11]

This bodes well for the full professor.

Sources and Amount of Pressure

Moving from comparisons between ranks to those between periods, when one considers the source of pressure and the amount applied to the complainant, additional evidence relating to the broader authority-subordination question comes to light. An attempt was first made to

Table 6.5. Sources and Amount of Pressure Precipitating Dismissal, 1916–62

Period	Amount of pressure	Central administration		Regents or trustees		Community and others outside the institution	
		%	N	%	N	%	N
1916–32							
	A great deal	19.4	(13)	26.9	(18)	14.9	(10)
	Some or not very much	49.3	(33)	43.3	(29)	34.3	(23)
1933–44							
	A great deal	31.3	(15)	25.0	(12)	2.1	(1)
	Some or not very much	56.3	(27)	66.7	(32)	56.3	(27)
1945–62							
	A great deal	44.0	(22)	56.0	(28)	18.0	(9)
	Some or not very much	20.0	(10)	28.0	(14)	52.0	(26)

determine whether any of the four levels of the college or university where policy might be made had become more or less actively involved in these matters over the years. The data do not reveal any notable changes. The proportional number of cases affected by each level—the department, 8 percent; the division or college, 23 percent; the central administration, 78 percent; and the trustees or regents, 80 percent—remained constant for the first three time periods.

Looking next at the three sources of pressure that could bring about action forcing a dismissal—the central administration, the regents or trustees, and the community and others outside of the university—the pattern is somewhat obscure. Pressure from within the institution was most evident during the second period, when the need to run the schools economically was most pressing; and pressure from outside the institution was greatest during the third period, when institutions were most sensitive to the community's concern that their faculties not undermine the faith of young people in the American political and economic systems.

However, if one looks, in table 6.5, at the intensity of pressure that is applied by these three sources, it becomes clear that there are true differences among the first three periods. It is of special significance that the intensity of pressure from the central administration and regents or trustees dramatically changed over the years. In the third period a considerably larger percentage of both exerted a great deal of pressure to have dissident faculty removed. This would indicate that

Table 6.6. Sources and Amount of Pressure Precipitating Dismissal, 1963–70

| | Sources of pressure | | | | |
Amount	Depart-ment	Admin-istration	Trustees	Commu-nity	Legis-lature
1963–66					
A great deal	0	8	7	3	2
Some	0	8	1	0	0
Subtotal	0	16	8	3	2
1967–70					
A great deal	2	18	15	3	1
Some	0	15	0	0	0
Subtotal	2	33	15	3	1
Total	2	49	23	6	3

up to the time of the outbreak of campus unrest in the early 1960s the central administration and governing boards were taking an increasingly active role in academic policy decisions that directly affected faculty.

It can be seen from table 6.6 that between 1963 and 1970 the source of most pressure, once again, was internal, with the administration applying pressure in essentially every case and manifesting considerable determination, as often as not, to rid themselves of unwanted faculty. These additional data bear out the thesis that there has been an intra-institutional struggle in recent years.

Although the years 1967–70 saw added pressure from the central administration, it is worth noting that the incidence of trustee intervention in the dismissals also rose. Since nearly all cases saw the trustees and the administration on one side of the dispute and the faculty on the other, it would appear that the former worked in concert to maintain the status quo. This is a marked departure from the expectation that one of the primary functions of administrators is to protect faculty from the unordained or unsympathetic laity. Finally, the incidences of community intervention in the affairs of the institution did not increase during the latter part of the 1960s; even trustees were not inclined to meddle unless it was clear that administrators expected them to do so. This finding runs counter to the popular notion that repressive forces outside the academic community mobilized to squelch antiwar sentiment and campus unrest.[12] At least for the cases in this sample, interest in the internal affairs of the university by a legion of fervid reactionaries remained relatively constant during the 1960s. It could be that in countless unreported instances administrators moved in to protect faculty from such assaults, or it may be that individuals involved in this sort of discord are going directly to the courts or to organizations such as the New University Conference and bypassing the AAUP. If either of these suppositions is valid, it is most likely the latter.

Between 1963 and 1970, 53 percent of the dismissals in which the administration was active were accompanied by a great deal of pressure. Thus, we see that the amount of pressure being applied by administrators in each period has steadily grown—from 19 percent to 31 and 44 percent to the 53 percent figure. It is possible that this constant increase in part also reflects more edginess on the part of administrators. Following this line of thinking, one can see (table 6.4) that as pressure in the 1960s intensified and the reasons for dismissal focused on the issue of governance, more reasons were offered to justify each incident. This may be but another example of the administration attempting to bolster its position; when it was simply a matter of getting rid of a fellow traveler, as it had been for the previous twenty years, less pressure and fewer reasons were brought forth to explain a dismissal—the insinuation that someone was un-American was quite enough.

THE COMMANDING ROLE OF ADMINISTRATORS

Thus, a review of over two hundred contested dismissals from 1916 to 1970 reveals that faculty may play an insignificant role in determining who is finally purged from the academic community. These decisions seem to rest with administrators, who appear to be interested in questions other than merit.[13] It is possible that the expanding role of academic-administrators may be due to the greater size and complexity of many contemporary institutions; however, the data here indicate that more than mere physical growth is involved.

The ideological position of faculty has been the central bone of contention in these disputes since World War II (in only 13 of the 217 dismissals was there even a suggestion of incompetence in either teaching or research) a consequence, no doubt, of the growing interrelationship between the larger society, especially what is commonly referred to as the military-industrial complex, and academic institutions. While the importance of political ideology has remained relatively constant during these years, the question of university governance has become increasingly important. Since none of the cases analyzed here indicated that questions relating to students were central to any controversy, it is reasonable to conclude that conflicts resulting in the unplanned exodus of those who have annoyed someone whom they should not have annoyed are generally limited to disputes between faculty and administrators, although the spate of suspensions of student activists in the early 1970s would indicate that they too were beginning to get on some people's nerves.

Governing boards have never been reluctant to intercede in intramural affairs. The data show, for example, that they were primarily responsible for initiating 52, or 31.5 percent, of the 165 dismissals in the first three periods. Further, in other instances when the conflict was between the central administration and a faculty member or, more rarely, between two faculty members, they were quite willing to assume an active part in the controversy, most of the time supporting the position taken by the administration. Robert MacIver's observation that in some institutions "the governing board is still ready to think of the faculty members as its employees, its hired men"[14] is probably generally correct.

What MacIver meant is epitomized in the behavior of a regent from one of the schools from which an individual in the sample had been discharged in the 1950s for simply voicing disagreement with the administration over a relatively minor matter. At a reception after a meeting of the local chapter of the American Association of University Professors in 1960, the regent told three young psychologists that if they or "the staff didn't like it [the University's policy on salary] they could leave, as the University could always find others to replace them." The following year he insisted that the political science department hire for an academic position someone who had had only one year of college training and had been prematurely retired from the State Department for his affiliation with politically conservative groups. Subsequent to this, he initiated action to have promoted to a deanship a psychologist who was employed part-time (moonlighting) at the state mental hospital. What is striking is, not that this was done, but that it was done openly and that the regent felt that it was proper.

A trustee of Harvard University remarked in 1954: "The men who become full members of the faculty are not in substance our employees. They are not our agents. They are not our representatives. They are a fellowship of independent scholars answerable to us only for academic integrity."[15] However, ten years later the chairman of the trustees of a state university said in discussing the vacancy of a university president: "I wouldn't send an academician to do it . . . you get it [money to run a university] by a fellow who knows how to marshal arguments."[16] Yet, strangely enough, there did not seem to be a flood tide of outside intervention by governing boards or anyone else during the turbulence of the 1960s. In spite of the activities of campus militants and the corresponding reaction by the more conservative elements in society, there is little evidence to suggest malevolent repression of faculty. There is also no reason to suppose that administrators are doing the dirty work of either trustees or the Yahoos. If anything, most people in the atomized and autonomous society do not really know or care about the state of affairs within institutions of higher learning as long as the semblance of peace and order is maintained (and their children and other kinfolk can gain admission). Having fewer constraints on them in the most recent past, administrators seem almost intent on suppressing any and all opposition.

The combination of ideological position and university governance as the dominant theme in the late 1960s suggests that a distinction had begun to be made between what might be called a safe radical and one who was perceived as a threat to the power structure within the university. A faculty member who was opposed to the country's policies in Southeast Asia, who supported civil rights movements, or who had liberal attitudes toward sex was more likely to suffer recriminations prior to 1966 than after. In the absence of any widespread notoriety, such preoccupations had become defined as extraneous to the academic-administrator's dominion. If in the later period these views were part of a more general philosophy that went beyond specific issues and raised questions about the existing distribution of institutional power, then conflict was likely to result. Thus, the campus in recent years might then be seen as an arena where some faculty were challenging administrative supremacy. The identification of some of the most celebrated and vocal old-guard and old-left professoriate with the administration's side on most questions has served to veil the struggle, and their collaboration may partially explain the disproportionately high dismissal rate among junior faculty that has accelerated and continued into the 1970s.

Academic-administrators have been able to defend their position vis-à-vis students by combining token concessions with outright force. They have not been as successful with faculty. This does not mean that the faculty have effectively restructured the university. Nevertheless, there is no evidence to indicate that the struggle is abating, so that in the unlikely event that the university is transformed during the 1970s, faculty will be in the ascendance, not students. There is little to suggest that administrators are going to be easily divested of their power. Administrators, even though they are former academics, do not have an impressive record of protecting academic freedom. To the contrary, the evidence suggests that in the face of opposition they will sacrifice academic freedom to retain their power.

Between 1963 and 1970 only one-third of the institutions involved in disputes concerning academic freedom had an established faculty grievance procedure; an even smaller percentage afforded the complainants due process. In most cases, administrators operate from the premise that institutional needs take precedence over those of the individual. Questions of governance can easily be interpreted as a threat to institutional stability. As a consequence, the academic who has had a brush with a dean or one of the countless vice presidents who have colonized the American campus may be in more danger than if he harbored extreme views on more general social or philosophical issues.

Needless to say, administrative high-handedness is not a simple *trahison des clercs* or even a recent phenomenon. From the infancy of the colonial colleges up until the years between the two world wars, an institution's president and his deputies had firm control over both academic and nonacademic affairs. Veblen's "captain of erudition," marked, like the businessman, by "quietism, caution, compromise, collusion, and chicane,"[17] in addition to an abundant ego and brimming arrogance, is probably more unbearable as far as most faculty are concerned than the contemporary "Pragmatist" and "outgoing activist and analytical problem-solver," as Kingman Brewster of Yale University has been described.[18] No administrator today would talk to faculty as William Rainey Harper of the University of Chicago or Nicholas Murray Butler of Columbia University did in the days before the AAUP was founded:

> Your speech . . . has caused me a great deal of annoyance. It is hardly safe for me to venture into any of the Chicago clubs. I am pounced upon from all sides. . . .[19]

> So soon, however, as the nation spoke by the Congress and by the President, declaring that it would volunteer as one man for the protection and defense of civil liberty and self-government, conditions sharply changed. What had been tolerated before becomes intolerable now. What had been wrongheadedness was now sedition. What had been folly was now treason.[20]

As a study for the Carnegie Commission on Higher Education revealed, in the age of the multiversity there is typically more emphasis among administrators on "conflict management."[21] The successful administrator "efficiently and effectively" does what needs to be done to insure institutional survival: a comprehensive set of rules can be framed to restrain those who would threaten what any sensible person would agree are legitimate ends.

The increasing size and complexity of institutions of higher learning and the concomitant development of a bureaucratic organization at the expense of the traditional collegial organization has created a situation which surely must account for some of the greater control of academic matters by the central administration, and to a lesser extent governing boards, in recent years. The potential power generated as the structure of institutions grew and changed was not secured by the faculty and consequently fell into the lap of others. This fact, coupled with the belief that since a larger proportion of the population are becoming committed to higher education, the public should become more active in guiding activities within institutions of higher learning has led most to accept the idea that colleges and universities should not necessarily be governed by their faculties. It has even been suggested that a faculty-controlled institution would be a form of pure syndicalism not found elsewhere in American society (and would, therefore, be un-American).

Lazarsfeld and Thielens have written that "the professional pride of the college administrator" will give his actions "autonomy," so that he will be unwilling "to sacrifice good teachers in the interests of possibly temporary cycles in ideological mood."[22] This might only be wishful thinking, however, as it assumes that college administrators value the norm of academic freedom. It might be well to consider Veblen's comment that "as competitors for the good will of the unlettered patrons of learning the university directorates are constrained to keep this need of a reputable notoriety [publicity] constantly in mind. . . ."[23] Quite simply, the desire not to offend the public at large may be one of the overriding considerations in the management of institutions of higher learning. We would agree with MacIver that "since the twenties there have been increased manifestations of a tendency in the universities to adopt the same predominantly utilitarian attitude toward knowledge that pervades the country as a whole."[24] This combination of the concern with maintaining a proper image and the proclivity toward pragmatism does not appear to be conducive to an atmosphere in which academic freedom would be able to flourish if it were put under attack.

ACADEMIC FREEDOM: SOME PERSPECTIVES

The ideal of academic freedom, which presumedly frees each person dispassionately to search out the truth, has been in force in American institutions of higher learning only since the early 1900s. Those who have advanced this concept have held that nothing other than scholarly standards, conscience, and the obligation not to interfere with the freedom of others should impede the scholar in pursuing his career. There is an assumption that those who plod along unbeaten paths may appear unreasonable or disloyal and will need distinctive and explicit protection for holding or expressing unconventional ideas.[25] Yet, perhaps because it has a relatively short history in American institutions of higher learning, the commitment to academic freedom by faculty is clearly limited, and for this reason it is especially vulnerable.

For only a little more than one hundred years has it been generally recognized that the faculties of American universities need freedom of activity and expression if they are satisfactorily to perform the dual function of creating and transmitting knowledge.[26] This notion of academic freedom "has been developed by men who have absorbed analogous ideas from the larger life of society."[27] Unfortunately, however, this does not seem to include most faculty, although it is widely believed that they all hold academic freedom dearly; it is generally assumed that, even though faculty may be menaced by administrators and trustees, they are committed to creating an environment in which academic freedom can flourish. The survey of faculty considered below suggests that the tenuous hold of academic freedom stems as much from a lack of support by faculty as from assaults by administrators and governing boards.

The data upon which this brief section is based are from questionnaire responses from the faculty of a northeastern American state university. In the fall of 1964, a questionnaire was mailed to the entire full-time faculty of this rapidly growing, urban university. Five hundred and thirteen, or 56 percent, of the 915 faculty in residence completed and returned the questionnaire.[28] The institution from which the sample was obtained had an enrollment of over ten thousand full-time day students. It offered degrees to undergraduate, graduate, and professional students in as many fields as the typical state university, with the exception that it had no school of agriculture.

The respondents were asked a series of questions about three facets of academic freedom: adherence to its principles, the wisdom of its being practiced, and how resolutely and under what conditions (for example, if a religious, economic, political, or moral issue were in question) it should be defended. In all, there were twelve items on which the respondents were to indicate their degree of support. For each item respondents were divided according to whether they firmly supported academic freedom or gave it qualified support. The distributions on all items by discipline are shown in table 6.7.

The first noteworthy datum in table 6.7 is the finding that there is

Table 6.7. Support of Academic Freedom, by Disciplines

	Behavioral and social sciences (N = 112)	Humanities (N = 66)	Physical and life sciences (N = 143)	Professional (N = 140)
Adherence to principles of academic freedom—percentage who strongly agree that a faculty member should be free . . .				
To investigate any subject	80.4	86.4	64.3	50.0
To make known the results of his research	83.0	78.8	66.4	52.9
To take part in any public controversy	77.7	81.8	56.6	50.0
From repressive measures that could result from opposing powerful interests or jostling established prejudices	67.9	75.8	48.3	42.1
Belief in the practice of academic freedom—percentage who feel that a professor who can defend his position should definitely argue in the classroom for a change in the following American policies . . .				
Nonrecognition of Red China	54.5	50.0	30.8	28.6
Continuation of the arms race	55.4	51.5	32.2	29.3
Private ownership of public utilities	55.4	48.5	34.3	27.9
Belief that academic freedom should be defended—percentage who believe a university should defend persons who espouse a controversal view regarding . . .				
Contemporary religion	61.6	59.1	37.8	29.3
Injustices in the tax system	63.4	62.1	35.7	30.7
Socialized medicine	67.9	65.2	37.8	32.9
American foreign policy toward Cuba	58.0	59.1	28.0	25.7
Sexual behavior of adolescents	49.1	45.5	21.0	24.3

little unqualified commitment to academic freedom among the respondents as a whole. This does not mean, however, that in general faculty do not support some form of academic freedom; on the twelve items the expression of favorable sentiment ranged from a low of significantly less than 50 percent (espousing a controversial view regarding adolescent sexual behavior) to a high of about twice this proportion (being free to make known the results of research).

The finding that there is a general lack of support for academic freedom is due, of course, to the relatively small number in the professional disciplines and, to a lesser degree, in the physical and life sciences who unequivocally subscribe to it. Second, all four items on which over half of the faculty definitely approve of academic freedom reflect a belief in its principles and not in its practice. Also of some interest are the obvious and consistent differences between those in the behavioral and social sciences and the humanities, on the one hand, and those in the physical and life sciences and the professional disciplines, on the other hand; for eleven of the twelve questions, those faculty who consider themselves to be professional are least likely to sanction academic freedom.

The differences observed in table 6.7 are of additional interest because they bear on conclusions of Lazarsfeld and Thielens that pertain to the degree to which liberalism has permeated American institutions of higher learning. On the basis of their sample of social scientists, Lazarsfeld and Thielens characterized the academic milieu as permissive,[29] an environment in which individuals "were interested in new ideas themselves and tolerant toward people who held unorthodox views."[30] Yet, because the climates of opinion among academics in various disciplines are so dissimilar, the value of such a generalization is obviously limited.

Commentary and Clarifications

The diversity of opinion regarding the extent to which faculty are thought to be responsible to ideas rather than to men or institutions is also evident in the marginal commentary of many respondents. Aside from what the content of the remarks revealed, it was found that most comments were volunteered from those persons in the behavioral and social sciences and the humanities who strongly favored academic freedom and those persons in the physical and life sciences and professional disciplines who strongly opposed academic freedom. Both categories of respondents were taking the view accepted by most of their colleagues and were simply elaborating on this for the researcher. That is, they apparently did not consider themselves at bay but were matter-of-factly replying to what they saw as a gratuitous series of questions. The statements were overwhelmingly circumspect; persons did not appear to be anxiously trying to defend what they might suspect to be an untenable position but seemed instead to be prudently clarifying self-evident conclusions. Even the elucidations of those who took polar positions with regard to a commitment to academic freedom indicate this. For example, an associate professor of humanities and social science whose response pattern indicated that he was firmly in favor of academic freedom stated: "The university should have a place for extremes of thought on almost *any* question." And he continued: "Ideally, I personally might be careful in what I say if I felt the climate was not sympathetic—but in principle, the freedom [to make known the results of research] is basic, and I would support others who risked themselves." The converse of this position, that of opposition to the idea of academic freedom, was held because of the belief that "the university is no place for public debate"; that "its [the university's] business is teaching and research, not political or semi-political controversy"; or that debate over the arms race or American policy toward Red China "should not take place in the classroom."

Of course, not all respondents gave such measured reactions. On the question of defending faculty who advocated provocative views, one professor of social science did not even feel that such superfluous questions merited answers, and added: "They damn well better *had*— on any controversial view in any field, if they want to remain a university." However, an associate professor of life science reacted differently to the issue of defending controversial faculty: "The university does not have to *defend* anyone. The question is one of *prosecution.*"

The commentary not supportive of academic freedom seemed to be of eight types. First, there were some who were suspicious of the research project. An assistant professor in the school of medicine reflects this skepticism about the objectivity of the study:

> Sections XXVI–XXIX [items on academic freedom] are so obviously slanted as to be both rediculous [sic] and invalid. I hope no "critical" analysis of such questions will be reported. They [the questions] appear to be expressly designed to provide a club with which to beat policy makers.

Mistrust possibly lies behind the actions of the eight persons who ripped pages from their questionnaires before returning them and the average of ten persons who did not take a stand on each of the twelve items.

Second, some faculty felt that they might put themselves in jeopardy by defending academic freedom. Some talked about "strategy," and it was mentioned that the matter of academic freedom "depends on circumstances and what procedures are being jostled." An associate professor in the school of medicine would not take any stand on the institution's defending an individual who becomes embroiled in a dispute over socialized medicine because "I am an M.D. and consider this too dangerous to answer."

There was also a large number who believed that academic freedom should be secondary to the interests of the institution. A professor of engineering felt that the principles of academic freedom should be curtailed "to the extent this might affect his employer," and a humanist felt that the principles should be adhered to "not at the price of reputation to [of] the university." An associate professor of life science felt that academic freedom should not be defended "against violations of law or university regulations," and an instructor of education could not decide whether it should be defended until it could be determined "how much" financial support the institution might lose. A few raised a related question of whether national-domestic and foreign-policy interests should supersede academic freedom. It was asked, for instance, whether it was "now proper" (in 1964) to examine U.S. policy toward Cuba.

Many contended that academic freedom should be restricted because students are "young people" and "need some protection." Others took this position because they believed that academics had more public responsibilities than most people and therefore should not exercise their right of free speech. One individual, for example, was of the opinion that a faculty member was not free as a citizen "if it would involve the University."

Others held that they could not unequivocally defend the idea of academic freedom unless persons involved in particular incidents were clearly shown to be blameless. A professor of physical science was of the opinion that no repressive measures should be applied to an individual "provided his position is defensible." Another professor of physical science agreed with this and added the proviso that the "sanity and emotional maturity of the faculty member" are "rational limits" that must be considered before it can be decided that sanctions are unnecessary. An assistant professor of social science felt that a faculty person should have academic freedom to investigate any subject "as long as it is relevant to his discipline."

Finally, there were those who expressed an overall qualified endorsement of academic freedom. An associate professor of dentistry indicated that a person should adhere to the principle of academic freedom "as far as it [did] not interfere with his job." An assistant professor of medicine felt that a professor was right to discuss private ownership of public utilities "if he is being employed at a private institution" but that he should not do so "if he is being employed at a tax-supported institution." And there was a large aggregate, almost 20 percent of the sample, who explicitly declared that there should generally be limits on various aspects of academic freedom.

THE CHALLENGE TO ACADEMIC FREEDOM

In his book *Academic Freedom in Our Time*, Robert MacIver analyzes features of contemporary America in order to determine why "attacks on and violations of academic freedom . . . [seem] to be peculiarly characteristic of our society."[31] He is convinced that a "large part of the answer lies in the relation of two distinctive phenomena . . . the special form of academic government . . . [and] the character of public opinion."[32] In a later chapter he writes: "If the control of educational policies were in the hands of the faculty, academic freedom would on the whole be secure, save for minor infractions that can best be dealt with by its own discipline, conjoined with that of its administrative officers."[33] Unfortunately, this is probably untrue. This survey would lead one to believe that a decisive reason why academic freedom is so open to attack is that faculty do not vigorously want this shield or do not see themselves as having the right to it.

There are many possible ways to explain the differences found among the faculties of various disciplines. It appears that those who are most threatened and most in need of protection and whose control over their own lives is consequently most essential are those most in favor of academic freedom. We know from the research of Lazarsfeld and Thielens that those academics who feel the most vulnerable are the most apprehensive about the consequence of their political opinions and are the most concerned about civil liberties.[34] It is the faculty in the behavioral and social sciences and the humanities who—because of the nature of their disciplines, which make them de facto critics of their society, or because of their self-alienation—are most likely to be subject to attacks by university administrators or the public.

If all of this is correct, it might mean, among other things, that on the whole university faculty did not feel any impending danger at the time these data were gathered,[35] which could mean, of course, that their teaching was a sort of profession of faith the imparting of which would not result in their positions being endangered. In any case, given this profile of opinions, it is questionable whether academic freedom would be able to tolerate even the most mild, but systematic, sort of administrative (or trustee) aggressiveness.

THE CHALLENGE TO ADMINISTRATIVE AUTHORITY

In the spate of books, articles, and speeches regarding the campus unrest of the 1960s, attention invariably focused on students' dissatisfaction about their disenfranchisement and on their unshakable conviction that they should have a greater voice in planning their education. While student restiveness was a serious matter, it may be that, hidden behind a screen of demonstrations and sloganeering, a more profound condition was unfolding: Perhaps the significance of the 1960s as far as university governance was concerned was in a challenge by some faculty to the concentration of power vested in the office of the academic-administrator, and the reaction to this threat. The homage paid by social scientists and journalists to student activists may have missed a more important development of the decade; it appears that during this period faculty may have been more centrally involved in an intra-institutional struggle with administrators over the governance of the university than were students. In this regard, one might question the lament of most academic-administrators that relative to faculty they have little power in matters of university governance. For example, Clark Kerr's argument that an administrator merely carries out the wishes of faculty in order to make them more productive is debatable.[36] There is no evidence that administrators have turned over their institutions either to faculty or to students; the struggle for control within universities may continue for years to come, and the outcome is not at all clear.

While it is undoubtedly true that in the late 1960s students were given a greater voice in the governance of the university, their voice was at best muffled. Often student protests were met by offering more courses with flexible grading procedures, by adding one or two students to each of the standing committees of the faculty senate (limiting their number assured that they would have no more than a voice), by allowing students to attend faculty meetings, and by dropping certain distribution requirements (actually, there was little in the way of substantive change, since the hours required for graduation remained the same, and nearly all of the courses were taught in the same manner). This tokenism is not so striking; what is striking is the fact that faculty often either worked against student demands or were silent witnesses to the rout. Faculty are primarily concerned with their position relative to the administration and, as a result, are not particularly receptive to the intrusion of a third party. This in part may explain the lack of support for student activism.

On the other hand, it is interesting to note that students also generally failed to consider seriously the role of the faculty; almost invariably they fixed their attention on the administration, presuming that at least the more liberal faculty supported their efforts. This inference was probably invalid since, in the long run, the concerns of faculty and students are not similar, although at one time or another there might be a coincidence of interest in minimizing the power of the administration. Thus, in spite of all the attention lavished on students during the 1960s, they remained essentially second-class citizens, and the real challenge to administrators, insofar as there was a real challenge, came from some faculty.

In any case, the significance of the 1960s for the management of universities seems to center on an incipient intra-institutional struggle for power between the administration and some spirited faculty. As the struggle continues, it may well be that the most insidious threat to academic freedom will originate from academic administrators rather than from sullen and fearful forces of repression within the society at large. Or, perhaps, as the dissension on campus becomes more formal in character, faculty will conventionally seek to settle questions about academic freedom will originate from academic-administrators rather should insure that neither administrators nor faculty nor academic freedom—nor merit, for that matter—will be in the ascendance. It is of interest that with increased internal pressure, faculty have in greater numbers turned to other institutions, namely, organized labor, and, to a lesser degree, to the courts for relief. To formally counterpose faculty and administrators, completely and finally, on opposite sides of the bargaining table or the courtroom, shatters the notion that the academic community is a *community* in every sense of the word. As a president of the AAUP has observed:

> In dividing the university into worker-professors and manager-administrators and governing boards . . . [collective bargaining] imperils the premise of shared authority, encourages the polarization in interests, and exaggerates the adversary concerns over interests held in common. . . . Moreover, the process itself as it functions tends to remit issues which faculty should themselves determine to outside agencies, such as state and federal boards, arbitrators, and union bureaucracies. In addition, since unions rest on continued support of their constituency, the process becomes susceptible to essentially political rather than essentially academic decision-making.[37]

THE UNIONIZATION OF FACULTY AND SOME OF ITS CONSEQUENCES

It hardly needs to be pointed out that a fundamental belief that has nurtured the growth of industrial unions is that there is an inherent conflict of interest between managers and employees. If there were no competition for scarce resources, it would be difficult for anyone to justify the need for unions. Although the functions of faculty differ from those of blue-collar workers, there is no reason to believe that they are so different that collective bargaining in institutions of higher learning will not in the end embrace many elements of this model, including the assumption that adversary relationships are in the nature of things. Since there are no legal distinctions between faculty and other types of employees, it is not unlikely that the perceived basic division between management and labor will further tax what seems to be the already strained relationship between administrators and faculty. Already a union chapter has "instructed" faculty as individuals to refrain from giving any information to the administration that would contribute to or facilitate decisions on merit, salary, promotion, tenure, or retention while negotiations were being conducted.[38] One must not give aid and comfort to the enemy.

Moreover, it is worth noting that since collective bargaining is usually understood to constitute a form of confrontation between competing parties, its consequences are often the product of coercion rather than of reason. This final appeal to power, with the strike or lockout as an ultimate weapon in the event that compromise, intimidation, self-interest, or fatigue does not lead to an agreement, even further reduces the possibility that academic decisions will be made on academic grounds. Granted this is too seldom the case, but the recourse to power will clearly not alter this balance and is, therefore, not the solution.

On the other hand, along with their customary concerns for economic and general working conditions, unions sooner or later may well devise formulae to protect academic freedom. In the mid-sixties the AAUP, the American Council on Education, and the Association of Governing Boards of Universities and Colleges reaffirmed the principle that "the faculty has primary responsibility for such fundamental areas as curriculum, subject matter and methods of instruction, research, faculty status, and those aspects of student life which relate to the educational process,"[39] rights which unions are vitally interested in guaranteeing for faculty. In the negative this translates to mean that faculty are merely responsible to themselves, no matter how outrageously they may act; yet, these precepts are part of the scaffolding upon which both academic freedom and the principle of merit rest.

In addition, with unionization and collective bargaining, mechanisms for accountability surely will be introduced. If a decision had to be openly explained and defended, it could be expected that as much attention as possible would be paid to how it affected academic quality. The influence of the social ethic and ascriptive factors would undoubtedly be minimized. The decisionmaking process and its results would not only be more rational but might also be less capricious, less foolish, and less cruel. With increasing unionization and centralization, faculty would perhaps still establish the criteria for retention, promotion, the granting of tenure, salary increases, and so on, but they would not necessarily have a central role in carrying out particular decisions. These matters all would be implemented by means of procedures set up by the unions and extramural committees. Thus, there is a risk that another cumbersome layer of bureaucracy—with specially trained mediators, advocates, planners, budgetary experts, and organizers—would be introduced into the structure of the university to further obfuscate its central function of teaching and research and to further minimize the impact of individual merit.

It is already evident that these new components are not simply going to play a passive or peripheral role in academic matters but can be expected to become more and more directly involved in decisions that heretofore were in the purview of the faculty or jointly shared by faculty and administrators. In fact, there are instances where arbitrators have begun to do precisely this.

For example, in one case where the contract of a lecturer at the City University of New York was not renewed on the grounds that he had not completed his Ph.D., an arbitrator ruled that since the man held a teaching position which did not imply a research commitment, he could not be refused a reappointment. The nonrenewal, it was argued, "imposes a condition which was not negotiated by the parties."

> This arbitrator recognizes that scholarly research could be helpful to teaching effectiveness. He also recognizes that many academicians equate the possession of a Ph.D. with scholarly research. However, the contract bars the university from using the criteria of scholarly research and the lack of a Ph.D. as the *sole* grounds for denying reappointment.[40]

On a second City University campus, an instructor was denied reappointment which would have resulted in tenure, although his superiors failed to follow contractual evaluation procedures which involved classroom observations. In view of this irregularity, the personnel committees in the department and the college reconsidered the matter, but the prior negative judgment was reaffirmed. The arbitrator, nonetheless, ordered reappointment, which in effect conferred tenure.[41]

The appointment of another lecturer at City University was not continued because, according to his department, his academic output was meager. There were also unfavorable memoranda from faculty members who had observed the grievant's classroom performance. The lecturer contended that the true reason he was not kept on was that he was a union activist. Because he recognized the "interlacing of displeasure with the grievant as an official of the union and with him as a teacher," the arbitrator ruled that the departmental decision was "tainted by the department's bias stemming from disapproval of the union and his activities."[42]

Egalitarianism and Other Principles: Tenure, Merit, Seniority

This is not to disparage the notion of equity that is at the heart of the arbitration processes or even unions, which, after all, are service organizations concerned with the well-being of individuals. But because their orientation is service, unions, unlike professional associations, are not primarily interested in professional standards. As a consequence, they see the academic world from a single, although certainly not ignoble, perspective that has as its goal enhancing egalitarianism and the welfare of the majority at the expense of the vast array of potential privileges of the few. Academic traditions functioning to foster excellence accordingly have been reinterpreted.

For instance, unions have reduced the concept of tenure, a mechanism conceived to assure the individual scholar that he may study and teach free from secular interference, to be nothing more than another form of job security. Thus, a proposed union contract at the City University of New York stipulated that denial of reappointment on the basis of incompetence could only be made if previous evaluations clearly indicate unsatisfactory performance.

> No classroom teaching member of the instructional staff, full-time or part-time, shall be denied reappointment for reasons of professional incompetence unless he has been evaluated according to the provisions of this Agreement, and either the last two semester teaching evaluations and the last yearly evaluation are all rated "Unsatisfactory"; or the last three semester teaching evaluations are rated "Unsatisfactory"; or the last two yearly evaluations are rated "Unsatisfactory."[43]

One need not excel; he must only avoid being completely incompetent.

When the State University of New York was in the process of deciding what form their representation would take, a plank of one union's platform was that "tenure shall be conferred after an initial probationary period of not less than one year and not more than four years."[44] Tenure is redefined as entitlement to permanent employment, not as a measure devised to advance the search for the truth.

Consistent with this view, the New Jersey National Education Association argued during the 1972 bargaining election in the state college system that "if recruitment and selection procedures are sound, almost all new faculty members should qualify for tenure."[45] In the same year an affiliate of this union negotiated in its contract with the fourteen-campus Pennsylvania State College system "full tenure following three years of satisfactory service."[46] In the same vein, the

American Federation of Teachers contends that tenure decisions should not be competitive. An individual whose performance is *adequate* should be granted tenure, even though a better-qualified outsider, particularly *only* in terms of research creativity, may be available. It is the policy of this union that "there should be one standard definition of probation. If an individual meets the objective qualifications for a job, he is entitled to that job."[47]

Not only could the practice of collective bargaining grant tenure to someone on the basis of service alone, without regard to whether or not it was earned or necessary, it could deny it to someone who might have a legitimate claim to it. In those states, like Michigan, where the agency shop has been instituted as a legal device to protect unions and their members, it is not beyond the realm of possibility that some faculty with continuing appointments could lose these if they did not join or in some other way financially support the union. There have been at least a dozen court decisions in Michigan which allowed discharge of a faculty member with tenure who failed to pay the unions' service fee in an agency-shop situation.[48]

More directly relevant to the issue of merit is the unions' interest in reducing distinctions based upon not only administrative favoritism but also individual achievement, a matter in which they have been successful in both factories and government offices. "The American Federation of Teachers opposes 'merit-rating' systems of pay for teachers, on the basis that such systems cannot operate without the injection of personal bias and preferment":[49] essentially the union's position here is reasonable; economic rewards are probably more often than not granted or withheld for the wrong reasons. Furthermore, a convincing argument could be made that perquisites other than emoluments should be given to those who have the most persuasive bibliographies, who have the greatest disciplinary prestige, or who in some other way have made significant contributions to scholarship or science —that is, those who are the most meritorious. But to emphasize uniformity and standardization in performance, which is already done with respect to behavior, is to place limiting conditions on the actions of the wrong set of people—faculty rather than administrators. Yet, as a number of persons both within and outside the labor movement have pointed out, "collective bargaining is essentially an egalitarian activity."[50] This is why the president of the Rutgers Council of AAUP Chapters challenged a proposal by the president of the University "that an amount equal to a normal increment for each faculty member below the maximum of his salary range be '. . . awarded selectively to those members of the faculty who had demonstrated exceptionally meritorious performance.' " As another AAUP leader said, "prices rise for everyone, not just the meritorious."[51]

In considering the effects of collective bargaining in higher education, K. P. Mortimer and G. G. Lozier concluded that "bargaining agreements tend to substitute the 'objective' standards of seniority and time in rank for the principle of merit."[52] This inference is not completely far-fetched. An extensive analysis of the effects of collective bargaining found, among other things, that

> (1) the seniority principle sometimes has been carried to extreme limits. In many cases there are almost no exceptions to the application of seniority in promotion. . . . The simple principle appeals to union leaders; and the path of least resistance for management is to avoid making exceptions. . . . (2) The merit principle has tended to disappear and to lose meaning. Where rate ranges [in remuneration] exist, advancement to the maximum is more or less automatic.[53]

As if determined to play into their critics' hands, the United Professors of California, representing faculty in the California university and state college system, have argued (successfully) that once an individual has tenure, there should be no further evaluation of his work as a condition for advancement. In testimony, they outlined this position:

> UPC's plan . . . rejects merit evaluation as a condition of advancement from one step within a rank to the next higher step. If a faculty member is adjudged good enough to be retained, he is good enough to merit a 5% salary increase. . . . If they [associate professors] are good enough to keep, they are good enough to be rewarded for their additional experience with more pay. Since there is not enough money for all step 5 Associate Professors to receive a step increase, *the choice should be on some non-invidious basis, either seniority or by lot. Of the two possibilities, seniority seems preferable.*[54]

In light of such reasoning, what might otherwise be dismissed as only a reactionary polemic unhappily seems at some points to approach the truth.

> Elements of the faculty, dissident from the traditional modes of faculty representation because of their own mediocrity and lack of advancement thereunder, may seize upon this alternative [of unionization] as an ersatz avenue to academic "success." And since the majority of any group, however elite, is necessarily less elite than the most elite in the group, there is apt to be resort by the less-qualified majority to the political power result-

ing from numbers to achieve the ascendancy of "good fellowism," mediocrity, the less-demanding life, over high standards and excellence. The leadership of the faculty may shift from the most dedicated scholars and classroom performers to faculty politicians. The latter, to maintain their position as new leaders, must appeal to where the votes are, and in the "one-man, one-vote" context of democratic unionism the vote is not apt to be delivered by a program of incentives toward excellence, but by a program of immediate acoss-the-board benefits for the existing majority. The product of these forces might be expected to be a collective bargaining agreement containing standardized salaries, annual mandated increments, relaxed standards for tenure and promotion with primary reliance upon time-serving—in short, a surrender of the environment of excellence, of tough-minded application of high standards through the traditional joint agencies of faculty and administration.[55]

Unionization and the Autonomy of Faculty

If unionization of faculty means, on the one hand, curtailing the powers of academic-administrators and governing boards through explicit and rational principles of management, it might also mean, on the other, the ultimate abolition of faculty self-government. If the worst comes to pass, administrators will press for and gain managerial prerogatives heretofore not granted, and unions will assume some of the traditional functions of the faculty. If it remains the responsibility of faculty to set standards utilized in making decisions regarding admission and curricula, they may only lose what has been thought to be their traditionally vital role in helping to administer these matters. But if in the age of the multiversity this function has, in any case, been eroding, perhaps they will not, in fact, have lost much.

More than a quarter of a century ago, when Samuel P. Capen was chancellor at the University of Buffalo, he noted that in making their case for academic freedom, faculty differed from other professions and occupations in that they expected "to be protected against every form of reprisal" in exercising free speech;[56] others must accept the consequence of behavior from which faculty have asked protection. This immunity is justified, Capen maintained, "only on one condition. That is, that we shall be partisans of no organized interest within the state, not even of the organized interest of education itself . . . [for] if society is to have faith in our loyalty to the cause of truth, it must never have occasion to suspect that that loyalty is divided."[57] Participation in unions, namely, organizations conceived mostly for the material benefit of academics, raises the additional question, given Capen's argument, whether in fact a justifiable case can be made to continue to support the professoriate's claim for academic freedom.

Thus, a violation of the principle of academic freedom not only implies a violation of the principle of merit; but in the long run, the structures that develop to protect immediate interests in the face of such violations could well result in the complete erosion of both principles.

7

Bureaucracy and Meritocracy

This chapter focuses on the expanding bureaucracy in institutions of higher learning wherein faculty resemble civil-service employees, an ambitious class of functionaries thrives to hold them on course, and careers have come to depend as much on service, longevity, and age as on merit. One consequence of this development is that the definition of how institutions of higher learning should serve society has been recast, so that the expectation is that the more academics dabble in nonacademic matters on and off campus, the more successful they are thought to be. To the degree that the time and interest to concentrate on teaching and research are curtailed by the infinite horizons occasioned by a university which has taken on a vast repertoire of obligations, the principle of merit is weakened. Student unrest in the 1960s was the most perceptible signal that the bureaucratization of institutions of higher learning, in both directly and indirectly enfeebling the academic enterprise, had become dysfunctional.

ACADEMIC BUREAUCRACY AS A GENERATOR OF CAMPUS UNREST

It would seem that there are as many explanations of why the mood on American campuses turned so grim in the 1960s as there were persons writing on the subject. Campus unrest was sometimes diagnosed as a morbid condition of a slightly unhinged society that had fostered young anarchists, nihilists, artless idealists, and embittered blacks who were unable or unwilling to leap the generation gap into suburbia. Disorder on campus was seen mostly as a reflection of disorder in society.

At some point most conjecture touched upon the theme that students became frustrated and disillusioned about the interminable war in Southeast Asia and merely turned on that institution that happened to be close at hand, where, after all, they were dangerously packed together. A corollary of this argument was that universities, with their tradition of working hand-in-glove with other American institutions, were prime targets for the wrath of those unhappy with the American way of life as defined by national leaders. Stop the war, it was said, and young activists will go back to stacking telephone booths, purloining underwear, guzzling bear, swallowing goldfish, or hazing each other. As the war in Vietnam wound down, so, indeed, did the activities of the Students for a Democratic Society.

Some of the turmoil was also traced to the fact that a growing number of students neither respected nor trusted those whom most young people usually look up to—teachers and other professionals, successful men of affairs, or community and government leaders. There was said to be a belief among students that America must reshuffle its priorities; many were convinced that the New Frontier/Great Society/Just Society was an empty charade of unfulfilled promises, and the prevailing view was that those in positions of authority lacked the humane convictions needed to bring about significant constructive changes. With the passing of the 1960s, students became more phlegmatic, a sign to some that this manifestation of what was called the new consciousness was only fleeting.

The simplicity of this sort of analysis is indeed appealing. To be sure, the assumption that students were off on a lark (which may have momentarily turned sour) is reassuring. Obviously, however, a great deal more can be said about this entire matter.

Most simply and apparently, students were less than happy with many actions carried out in the name of institutions of higher learning. As far as many of them were concerned, universities were accessories to a vast array of social injustices. Nonetheless, a key word here is *accessories*; this is the extent of the involvement of universities, and students knew this. To phase out ROTC programs or terminate classified research for the military might in the short run remove the most visible irritants, but universities are part of American society and, short of becoming counterinstitutions, they must by definition "support" what goes on. That all parts of society ultimately contribute to its character is a point easily grasped and was, of course, commonly acknowledged by a large number of students. Why, then, was there so much campus disruption? Why was there so much fury directed at perhaps the least culpable institution in society? Why at the height of the unrest was almost all of the rancor of students directed toward universities rather than toward secular institutions?

It is the thesis here that this was in large part due to the fact that although universities were not malevolent, they were particularly vulnerable because they were trying to pass themselves off as something that they were not. Again and again the claim was made that how one served learning was what really mattered in universities; that the principle of merit enriched life in the academy. Yet, the truth of the matter was that institutions of higher learning had been evolving into bureaucracies in which other precepts, such as the impression one made on others, had become more influential in the strategics of career advancement. Institutions of higher learning in which so much was going on that the heart of the academic enterprise was eclipsed and lost to some were more vulnerable to the new militancy than they might otherwise have been. Who could blame a twenty-year-old for not knowing what academic life was all about and how fragile the social bonds were between professor and student, teacher and teacher, and student and student in multiversities of thirty thousand students and as many rules, routines, functionaries, and miles of red tape?

It would thus appear that by taking on some of the surface features of government and resembling such bureaucracies universities ensnared themselves—by presenting themselves as something less than warm to students they invited more than a response in kind; by metamorphosing from putative meritocracies to recognizable bureaucracies they laid at the feet of students something concrete on which to displace their festering hostility. What had been going on in administrative offices and in the classroom had made the substitution natural and easy. Universities were not merely innocent (or partially guilty) and handy, but by embracing such features of bureaucracy as porkbarreling, sandbagging, logrolling, and railroading, they could not help but become targets. The college president, for example, was abused, not because he was a father figure and young people were struggling to resolve oedipal ties, but rather because, with his office of public relations, with his coterie of eager assistants, and with his preoccupation with calming the waters and staying in office, he could well have been a highly placed governmental official. Likewise, it was not simply the putative generation gap that led students to attack professors: the latter, like the archetypical bureaucrat, had confused means and ends—seemingly unaware of the ends of education, these professors, with passion and dispassion, pursued the means. They went through the acts of teaching and research, but the rituals were empty of meaning and ideas; they seldom engaged each other, never students. In short, students were lashing out at a pervasive bureaucratic structure and were accelerating the subversion of institutions of higher learning *as* institutions of higher learning that had already been well advanced by this selfsame structure.

FROM THE BUSINESS MODEL TO OFFICIAL BUREAUCRACIES

Over fifty years ago Thorstein Veblen trenchantly demonstrated how the norms and conduct of business had permeated the academic world, beginning with the governing boards and extending through the administration to the classroom. Because of their link with men of commerce, universities, Veblen argued, were becoming similar to commercial organizations.[1]

The concern about American universities losing their traditional purpose—the dispassionate search for truth—had, of course, been abroad prior to Veblen's analysis. He was warning of an old principle, "he who pays the piper calls the tune," applied to a phenomenon almost uniquely American: the entanglement of business and higher education. And his argument was simple: universities could not expect to be so closely tied with the world of commerce without, first, taking on some of its characteristics and, second, in the long run, serving as its handmaiden.

It hardly needs to be said that subsequent to World War II, government replaced business as the prime supporter of the American university's endless battle to expand and yet remain financially solvent. First millions, then billions, of dollars have been channeled into universities to underwrite research, building, and educational programs. The praise of federal subsidization from the liberal sector of the public, from rapacious academic-administrators, and from jet-set professors has been loud and unending.

At the same time, some dissidents, mostly traditionalist and neglected faculty from the humanities, have been alarmed that others were engaged in research clearly designed to further governmental policy. Even right-minded activities, from research on social problems to the development of clean thermonuclear weapons, they argue, are nothing more than reciprocation for government financial aid; they thwart the educational ends of universities, and they are the type of servitude, for a different master, about which Veblen warned. The standard response to this is that one of the functions of universities has always been to contribute directly to the public welfare. A more muted response is that every financial subscription, no matter what its purpose, in the end helps all faculty: the overhead that the university deducts from research grants can be utilized for the less marketable pursuits of the humanistic scholar. In addition, it is argued that the inflated salaries of those involved in subsidized research ultimately serve as a catalyst to elevate all faculty salaries. Some critics have been silenced by these explanations, either in the hope of personal gain or from perplexity at the specious logic.

Everyone would agree that government establishments are bureaucracies and that universities are well on their way to becoming full-fledged bureaucracies, with a hierarchy of offices from directorial levels of authority to more modest positions that have only implemental responsibilities and by a span of influence in which each level is controlled by and answerable to the one just above it. From this, a somewhat superficial causal argument can be advanced, and the case may be made that universities are bureaucracies. However, the complexity of the problem and its ramifications demand that it be connected by more than this one tenuous thread. It is not just a matter of bureaucratization but one of fundamental changes in universities away from the business model in the direction of the official bureaucracy.

The transformation in universities that has gained the widest attention in recent years is that of the treatment of students. Between the two world wars, in the days of raccoon coats and the Charleston, when football and fraternities dwarfed all other pursuits, student goodwill was cultivated on campus. Even at schools not short of students the business ethic prevailed, and the customer was pampered.

Lately students have been treated as clients. University personnel, like government officials, have generally ignored or have been insensitive to the needs of those whom they serve. It is not simply that big-time athletics no longer dominate campus life at many of the better schools or that some institutions have banned Hellenic organizations. Nor is it that from the beginning the process of class enrollment is a prolonged, bewildering, frustrating exercise of wandering from one interminable line to another merely to wait for evasive answers to what are momentarily urgent questions. The disregard for the student has penetrated more deeply; it has moved into the classroom. Many faculty now look upon the teaching of undergraduates as an execrable interference with their more important functions—intriguing in intramural politics, playing bridge, occasionally writing trifling journal articles for interment between the dissertations and the dust in the library, and so on—and many academic-administrators see it as a hollow but hallowed charade that must be engaged in if students are to amass enough credits and obtain the proper distribution of courses to receive their diplomas. As has been pointed out: "The bureaucrat, most conspicuously, is more concerned with solidifying his position and extending his authority than in performing a public service [in this case teaching]. Indeed, to the true bureaucrat, public service becomes merely an object of exploitation."[2]

In the 1960s students began excitedly to demand more extensive contact with faculty; the agitation at the University of California at Berkeley beginning in 1964 and much subsequent unrest at other institutions were in large part a desperate call from young people for a more significant and closer community with those who teach. Likewise, the appearance of the hippies and the free universities in the latter half of the decade can be seen as an attempt by some to find meaning through relating with others. It would be fallacious to conclude that one of the purposes of a university is to satisfy the drive of gregariousness, or other-directed needs, of students. Other-directedness is an affliction of young and old alike in American society and is probably insatiable. It is the elemental responsibility of academics, however, to instill in students the value of the life of the mind. This is the essence of the teacher's role; other postures, whether domineering or avuncular, defraud the student. Indeed, the communication of ideas, itself, is a personal act, and the satisfaction of an individual who has been taught something creates a warmth that is at the core of human relationships.

Yet, important teaching assignments in universities are often left to eager but ill-prepared graduate assistants. The teaching load for senior faculty has dwindled. One hears reports of lectures delivered from notes yellowed with age. Ideas that lack reflection and profundity are extended. University faculties have freed themselves from high-handed and benevolent interference with students' personal or parietal lives only to disdain them in the same manner that a Kafkaèsque clerk might neglect someone. Like civil servants, faculty worry as much about matters of tenure as about satisfactorily performing their work roles. The infrequent, serious attention a student receives may have more to do with vocational training than with the basic problem of how to think.

It should come as no surprise that the modification of universities from prototypes of businesses to official bureaucracies has begun deeply to affect their entire organizational arrangement. Business establishments are structured into a unified whole; the various divisions of a store or factory are ordered so that all are working for a common goal. On the other hand, the units of a governmental office commonly compete and work against each other. Thus, a mark of business is efficiency, while two features of official bureaucracy are secrecy and duplication.[3]

In times past, we are told, academics were evaluated and secured advancement mostly on the basis of qualification, competence, or effectiveness.[4] Those who excelled in the classroom or attained renown as scholars had the most successful careers. Today, as we have seen, other criteria are as important to occupational advancement. The dictum to publish or perish, which at best seems to operate in only a handful of major universities, is mostly a fiction used to explain away the demise of the social misfit, the ideologically deviant, the candid, and the ingenuous. Those who engage in what is broadly called community service and those who contribute to the institution's robustness through administrative duties have academic careers as successful as those who are occupied with scholarship. This has resulted in incompetents swelling the higher academic ranks, and more and more peripheral tasks and positions have been created to justify their existence. Consequently, universities have become top-heavy with a wide assortment of vice-presidents, provosts, deans, directors, and miscellaneous assistants to all of these, the uninterrupted growth of which is a clear indication that universities are becoming too large and complex and are simply trying to do too much. Indeed, it is getting to the point where universities are oversupplied with men who traffic in power. How else, for example, can one explain the multiplication of what are known as research institutes (often the operations of restless and aspiring campus executives who are granted the directorship for want of other administrative positions)?

One need look only briefly at universities to find the insidious effects of intraorganizational competition. Faculty contend for salaries, administrative favor, prestige, and publicity. Departments vie for large enrollments, majors, and money. Departmental allegiance is deemed more important than institutional loyalty. It is not uncommon to hear someone reverently referred to as an empire builder. Under the banner of academic freedom a reckless and confused profusion of courses that rest on no pedagogical philosophy is offered. All of this, naturally, is divisive; rivalry only isolates one group from another, and pettiness among colleagues is carried to the classroom and conveyed to the student.

The waste of time and motion that has made remarkable progress in inundating the campus in recent years is also a quality of governmental officialism, which has been thoughtlessly embraced by universities. When universities were like businesses, the learned profession was wickedly exploited, performing myriad duties at a beggar's salary. As good executives, those who managed institutions got the maximum amount of work with a minimum outlay. When faculty were not teaching, they were maintaining discipline, correcting assignments, and offering spiritual and moral guidance.

In the post-Sputnik days of relative affluence, another mark of bureaucracies, the specialization of personnel, can be stretched to interminable limits, and secretaries, administrative assistants, technical specialists, and graduate students carry out many functions that traditionally belonged to the academic man, and he has had little to do and much time in which to do it. Accordingly, uncanny ways of keeping busy have been developed. Nonessential work serves to provide a useful outlet for excess energy, both in reducing the chances that faculty will become restive and in affording an opportunity for appearing to build an impressive record of accomplishments. The administration also benefits, since this activity keeps the faculty absorbed while important decisions are made on educational policy and on other heretofore faculty spheres of responsibility.

Committee work and faculty assemblies allow for the widest variety of diversions. With the array of committees on the departmental, divisional, and institutional levels, there is hardly a chance that anyone, regardless of personality defect, will not find something to keep him busy a few afternoons a week. At the pinnacle of committees is the senate, often presided over by the president, who has guaranteed places for enough deans and other administrators to assure a voting majority in the unlikely event that the faculty representatives become contentious. A cherished committee for an unusually officious person might be one dealing with recruitment, tenure, and promotion. Here there are unprecedented opportunities to hector, gossip, set unrealistic standards, or hinder the careers of young men whose achievements threaten to surpass those of senior faculty. Undergraduate curriculum committees, which spend months, sometimes years, debating pedagogical reform, are ideal for the more prudent, who might well know that the teaching program follows no educational principles but who really do not want changes that could lead to more work for everyone.

Even faculty research has become less often an individual effort than a shared enterprise. Fewer individuals spend their hours doggedly working through an intellectual problem, and more research teams spend their afternoons writing progress reports, cultivating stratagems to assure the refunding of a project, and ordering about research assistants.

Given the abundance of collectivities of all forms, it is not uncommon for one seeking information about a decision affecting his future, the program of instruction, or general policy to be referred to some group decision for which no one is willing to take responsibility and about which almost everyone attests his ignorance and innocence.

If one has a few moments free from various legislative duties, he can assist students in their semiannual task of answering questions on almost a dozen information cards that must be meticulously completed before the students are considered officially registered. Much time can also be spent filing grant or fellowship applications or fabricating progress or activity reports for some office or campus newsletter. Vacant hours can also be filled by writing letters of recommendation to graduate schools attesting that a half-forgotten student is highly motivated or to superintendents of schools certifying that a former advisee who may have stopped in to have his program signed twice a year is merely fond of children and is neither gay nor subversive. Finally, there are convocations, baccalaureates, commencements, lectures, presidential teas, departmental get-togethers, and other ritual events to attend, some with, some without cap, gown, hood, and tassel.

Above all, governmental bureaucracies are expected to maintain a neutral stance. This is necessitated not only because the nature of their impersonal operations demands impartiality but also because they must respect the diversity of opinion that divides members of any society. This is also a requirement of the university, which ideally is guided by the spirit of disinterested inquiry. The dispassionate pursuit of knowledge is encouraged to protect institutions of higher learning against special interest groups—private or public.

As universities have taken on more and more features of governmental bureaucracies, they have more strenuously reaffirmed their impartiality by tolerating any group, any idea, and any form of behavior on campus. To do so is thought to be tantamount to providing undergraduates with a well-rounded education and guaranteeing faculty their academic freedom. Some go to great pains to advertise that they take no stand on issues of war and peace, communism and socialism, fascism and democracy, morality and immorality. In their efforts to reflect the posture of fairness of the governmental bureaucracy, academic men have confused nonpartisanship with either intellectual irresponsibility or mindless indifference. Countenancing wickedness is not an indication that one is open- or fair-minded. Besides, it is idle to talk about the neutrality of institutions of higher learning because in actuality this rule has never been abided: the resources of the American university have been used to serve governmental purpose from the time of the founding of the land-grant colleges through the development of ordnance-research centers following World War II to the social-betterment programs of the reformation of the 1960s.

In sum, academic institutions which may have been the last sanctuary for individual initiative in a society dominated by a corporate psychology have become havens for impression management, patronage, committee decision, conviviality, callousness, and provincialism. American universities have undergone control, and still bear the marks, first from puritanical religion, then from business, and more recently from government. As a consequence of the search for allies and adequate funding, the basic functions of the university have often been forgotten, and a cadre of grey men have become well entrenched on campus, many but by no means most becoming academic-administrators.

THE NEED FOR ACADEMIC LEADERSHIP

It has been common to point to careerism, moral insensitivity, or intransigence on the part of the administration when specifying the conditions within academic institutions that make students unhappy and restive. This may or may not be true. However, the case being made here is that there is more to the story: that academic-administrators may have been able to give administrative leadership to their institutions but not academic leadership. For example, while academic-administrators have attested to the need for adequate facilities to produce a well-educated public, academic-administrators throughout the country have overburdened their campuses with a wide assortment of nonacademic activities, such as facilitating vocational training and recruitment for business and government, explained by one university president as having "a large educational component."[5] While academic-administrators have called for the national goal of excellence, throughout the country they have developed and supported educational programs that have cultivated a uniform mediocrity. While academic-administrators have deplored the lack of competent and dedicated faculty, throughout the country they have dissipated a disproportionate amount of their limited resources pursuing and catering to a handful of celebrated, and sometimes aged, scholars, nonscholars, and scientists.

It is true that the primary function of administrators in general is to coordinate work activities in organizations in order to assure a high

degree of effectiveness, but it is not altogether clear how much central-
ized planning, a basic feature of bureaucracies, universities in fact
need. There is no way of organizing either of the two essential tasks of
university faculty—research and teaching—in order to maximize success. Much research is an individual endeavor, not subject to extraneous control; for that research carried out by teams, outside direction
can help increase input but has not been shown to have much impact
on output. The activity of teaching itself cannot be regulated, and all
that can be done with reference to it is to make sure that there is a
wide selection of courses available to the student, that these are not all
offered at the same hour, and that there are well-ventilated, well-
supplied classrooms, so that distractions are minimized. Yet, as anyone
who has taught will attest, even these simple requirements often are
not fulfilled.

Since few would dispute the contention that not as much learning
occurs during the undergraduate years as ideally might, academic-
administrators cannot be judged successful in promoting the education
of students. This is not to say that they alone are to blame for the fact
that young people are almost as ignorant upon graduation as they
were as freshmen; surely faculty are more to blame for this depressing
condition. Yet, if one holds faculty totally responsible for this, then it
follows that academic-administrators should have no authority: it
makes little sense for such to be conferred on individuals for control,
which they do not and cannot have, over processes that occur but
sporadically. Like many faculty, academic-administrators do not appear to be overly concerned about what goes on in the classroom.
When asked about the preparation of graduate students to instruct
undergraduates, an associate dean of a graduate school casually re-
plied, "You say a few prayers."[6]

Thus, if academic-administrators are not to be first among equals as
scholars, which few clearly are, then they need only to provide space
and equipment to enable students (scholars)—young and old—to pursue their activities; it is not necessary for them continually to introduce
new sideshows to an already centrifugal campus merely to justify their
existence.

Taking the cue from the larger community, some academic-administrators are of the opinion that universities should provide more than
formal and scholarly learning to students, that they are doing this, and
that consequently they are satisfactorily meeting their obligations. Yet,
it is doubtful whether universities should take on these additional
activities, particularly in light of the fact that they have had such poor
results in attempting more basic duties—instruction in the arts, letters,

and sciences, for example. And they are probably failing here too. Given the low morale of students as manifested in what has been called discontent, defiance, insurrection, and all the rest, it would be difficult to make a case for administrative accomplishment (although on the basis of this no one can make the case for administrative failure). Further, the standard measure of low morale is high turnover, and, in spite of sanguine interpretations of statistics showing that many university dropouts eventually return to school, an alarming number of students do disrupt their program of studies. In addition, the findings of Philip Jacob[7] and of Kenneth Feldman and Theodore Newcomb,[8] after reviewing a massive number of research reports, that the long-range effects of higher education on students' values is almost nil should be considered here. At most, university education is preparing some young adults to fit into a ready-made, but far from perfect, society. This is a dubious achievement. In sum, academic-administrators really have little to do and, although they spend a good deal of time at it, they do it rather poorly.

It might be argued that the reason academic-administrators frequently flounder is that they are not trained as managers—at bottom they are not really bureaucrats. This is a valid point and is thought to be a blessing: if nothing else, it has helped prevent universities from becoming overly organized. Although it sounds reasonable, this proposition is probably false.

That there is less bureaucracy in universities than in other organizations is due to the nature of its functions, not its leadership. As has already been suggested, it would not be an easy matter for anyone to establish hierarchical control over the actual processes of research and teaching. Where it has been possible to introduce routine, this, in fact, has been done. Students must attend so many lectures a week for so many weeks for so many courses in order to earn a certain grade-point average to graduate. Faculty must also make so many appearances in the classroom, must teach a uniform number of courses, and are expected to give some distribution of grades. In addition, they can rarely induce the university to provide extraordinary equipment or facilities that might be necessary for a research or teaching program and must practically undergo trial by ordeal in order to obtain even the smallest sum of money needed to conclude some research, unless they are physical scientists or can show that their work can help someone make money. Prerecorded, televized lectures and scheduled reports demonstrating progress in research are the most recent innovations in the bureaucratization of universities.

Thus, the "muddling through" that is the mark of university decisionmaking is not an auspicious idiosyncrasy or a small price that must be paid for democratic rule but a cover-up for administrative ineptitude, which results from a lack of executive ability. The incompetence of one administration was highlighted not long ago when in a university which boasted a president, four presidential assistants and two advisors, an executive vice-president with two assistants, seven other vice-presidents, a score of provosts and deans, and an assortment of directors and coordinators, several large departments were removed during registration and the first week of school to a partially constructed "interim campus," which lacked furniture, a completed plan for space allocation, telephone facilities, and so on. Before the dust finally settled the semester was nearly over.

Universities undoubtedly need someone to lead and guide them. Yet, it is primarily academic leadership that is needed, not administrative leadership. This would require that present-day administrators be completely removed. Those now managing universities are too highly trained in other areas to perform the clerical functions that would still demand attention. On the other hand, they have clearly not demonstrated the capacity for reflection, and most do not have the scholarly accomplishments to provide an appropriate and acceptable example and inspiration to younger or more moderately endowed academics. Individuals making notable contributions to scholarship or science perhaps would have continued in these happy pursuits and would not readily have opted for positions of power. And if they had had the ability of original thought, the institutions in which they have been conducting affairs might have attempted to follow new (really old?) directions, reducing the emphasis on vocational training, applied research, continuing-education programs, and services for commercial interests. Is there a need for any university to expend effort to offer instruction in "Retail Merchandise and Management," "Introduction to Supervisory Skills," "Seminar for Widows and Divorcées," or even "Advanced Municipal Accounting," to use examples from the continuing-education listing of one large state university?

There are some who contend that the faculty need more than scholarly models, that they are incapable of handling their own affairs, such as recruiting and promoting colleagues or developing curricula, and, in fact, require some structure to contain their impulsiveness, guile, and petulance. If the faculty cannot manage their affairs, it might be because they lack experience in doing so. Many times apathy about such matters on the part of faculty is the result of years of disappointment and frustration at trying sensibly to affect their own affairs.

From years of deprivation, deference, and habit, faculty seem fairly well adjusted to the distribution of authority in universities. Many, both old and young, are aware that languor in research and publication, which might be penalized under an administration of scholars or scientists, is not a distinct disadvantage under present conditions and may even be rewarded if enough misappropriated time (which could best be spent in the library or the laboratory) is devoted to a variety of social amenities. As institutions are now managed, those who have little time for exhibitionism, oftentimes dedicated scholars and scientists, seem to be the ones who are neglected or undervalued.

The poor quality of academic-administrative talent can be traced to the process of selection. Those who reach the pinnacle of authority arrive there by being deemed capable by those who make such recommendations, that is, those who are already there. The surest way to be judged fit for a high administrative position is to carry out secondary administrative and committee assignments with enough flair to gain wide recognition. High visibility and some resemblance to those in high positions, then, are necessary conditions for moving up the administrative ladder. This facilitates the advancement of the faithful, the person with long service, and the sycophant—the good bureaucrat.

Thus, almost completely passing from the scene are Thorstein Veblen's iniquitous but self-righteous captains of erudition. Appearing in their place are practical conciliators bent on consensus, balance, and harmony. Here is how one of the more successful academic-administrators describes those to whom the scepter has been passed:

> The president in the multiversity is leader, educator, creator, initiator, wielder of power, pump; he is *also* officeholder, caretaker, inheritor, consensus-seeker, persuader, bottleneck. But he is mostly a mediator.[9]

Like their counterparts in other bureaucracies, these experts of delicate negotiations surround themselves with an assortment of lawyers, accountants, and public-relations directors to assist in determining how politic, safe, and expedient each alternative of any decision might be. It is rare indeed when a university administration takes a determined but potentially unpopular stand without first assessing the sentiment and possible reaction of a governing board, political leaders, and/or community pacemakers.

THE CALL TO PUBLIC SERVICE

In their attempt to win public—and financial—support, academic-administrators have allowed universities to assume more and more functions not central to education. The drift has reached the point where many universities now acknowledge that they have three equally relevant functions—teaching, research, and *community service*. But just as an emphasis on instruction perhaps fosters the social ethic and an emphasis on research fosters individualism, the accent on service promotes bureaucracy. It is no mere coincidence that the Wisconsin Idea of Van Hise (which places the university in partnership with the state for political reform, economic and social improvement, and human welfare) and the conception that academic administration is complex and must be elaborate were introduced at about the same time, with the latter becoming bulkier as institutions of higher learning have evolved more and more to resemble public utilities.

Because of special conditions operative in the local and national power structures, programs available to all of the people have recklessly multiplied. In contemporary America, neither large business nor small business nor agriculture nor labor nor industry nor the military nor government dominates the process of decisionmaking. And concerned about placating various pressure groups, universities spent the 1960s attempting to present themselves as allies to all: they sponsored agricultural extension programs, assisted the Selective Service in its activities by transmitting the class standings of students, aided business in its recruitment programs, helped insurance agents pass examinations to become licensed underwriters, offered degrees in industrial and labor relations, supported urban redevelopment and uplift, instructed in military science, engaged in contract research, and so on.

Most urban institutions continue to dole out instruction to those who wish to further their careers or solve some personal problem. Through afternoon, evening, weekend, or summer activities, public relations are improved, and the notion is promoted that in general the community is also being improved. It is problematic, however, if much ignorance is eradicated in having a tired, undermotivated instructor perform before a tired, career-oriented, white-collar worker two evenings a week.

Another way in which the community has long been brought into contact with universities is through intercollegiate athletics. These programs, with their handsomely remunerated head coaches and specially tailored academic programs permitting subsidized athletes to receive degrees with a minimum of scholarly effort, are obviously sustained to entertain sports-minded citizens. In the same manner, alumni- and community-affairs offices are established to make the larger society more hospitable toward institutions of higher education.

By means of such functions, a constant attempt is made to involve the community in the institution, and vice versa. But each has sort of befouled the other. For example, universities have encouraged communities to undertake urban redevelopment ostensibly for the betterment of both. This has sometimes resulted in helping commercial interests and in working hardships on the economically depressed. Furthermore, educational programs fashioned to assist some municipality in alleviating an undesirable situation often lead community leaders to believe mistakenly that important steps have been taken to solve their problems. As a consequence, little else may be done to try to eliminate them. Since such programs must still be proven effective, conditions can generally be expected to deteriorate even more.

In any case, the intermingling of educational institutions and the community has not been useful to either and has only served to enable the leaders of both to expand their influence. Academic-administrators are placed on the governing boards of local, national, and international profit-making institutions, while business executives are made trustees of institutions of higher learning. In forming the values he applies in managing his institution, the university president who is a bank director or who has recently received a local citizenship award must be affected by those with whom he interacts and who honor him.

A result of the special relationship with the world of affairs is that a university's success is now measured, not by the conversion of ignorance into learning, but by endowment, enrollment, number of degrees awarded, ability of faculty to obtain grants from the federal government or the large foundations, graduates in *Who's Who*, number of Ph.D.'s on the faculty, number of faculty who have won awards, number of merit scholars enrolled, and so on. Such standards are more appropriate to a commercial or governmental bureaucracy and have little to do with determining how well institutions of higher learning work. An even more insidious consequence is that vocational training has become an essential part of the course offerings of all institutions, so much so that the largest aggregate of full-time students pursuing undergraduate degrees are now enrolled in such programs.

Mostly without design, community influences have been effective in stifling freedom of thought and expression within institutions of higher learning. Sometimes community leaders press administrators to make decisions that, in the long run, can be detrimental to the institution; sometimes administrators act in anticipation of the public's response to their actions; sometimes the administration and influential citizens act in concert to attain a mutually satisfying goal. No matter what the conditions leading to an administrative decision, a close association with the community can act to impede complete academic freedom. In reference to a publicly supported institution, each tax-payer, because he seems to be so closely related to so many of its extramural activities and is helping to maintain the school financially, is led to believe that he should have a voice in making its policy and directing its operations. Too few academic-adminstrators have made an effort to inform the public that they do not have this right; their actions, in fact, would seem to encourage the thinking that the tax-payer ought to have his say. Thus, the public seems willing to permit indigenous representatives to oversee other public institutions, those in the domain of medicine and law, for example, but wants to influence directly the day-to-day activities of education. With reference to pri-vate institutions, it is mostly alumni and benefactors who seek to mod-ify policy.

This uneasy alliance between persons outside institutions of higher learning and those within has brought other mundane ideals into the classroom. For instance, the ethic of competition, so widespread in the community at large, has deeply penetrated the student moral code. The struggle for grades is perhaps the most divisive activity in which students engage, and research has shown that many are not happy about this. Not only is competition inevitably frustrating, it is a diver-sion from learning.

Businessmen and government officials have also been invited to carry their activities onto the campus. This is in no sense a fresh and unwelcome encroachment. It has, of course, been traditional for Amer-ican educational institutions to provide for the needs of influential citizens and organizations: Harvard has long had its graduate school of business administration, Columbia its school of journalism, Cornell its school of hotel management. It is not only that this practice has now reached calamitous proportions nor that there is now a qualitative difference in the demands made upon universities, placing them in the position of captives, so that, among other things, their presidents are kept ignorant of top-secret faculty research; rather, a more crushing but perhaps less readily apparent effect of the mutuality of academics and nonacademics is a blurring of the line between the academic and the nonacademic. Faculty and students no longer know what is prop-erly and logically in the realm of the university.

The Relentless Transformation of Academic Culture

In the first place, the value that those faculty who now offer their services to the highest bidder place on action, to some extent at the sacrifice of thought, extends to the classroom. In teaching, there is often excessive emphasis on *how* rather than on *what* or *why*. Efforts are made to train men who are technically competent. The end has been more vocationalism and less attention to nonutilitarian pursuits. One dean's despairing explanation for this is that "teaching the young to be intelligent, imaginative persons of high character is simply not a high priority among our national goals any longer"[10] is unhappily valid. And too many other administrators, and faculty, who have played a significant role in bringing this about readily assume that this is how it must or should be.

Not only is it no longer clear to many in institutions of higher learning what are and are not legitimate academic activities, few even understand that it might be necessary to be somewhat detached from day-to-day, worldly affairs if they are both to attain a proper perspective in their disciplines (Cardinal Newman's observation that "the common sense of mankind has associated the search after truth with seclusion and quiet" is no less true today than in 1852)[11] and, more fundamentally, not in the long run change the character of academic work. According to more than one student of the scientific community, this danger of a profound and permanent transformation may be no further away than a few more round trips to Washington.

> The values of the larger society, its greater interest in money, prestige, and perhaps in power or influence, may come also to play a larger part in the relations among scientists. When scientists begin to feel that their colleagues are more interested in these commodities, if only because such interests have become a more important part of their lives away from the laboratory, the commodity of competent response to creativity will be challenged by the commodities that are more negotiable outside the laboratory. A scientist's reputation may come to rest as much upon the amount of time he spends traveling about the country to meetings and as a consultant as upon the quality of his publications; it may be shaped more by the size of the research project he is administering than by the influence his work has upon the work of others. It seems possible, in other words, that the autonomy of the exchange-system of science may be weakened simply because scientists come to assume that their colleagues no longer value competent response so much more highly than other commodities.[12]

> Perhaps it is an inevitable development that once the notions of success in the business world to some extent invade the scientific, the same tools that promote success in one are sought after in the other. This raises the question, however, of whether the facile, the easily smoothed over, and the persuasion by personal manipulation, if such behavioral techniques become acceptable to the scientific community, will eventually prove destructive to the quality of scientific work.[13]

Given the validity of what psychologists call the law of effect, the inclination of individuals to repeat behavior that seems to lead to rewards and to discontinue behavior that is not rewarded or punished, we could predict with some certainty that the quality of scientific work would deteriorate.

The union of academics and power has been justified as a means of making campus life richer and the undergraduate experience more "relevant." But as far as undergraduates are concerned, the ultimate consequence of the coalition of the academic world and policymakers, and the bureaucracy this has fostered, is that they must turn away from universities in their search for what they consider an exciting education. The substitute education they receive from their worldly flurry is surely not without some value, but it can be obtained along with formal training, instead of in its place. The situation for students is, thus, not unlike that for their teachers: the jerry-built, officious structure is not conducive to intellectual work, which, if still pursued in spite of everything, has a pretty good chance of going unrecognized.

THE PROSPECTS FOR BUREAUCRACY

It is unlikely that the type of bureaucratic arrangements described here will persist; change will come, for there is a real possibility that Americans will lose interest in supporting institutions in which there appears to be an inverse relationship between both expanding the physical plant and developing "innovative" programs (that is, "programs of learning for those who hate learning") and the concern with education. Surely numerous suggestions for improvement will be forthcoming. If the advice of persons who advocate tightly organized bureaucracies is followed, then universities will have to turn to professional administrators. If, on the other hand, persons who favor the collegial principle have their way, then scholars and scientists can delegate administrative tasks to salaried assistants. Since this alternative might well increase the possibility that those who are engaged in cultivating qualities of the mind that would promote a more decent, humane, and liveable world would be successful, it seems to offer the most promise. As no one would be in the ascendancy, it would also make it less likely that anyone would use the university to further special interests, whether of labor or business, blacks or whites, those in power or those out of power, liberals or conservatives, radicals or reactionaries. If the concerns of university administrators were narrowly defined and nonacademic, if leadership on campus were a function of academic qualification, and if the force of power were moral persuasion, higher learning might approach a millennium, and America's future leaders would have been part of a democratic experiment upon which they would be able to model other institutions.

Such a community will not be attained easily—many from both inside and outside the university see it as only a utopian dream. In dismissing such an idea, one highly-placed academic-administrator wrote in 1967 that what is referred to as the company of equals "is, in fact, more likely an apathetic pseudo-democracy dominated by a few responsible individuals discussing trivial issues endlessly."[14] Such disdain will not miraculously vanish and can only be neutralized by success in collegiality. If academic-administrators were as concerned about the needs of the faculty as they are about those of politicians, the press, the clergy, the rich, the poor, and the like, the development of such a community would be immeasurably enhanced.

8

The Indispensability of Merit

MERIT AND DEMOCRATIC VALUES

Because the term "meritocracy" implies some form of social differentiation, it is neither value-free nor devoid of political meaning. The concept, in fact, is central to much of the long-standing and continuing debate among political theorists concerned with how societies should best be governed. For example, the idea that those with "virtue" and "talent" should be allowed to rise to positions of prominence has been a basic tenet of Jeffersonian democracy. For Jefferson, a durable system of merit is the keystone of an open, democratic society. What he called a natural aristocracy, government by those citizens who are the most capable, is the equivalent of a meritocracy. It was Jefferson's expectation that artificial aristocracy founded on wealth and birth, characteristic of so many other nations, would be supplanted in America by a natural aristocracy, those with ability: "the most precious gift of nature for the instruction, the trust, and the government of society."

Moreover, advancement that is a function of what one can do rather than of status, preferment, or irrelevant criteria is a logical complement to the Marxian doctrine "From each according to his ability." The idea, however, suggests nothing more; by itself, this precept would be consonant to either a socialist or a capitalist society. It should be underscored that a meritocracy presupposes neither "to each according to his need" nor "to each according to his ability"; both corollaries are consistent with the convictions that competence should determine movement in a structure and that equality of opportunity is necessary to facilitate this. It is apparent, as it was from the definition of meritocracy considered in chapter 1, that the term conventionally has implied differential power, prestige, and rewards, and given this common usage, what Paul Seabury has written is not surprising:

> Let us consider the idea of merit. As a conception of justice, it means "to each according to his abilities," or in another and closely related sense, "to each according to his works." In these two combined senses merit advances and rewards according to ability and accomplishment, rather than according to status, preferment, or chance.[1]

This definition of justice is too culturally bound; in societies where the ideal is something other than that power, prestige, and reward should generally be a function of performance, its meaning could be more abstract and benevolent. The pursuit of excellence that is the quintessence of the principle of merit is not the same as striving to increase one's power, prestige, or rewards.

Aside from these considerations, there might still be ideological reasons that would lead some to reject the idea that people should be dominated by a principle of merit. First of all, one concomitant of a meritocracy, individual initiative, could breed excessive competition, which many believe must in some way be checked if civilization is to reach its millennium.

More important to many imbued with the American creed of the equality of all men is the presumption implicit in the idea of merit that some people are in fact better than others, that all men are not created (with) equal (aptitudes). Merit does, however, imply an equality of opportunity. This is because equality and equality of opportunity are not the same; the former is concerned with ends (some biologically determined), while the latter is concerned with a process or means.

It cannot be reiterated too often that the sorting of people according to merit does not preclude equality of reward. The inequality which results from differential reward is not an inevitable consequence of differential merit. To reduce the differential rewards of those who succeed and those who do not would no doubt soften the impact of individual differences by reducing both competition and the distance between those at the top and those at the bottom. Yet, this would by no means eliminate them; history seems to indicate that some sort of division of labor and subsequent stratification is unavoidable. Granted that there is inequality, it could not help but be salutary if the most able people were in positions that required the most skill. It is not a question of whether some individuals should be on top but primarily one of who should be there.

Given what is being said here, there is really no need to take a position on the Tocquevillean view that the triumph of mediocrity, the resentment of excellence, and the dissolution of the life of the mind are some of the fruits of equality. The thrust of merit as it has been used throughout the book is relatively free of some of its conventional ideological overtones.

The question of merit does touch the critical issue of the polity of academia, particularly as it pertains to what, according to some, has been the unremitting collapse of order in universities. There are a number of reasons why the structure of authority in universities has been eroded to the point where many of the more traditional faculty picture the situation as nearly approaching anarchy. Five explanations come readily to mind. First, those who are granted legal control of universities, the governing boards, are selected not because of ability or interest in academic affairs but on the bases of political, financial, or public-relations considerations that cannot but diminish their influence over the primary functions of institutions of higher learning. Second, because academic-administrators are not elevated to positions of authority on the basis of their qualifications as scholars and scientists, they do not necessarily possess the special virtues that could keep the wheels of a university from jamming. For example, if the use of reason is a central value in institutions of higher learning, it follows that if those in influential positions were there by virtue of their superior rationality, they might well be effective leaders. Third, the fact that the jurisdictions of faculty and administration are distinct, the former being concerned with educational processes and curricular matters and the latter being responsible for managing property, the budget, extracurricular activities, and so on, not only renders certain that one or the other does not achieve absolute authority but creates a leadership vacuum in institutions that have lacked impressive leadership since the second world war. Fourth, the surfeit of students since at least the middle 1950s, many with little interest in or preparation for a college education, has made it nearly impossible for a cohesive community to mature that would help preserve the traditional academic authority structure founded on reason and knowledge. Fifth, it is students and the wider scholarly and scientific communities, and not those (administrators and senior colleagues) who have ultimate power over an academic man, who are primarily interested in the products of his labor. This lack of concern by those with formal power limits their influence over an academic's day-to-day activities. Given these factors, particularly the first two, it is more an informed assertion than a normative statement that a hierarchy predicated on varying degrees of competence would undoubtedly function to bolster the seemingly flaccid authority structure of institutions of higher learning.

Although one may find distasteful an ethic that pits one man against another and is founded on the premise that some people are superior to others, that is, one that appears to be a refutation of humane and democratic values, a compelling case can be made for adherence to meritocratic principles in an academic setting. It is not simply a matter of establishing a meritocracy in order to insure that the most deserving receive the weightiest prize. After all, ideally, academic man is motivated by the pursuit of knowledge for its own sake, and the relative size of one's recompense should not be a principal consideration keeping him preoccupied with his work. Only if someone is treated so unfairly and his situation becomes so punishing that he must dissipate a great deal of time and energy pursuing personal justice and vindication would the idea of receiving one's due be as important in an academic milieu as in other contexts. Most people on or off campus would agree with Seabury, who, in his analysis of what he sees as the decline of autonomy of academic institutions, has noted that:

> any occupation or profession, however inefficient or corrupt, at least must make a pretense of equitably rewarding, honoring, and advancing its members on some grounds other than caprice, favoritism, lottery, or automatic tenure principles; for were it otherwise, it is hard to imagine how it could even claim to be just or fair in its practices, or exempt from harsh complaints from victims of its shoddy practices.[2]

MERIT, TENURE, AND ACADEMIC FREEDOM

It seems that a social system, small or large, could eventually collapse under the damage generated by too many unfit members. In fact, this has been a central tenet in the explanation of the diminution of British industry, power, and empire. To wit, because appointments and advancement in the military and the civil service were gained primarily by wealth, nepotism, and connections, an individual's social class and family became more important to a government career than how effectively he could serve the nation. Such an arrangement could not survive when put to the test in a time of crisis: "A social system had been exposed by battle as decadent and uncreative. Jutland proves that already in 1914, when Britain and her empire had never seemed richer, more powerful, more technologically able, dry rot was crumbling the inner structure of the vast mansion."[3] The American university, to be sure, is not the imperial Britain of yesteryear, but the lesson might still be instructive.

Over and above all of this, the distinctive and cogent reason why it is essential to determine merit in institutions of higher learning is that the right of tenure, the bulwark of academic freedom, is predicated on the assumption that those who contribute most to the discovery, advancement, or transmission of knowledge can be identified and selected to be accorded this special right. When a teacher does more than retail what is known and when a researcher does more than elaborate on received dogma, that is, when conventional assumptions are challenged, the response of some members in the wider community or society at large is likely to be a redoubled effort to sustain the status quo. To deviate from tradition is to run the risk of provoking a negative reaction, and it is for this reason that tenure must be firmly rooted.

There has always been agreement that all academic men do not have a claim on tenure, that it should be granted only to those who have demonstrated their competency to their colleagues. As far as the AAUP, the force behind legitimating the tenure principle, is concerned, competency and integrity are the paramount criteria to be weighed in a decision about a continuing appointment. To the degree that it is possible to discriminate between a good and a not-so-good chemist or literary scholar, it is possible to establish relative merit. Thus, the need to grant tenure is the special consideration occasioning the establishment of the principle of merit in institutions of higher learning.

The contention of some critics of tenure that it undermines merit by providing a sinecure or by not casting aside the old guard for the scintillating young Turks is unfounded. Differential productivity according to age has still to be proven, and instances of a superfluity of those in decline barring the advancement of those still on probation are rare. When the market is tight, the mediocre would not be expected to move up as rapidly as when it is not, but the rate of promotion for the more talented would probably be fairly constant. This is not to say that tenure is never used to defend the fraud, the fool, and the indolent. But again, this, more than anything else, implies the need for careful selection according to merit.

In other words, the *sine qua non* for merit goes beyond the point made by Daniel Bell that: "there is every reason why a university has to be a meritocracy if the resources of the society—for research, for scholarship, for learning—are to be spent for 'mutual advantage,' and if a degree of culture is to prevail."[4] It is not simply a question of pursuing excellence or of the rational utilization of resources; it is more basic and concerns the survival of universities *as* universities.

According to the 1940 "Statement of Principles on Academic Freedom and Tenure" of the AAUP and Association of American Colleges, "tenure is a means to . . . freedom of teaching and research . . . ," and this freedom is "indispensable to the success of an institution in fulfilling its obligations to its students and to society."[5] Although sometimes overlooked in the endless debate about the relative advantages and disadvantages of tenure, it is its relationship to academic freedom that gives it its warrant—most other defenses are more or less beside the point. As Fritz Machlup has observed: "This one advantage—really the only justification for the system of academic tenure—lies in the social products of academic freedom, a freedom which in many situations . . . can be guaranteed only by the instrument of tenure."[6] And as Walter Metzger, one of the foremost scholars of the development of academic institutions, has cautioned: "[Academic freedom] is not only relevant to the modern university, but essential to it—the one grace that institution may not lose without losing everything."[7] A point to remember here is that academics cannot be free if they are incessantly threatened with economic reprisals. Tenure, after all, guarantees not only academic freedom but security and dignity. In sum, academic freedom needs to be sustained, not because of a particular solicitude for the professoriate, but to insure that society will receive the full benefits of critical and independent thought and analysis from those whose task it is to provide such.

It might thus be argued that tenure and due process are the first lines of defense of academic freedom. Ultimately, of course, as Jefferson instructed us, freedom lies not in institutional safeguards but in its effective exercise. Nonetheless, the position taken here is that there cannot be universities unless there is academic freedom; there cannot be academic freedom without proper protection to assure that a professor is removed "only for adequate cause" and is accorded a formal hearing and due process before he is terminated, which is the meaning of tenure; there cannot be tenure unless an individual has demonstrated that he is entitled to a permanent appointment: the determination of merit is essential to the vitality of the academic enterprise. By the same token, the individual cannot actualize or demonstrate his merit unless there is academic freedom; the fewer the constraints, the greater the probability of someone's working to capacity.

DIFFICULTIES IN THE DETERMINATION OF MERIT

It cannot be denied that those whose merit must be determined run a clear risk that their relative incompetence will be exposed. A situation where some people are downgraded not only increases inequality; it can also be psychologically painful to both winners and losers and undoubtedly also works to reduce feelings of security and freedom for many. Such effects, harmful as they may be, must be balanced against the need for academics to have their work examined and criticized. After all, a judgment of merit relates only to specific professional tasks. It is an assessment of someone's performance as a teacher or researcher, not of his worth as a human being. If tempered by respect and tolerance, it is the lifeblood of the academic enterprise, the way in which individuals can learn from one another and ultimately improve the quality of their work. Academic life would stagnate without it. The assertions of some that institutions need the inept, that the mediocre need someone less able than themselves to bolster their position, that a "rigorous application of the norm of performance" would undermine morale, reduce productivity, and rend the social fabric are only conjectures.[8] Groups may "not typically expose or expel their members for lesser achievement or talent,"[9] but the argument that to do so would be pernicious simply has no facts to support it.

Given the intensity of feelings—both positive and negative—generated among individuals in any work setting, it is understandable why considerations other than those purely academic enter into any decision regarding merit: "Frankly, he is very nice"; "He can be difficult at times"; "Everyone likes his family"; "He never hesitates when called upon to perform some service"; "She's one person who knows the real meaning of friendship"; "I, and a number of my colleagues, find his left-wing politics unfortunate." It might seem to be but idle optimism to expect a veridical evaluation of an academic from his departmental colleagues. And since objectivity is so unlikely, why bother with the pretense? Why not acknowledge that in this imperfect world men are never judged on the basis of their work alone?

Admittedly, the problem of determining the merit of any individual is most difficult. Not only is it too much to hope that most senior members of one's department will make a fair assessment of his or her qualities, but one also could expect to find less than complete agreement about what aspects of the multifaceted professorial role are central to the performance of academic functions and about the comparative merit of individuals. A comparison of the printed or oral reviews of most any book should be fairly convincing evidence of how nearly impossible it is to get consensus about the value of someone's contribution to the world of ideas.

Notwithstanding the complexities of determining merit, there are some procedures that clearly come closer to estimating it than others. A written review of someone's publications by one or more specialists in his field is a better method than having departmental colleagues—some close friends, some competitors, some not qualified—discuss in an ad hoc manner bits and pieces that may or may not be of particular interest. Parliamentary forms of decisionmaking, in which all relevant matters can be openly and fully considered, will lead to wiser decisions than will a Star Chamber tribunal. Formalized rules in which procedure and appeal rights are specified are eminently fairer than variable standards randomly applied. Yet, Clark Byse and Louis Joughin reported that less than one-half (46 percent) of the eighty institutions in California, Illinois, and Pennsylvania which they surveyed in 1955 specified the grounds upon which faculty were judged for promotion and tenure, and some of the accounts offered by institutions were vague and otherwise inadequate.[10] This is consistent with the studies cited in chapter 2 that indicated that the evaluation of faculty is a problem still to be solved.

MERIT AND THE FUTURE OF UNIVERSITIES

Although it may seem to be the case, viewed through the telescopic perspective of history, American institutions of higher learning have never really known a golden age. They have always been beset with one crisis or another: too few students or too many students; too much money or too little money; too much interest and meddling in internal matters by the church, by business, or by the government or too little interest and meddling in internal affairs by the church, by business, or by the government; too few qualified faculty or too many qualified faculty; too much concern on the part of students with social issues or too little concern on the part of students with social issues. The tide wanes and ebbs, and universities lunge from one precipice to another tenaciously holding on to life—and never recovering fully intact. There is constant pressure to redefine goals, bend standards, change coloration. What better way, so it seems, to win over what are always too few friends? And is it all that bad to serve some humanitarian need, for example, to form a partnership with those working to reduce pressing social problems? Is it not laudatory to expand the career opportunities of the disadvantaged by setting aside timeworn and restrictive requirements, such as by operating on quotas rather than qualification?

It is likely that institutions of higher learning will continue to experience good times and bad times, and it is also likely that, regardless of the state of their immediate popularity, they will be in need of powerful and influential allies and popular support. That is, there will always be the expectation that they should befriend the rich or the poor or those in between, that they will be most useful to society by becoming less of a university. The only possible defense university faculties have against forces working to subvert their calling as the guardians of culture is to observe those precepts which shield universities from becoming first-aid stations, bazaars, brothels, or temples for any number of seductive isms—philosophical, political, social, or economic. If nothing else, the pursuit of merit demonstrates that the professoriate believe that academic work *is* important and worth doing —and by virtue of this, they have their foremost safeguard against those who would make the university something other than a civilized and civilizing force.

Notes

PREFACE

1. Thorstein Veblen, *The Higher Learning in America* (New York: Hill and Wang, 1959), p. 119.

2. *Bureaucracy* has two meanings. It refers to a large-scale formal organization that with its highly trained experts and its emphasis on rationality, technical knowledge, and impersonal procedures may hardly be distinguishable from a meritocracy. It also refers to the administrative aspect or the hierarchical apparatus of control of a formal organization. It is used here in the second sense.

CHAPTER 1

1. James Bryce, *University and Historical Addresses* (New York: The Macmillan Company, 1913), pp. 160–63.

2. Talcott Parsons and Gerald M. Platt, *The American University* (Cambridge, Mass.: Harvard University Press, 1973), p. 124.

3. See Walter P. Metzger, *Academic Freedom in the Age of the University* (New York: Columbia University Press, 1961), pp. 21–22, 78. See also Earl James McGrath, "The Control of Higher Education in America," *Educational Record* 17 (April 1936): 259–72.

4. Frederick Paul Keppel, *Columbia* (New York: Oxford University Press, 1914), p. 7.

5. Charles Franklin Thwing, *The American and the German University: One Hundred Years of History* (New York: Macmillan, 1928), p. 42.

6. James Morgan Hart, *German Universities: A Narrative of Personal Experience* (New York: G. P. Putnam's Sons, 1874), p. 264.

7. *A Turning Point in Higher Education: The Inaugural Address of Charles William Eliot as President of Harvard College, October 19, 1869* (Cambridge, Mass.: Harvard University Press, 1969), p. 21.

8. W. H. Cowley, "Three Curricular Conflicts," *Liberal Education* 46 (December 1960): 473.

9. University of Michigan, *Catalogue, 1853–1854* (Ann Arbor, Mich.: S. B. Mc-Cracken, 1854), p. 20.

10. Bernard Berelson, *Graduate Education in the United States* (New York: McGraw-Hill, 1960), p. 10.

11. Ibid., p. 12.

12. These degrees were awarded on both sides of the Atlantic. Yale granted the first Ph.D. in America in 1861; in the years between 1898 and 1909 approximately three thousand were granted; the number in 1930 was 2,024 from seventy-four universities. See Walton C. John, *Graduate Study in Universities and Colleges in the United States* (Washington, D.C.: U.S. Office of Education, 1935).

13. W. H. Cowley, "European Influences upon American Higher Education," *Educational Record* 20 (April 1939): 183.

14. S. Willis Rudy, *The College of the City of New York: A History, 1847–1947* (New York: City College Press, 1949), pp. 285–86.

15. Allan Nevins, *Illinois* (New York: Oxford University Press, 1917), p. 241.

16. Thomas W. Goodspeed, *A History of the University of Chicago Founded by John D. Rockefeller: The First Quarter Century* (Chicago: The University of Chicago Press, 1916), pp. 318–19.

17. Richard H. Shryock, *The University of Pennsylvania Faculty: A Study in American Higher Education* (Philadelphia: University of Pennsylvania Press, 1959), pp. 34–35.

18. Reported in Laurence R. Veysey, *The Emergence of the American University* (Chicago: The University of Chicago Press, 1965), pp. 176–77.

19. Reported in Berelson, *Graduate Education in the United States*, p. 18.

20. Ibid.

21. Abraham Flexner, "The Problem of College Pedagogy," *Atlantic Monthly* 103 (June 1909): 844.

22. W. Carson Ryan, *Studies in Early Graduate Education: The Johns Hopkins, Clark University, The University of Chicago* (New York: Carnegie Foundation for the Advancement of Teaching, 1939), p. 126.

23. Michael Young, *The Rise of the Meritocracy* (Harmondsworth, Middlesex, England: Penguin Books, 1961), p. 189.

24. Ibid., p. 14.

25. Ibid., p. 15.

26. Ibid., p. 103.

27. R. J. Herrnstein, *I.Q. in the Meritocracy* (Boston: Atlantic Monthly Press, 1973), p. 215.

28. Ibid., p. 209.

29. Christopher Jencks and David Riesman, *The Academic Revolution* (Garden City, N.Y.: Doubleday, 1968), p. 12.

30. Ibid., pp. 12–13.

31. Ibid., pp. 18–19.

32. Ibid., p. 529.

33. Ibid., p. 530.

34. David Riesman, "Notes on Meritocracy," *Daedalus* 96 (June 1967): 899.

35. Zbigniew Brzezinski, "America in the Technetronic Age," *Encounter* 30 (January 1968): 16–28.

36. Jacques Barzun, *The American University* (New York: Harper & Row, 1968).

37. Pierre van den Berghe, *Academic Gamesmanship* (New York: Abelard-Schuman, 1970).

38. Theodore Caplow and Reece J. McGee, *The Academic Marketplace*, with a foreword by Jacques Barzun. Copyright by Basic Books, Inc., Publishers, New York.

39. *Digest of Educational Statistics, 1971* (Washington, D.C.: U.S. Department of Health, Education, and Welfare, 1971), table 113.

40. Seymour E. Harris, *A Statistical Portrait of Higher Education* (New York: McGraw-Hill, 1972), table 3.1–1.

41. Elbridge Sibley, *The Education of Sociologists in the United States* (New York: Russell Sage Foundation, 1963), p. 48, table 4.

42. Jonathan R. Cole, "Patterns of Intellectual Influence in Scientific Research," *Sociology of Education* 43 (Fall 1970): 383.

43. See either Oliver Fulton and Martin Trow, "Research Activity in American Higher Education," *Sociology of Education* 47 (Winter 1974): 34, table 2, or the original study, Martin Trow et al., *Technical Report: National Surveys of Higher Education* (Berkeley: Carnegie Commission on Higher Education, 1972).

44. *Digest of Education Statistics, 1971*, table 109.

45. *Education Directory, 1971–72, Higher Education* (Washington, D.C.: U.S. Department of Health, Education, and Welfare, 1973), p. xv, table 1.

46. *College and University Faculty: A Statistical Description*, American Council on Education Research Report 5, no. 5 (Washington, D.C., 1970). The figures are reprinted in *Digest of Educational Statistics, 1971*, pp. 81–82, tables 108 and 109.

CHAPTER 2

1. Barzun, *The American University*, p. 367.

2. H. S. Broudy, "Can We Define Good Teaching?" *The Record—Teachers College* 70 (April 1969): 583–84.

3. Kenneth E. Eble, "What Are We Afraid Of?" *College English* 35 (January 1974): 453.

4. John W. Gustad, "Evaluation of Teaching Performance: Issues and Possibilities," in *Improving College Teaching*, ed. Calvin B. T. Lee (Washington, D.C.: American Council on Education, 1967), p. 275.

5. Eble, "What Are We Afraid Of?" pp. 452–53.

6. Frank Costin, William T. Greenough, and Robert J. Menges, "Student Ratings of College Teaching: Reliability, Validity, and Usefulness," *Review of Educational Research* 41 (Winter 1972): 511–35.

7. Alexander W. Astin and Calvin B. T. Lee, "Current Practices in the Evaluation and Training of College Teachers," in *Improving College Teaching*, ed. Calvin B. T. Lee (Washington, D.C.: American Council on Education, 1967), pp. 296–311.

8. Ibid., p. 300, table 2. Robert Wilson, Evelyn Dienst, and Nancy Watson reported in 1973 that "despite the emphasis on colleagues' judgments of teacher effectiveness and the frequently important role these judgments play in decisions about promotion and tenure, there has been almost no reported research on the criteria used by college faulty members in evaluating one another or on the correlates of such evaluations" (Robert C. Wilson, Evelyn R. Dienst, and Nancy L. Watson, "Characteristics of Effective College Teachers as Perceived by Their Colleagues," *Journal of Educational Measurement* 10 [Spring 1973]: 32).

9. Astin and Lee, "Current Practices in the Evaluation and Training of College Teachers," p. 304, table 4.

10. Wilbert J. McKeachie, "Research in Teaching: The Gap Between Theory and Practice," in *Improving College Teaching*, ed. Calvin B. T. Lee (Washington, D.C.: American Council on Education, 1967), p. 212.

11. John W. Gustad, "Policies and Practices in Faculty Evaluation," *Educational Record* 42 (July 1961): 203, table 5.

12. Ibid., p. 203.

13. Astin and Lee, "Current Practices in the Evaluation and Training of College Teachers," p. 308.

14. Gustad, "Policies and Practices in Faculty Evaluation," p. 195.

15. Joseph Seidlin, "Evaluating Teachers: Eventually, Why Not Now?" (Paper read at the annual meeting of the New York State Association of Secondary School Principals, 1960).

16. Psychologists who have tried to calibrate intellectual capacity are criticized often for having reified their estimates—it has even been argued that what they are measuring is inherent and immalleable—and for having failed to see how social and cultural factors may systematically have influenced outcomes for both individuals and groups. Still, the fact that some psychologists have put too loose a construction on I.Q. test results does not mean that no assessment is better than even the crudest one.

17. Gustad, "Policies and Practices in Faculty Evaluation," p. 207.

18. Ibid., p. 208.

19. Ibid., p. 210.

20. Caplow and McGee, *The Academic Marketplace*, p. 127, from chapter 6, "Procedures of Recruitment"; used with permission of the publisher.

21. Harry K. Newburn, *Faculty Personnel Policies in State Universities*, [multilithed] (Missoula: Montana State University, 1959).

22. John S. Brubacher and Willis Rudy, *Higher Education in Transition* (New York: Harper and Row, 1968), pp. 216–17.

23. Martin Trow, "Undergraduate Teaching at Large State Universities," in *Improving College Teaching*, ed. Calvin B. T. Lee (Washington, D.C.: American Council on Education, 1967), p. 165.

24. Van den Berghe, *Academic Gamesmanship*, p. 19.

25. Barzun, *The American University*, p. 69.

26. *Woodrow Wilson Newsletter* (Princeton, N.J.) 4 (June 1966): 9.

27. Paul Woodring, "Must College Teachers Publish or Perish?" *Saturday Review*, 20 June 1964, p. 45.

28. Leonard Port, in *Spectrum* (State University of New York at Buffalo), 26 March 1965, p. 6.

29. Norman Care, "Yale's Tenure Trouble," *New Republic*, 27 March 1965, p. 14.

30. Caplow and McGee, *The Academic Marketplace*, p. 82.

31. Ibid., p. 83.

32. Lionel S. Lewis, "Publish or Perish: Some Comments on a Hyperbole," *Journal of Higher Education* 38 (February 1967): 85–89, challenges this assumption.

33. Logan Wilson, "The Professor and His Roles," in *Improving College Teaching*, ed. Calvin B. T. Lee (Washington, D.C.: American Council on Education, 1967), pp. 104–5.

34. Allan Cartter, "University Teaching and Excellence," in *Improving College Teaching*, ed. Calvin B. T. Lee (Washington, D.C.: American Council on Education, 1967), p. 160.

35. Such stories are rarer, although not unheard of, in university circles. Caplow and McGee even came across one example in their study of faculty from "nine major universities": "He came here as a young man, and at the time the head of the department forbade research—said that it destroyed a man's capacity to teach" (*The Academic Marketplace*, p. 84).

36. Brubacher and Rudy, *Higher Education in Transition*, p. 195.

37. Marcus W. Jernegan, "Productivity of Doctors of Philosophy in History," *American Historical Review* 33 (October 1927): 1–22.

38. E. J. Moulton, "Report on the Training of Teachers of Mathematics," *American Mathematical Monthly* 42 (May 1935): 265.

39. A. B. Hollingshead, "Climbing the Academic Ladder," *American Sociological Review* 5 (June 1940): 390.

40. Paul F. Lazarsfeld and Wagner Thielens, Jr., *The Academic Mind* (Glencoe, Ill.: The Free Press, 1958), pp. 397–98, appendix 2.

41. Nicholas Babchuk and Alan P. Bates, "Professor or Producer: The Two Faces of Academic Man," *Social Forces* 40 (May 1962): 344, table 2.

42. William C. Yoels, "On 'Publishing or Perishing': Fact or Fable?" *American Sociologist* 8 (August 1973): 128–30.

43. Lionel S. Lewis, "On Prestige and Loyalty of University Faculty," *Administrative Science Quarterly* 11 (March 1967): 634, table 3.

44. *College and University Faculty*. (The figures are reprinted in *Digest of Educational Statistics, 1971*, p. 83, table 109.)

45. Wilson, "The Professor and His Roles," p. 105.

46. Ibid.

47. David G. Brown, *The Mobile Professors* (Washington, D.C.: American Council on Education, 1967), pp. 68–73.

48. Kenneth G. Nelson, "Professional Publications of Teaching Faculty in Higher Education" (Paper presented to the American Association for the Advancement of Science, December 27, 1964).

49. Derek J. de Solla Price, "Nations Can Publish or Perish," *Science and Technology* 70 (October 1967): 87.

50. Ibid.

51. Derek J. de Solla Price, *Little Science, Big Science* (New York: Columbia University Press, 1963), pp. 43–46. In 1926 Alfred Lotka formulated his "inverse-square law" of scientific productivity. From a sample of articles published in physics journals in the nineteenth century, he observed that the frequency distribution of scientists by number of published papers could be approximately described by the function $F(n) = k/n^2$, where n is the number of papers, $F(n)$ is the number of scientists publishing n papers, and k is a constant (Alfred J. Lotka, "The Frequency Distribution of Scientific Productivity," *Journal of the Washington Academy of Sciences* 16 [June 1926]: 317).

52. Ibid., p. 49.

53. Bernard H. Gustin, "Charisma, Recognition, and the Motivation of Scientists," *American Journal of Sociology* 78 (May 1973): 1119.

54. APA—PSIEP, "Networks of Informal Communication among Scientifically Productive Psychologists: An Exploratory Study" *Reports of the American Psychological Association Project on Scientific Information Exchange in Psychology*, vol. 3, no. 21 (Washington, D.C., 1969).

55. Bernard Berelson, *Graduate Education in the United States*, p. 55. Copyright McGraw-Hill Book Company, 1960. Used with permission of McGraw-Hill Book Company.

56. Ibid., p. 127.

57. Harold Orlans, *The Effects of Federal Programs on Higher Education* (Washington, D.C.: The Brookings Institution, 1962), p. 158.

58. *College and University Faculty*. (The figures are reprinted in *Digest of Educational Statistics, 1971*, p. 83, table 109.)

59. Ibid.

60. Brown, *The Mobile Professor*, p. 67.

61. *College and University Faculty*. (The figures are reprinted in *Digest of Educational Statistics, 1971*, p. 83, table 109.)

62. Cited in Spencer Klaw, *The New Brahmins: Scientific Life in America* (New York: William Morrow, 1968), p. 96. Cf. figures in Orlans, *The Effects of Federal Programs on Higher Education*, appendix B.

63. Hollingshead, "Climbing the Academic Ladder," p. 393.

64. F. Stuart Chapin, *Contemporary American Institutions: A Sociological Analysis* (New York: Harper, 1935), p. 157.

65. Gustad, "Policies and Practices in Faculty Evaluation," p. 200, table 3.

66. Ibid., p. 201.

67. Ibid., p. 200.

68. David G. Brown, *The Market for College Teachers* (Chapel Hill: The University of North Carolina Press, 1965), p. 152.

69. Ralph E. Balyeat, "Factors Related to the Promotion of University Personnel," University of Georgia Cooperative Research Project S-107, mimeographed (Athens, Ga., n.d.), pp. 5–6.

70. Alvin W. Gouldner and J. Timothy Sprehe, "The Study of Man: Sociologists Look at Themselves," *Trans-action* 2 (May/June 1965): 43.

71. Fred Luthans, *The Faculty Promotion Process: An Empirical Analysis of the Management of Large State Universities* (Iowa City: Bureau of Business and Economic Research, College of Business Administration, University of Iowa, 1967), chaps. 4 and 5.

72. Quoted by Robert L. Ketter, "It ain't necessarily so . . . ," *Ethos* 6 (July 1972): 9.

73. David A. Katz, "Faculty Salaries, Promotions, and Productivity at a Large University," *American Economic Review* 63 (June 1973): 469–77, esp. 472, table 1.

74. Ibid., p. 472.

75. John J. Siegfried and Kenneth J. White, "Financial Rewards to Research and Teaching: A Case Study of Academic Economists," *American Economic Review* 63 (May 1973): 313, table 1.

76. Richard Doering, "Publish or Perish: Book Productivity and Academic Rank at Twenty-six Elite Universities," *American Sociologist* 7 (November 1972): 13.

77. William M. Stallings and Sushila Singhal, "Some Observations on the Relationships between Research Productivity and Student Evaluations of Courses and Teaching," *American Sociologist* 5 (May 1970): 141–43.

78. Allan M. Cartter, *An Assessment of Quality in Graduate Education* (Washington, D.C.: American Council on Education, 1966), chap. 4.

79. Personal correspondence, 13 March 1967.

80. Walter Hirsch, *Scientists in American Society* (New York: Random House, 1968), pp. 23, 28–33. Copyright © 1968 by Random House, Inc. Reprinted by permission of the publisher.

81. How little attention was paid to doing science during this day becomes most apparent when this narrative is compared to the account of someone who seems more immersed in his work. Here are the highlights that relate to professional activities of "a typical day" reported by a world-class scientist who has obviously ordered his life to insure productivity: From 4:30 to 5:00 A.M. he has a "conversation" with himself about his research problem of calciphylaxis (a question he considers again in the evening before retiring). By 6:30 A.M. he is at his desk dictating a book he is writing, which continues for two and one-half hours (with a ten-minute interruption). At 9:30 A.M. he is in his laboratory observing experiments, and at 10:30 A.M. he is performing autopsies for his research staff. During lunch he reads the previous day's dictation for his book, and after lunch he reads a thesis until he begins his two-hour study of the day's histology and preparation for the autopsy conference for the following day. The final half-hour at his office he reads copy. (Hans Selye, *From Dream to Discovery: On Being a Scientist* [New York: McGraw-Hill, 1964], pp. 117–20.)

CHAPTER 3

1. Richard H. Tawney, *Religion and the Rise of Capitalism* (New York: Harcourt, Brace & World, 1926), p. 211.

2. Jencks and Riesman, *The Academic Revolution*, p. 529.

3. Talcott Parsons, "The Professions and Social Structure," *Social Forces* 17 (May 1939): 460.

4. Lionel S. Lewis, "Students' Images of Professors," *Educational Forum* 32

(January 1968): 185–90; and Kaoru Yamamoto, ed. *The College Student and His Culture: An Analysis* (Boston: Houghton Mifflin, 1968), pp. 300–302.

5. Talcott Parsons and Gerald M. Platt, "The American Academic Profession: A Pilot Study," mimeographed (1968). See also their more recent *The American University*.

6. This simply refers to "the normative pattern which obliges an actor in a given situation to be oriented toward objects in the light of general standards rather than in the light of the objects' possession of properties. . . . [T]he role-expectation [is] that, in qualifications for memberships and decisions for differential treatment, priority will be given to standards defined in completely generalized terms . . ." (Talcott Parsons and Edward A. Shils, eds., *Toward a General Theory of Action* [New York: Harper Torchbooks, 1962], p. 82).

7. Jacques Barzun, "The Cults of 'Research' and 'Creativity,' " *Harper's Magazine*, 221 (October 1960): 70.

8. Theodore Roszak, ed., *The Dissenting Academy* (New York: Pantheon Books, 1968).

9. Logan Wilson, *The Academic Man* (New York: Oxford University Press, 1942).

10. Caplow and McGee, *The Academic Marketplace*, p. 10.

11. Alvin W. Gouldner, "Cosmopolitans and Locals: Toward an Analysis of Latent Social Roles—I and II," *Administrative Science Quarterly* 2 (December 1957): 281–306 and (March 1958): 444–80.

12. Diana Crane, "The Gatekeepers of Science: Some Factors Affecting the Selection of Articles for Scientific Journals," *American Sociologist* 2 (November 1967): 200.

13. Cartter, *An Assessment of Quality in Graduate Education*, p. 42.

14. Of course, various constructions can be put on much of what is in these letters. Vic Doyno, an associate professor of English, for example, has argued that a great deal of the actual meaning in recommendations for graduate students is cloaked by a string of clichés:

> For example, the professor who wrote, "He is a very educable person," reveals his kindness, seeing good even in the student's ignorance. Less admirable self revelations also occur, such as: "Mr. X is tall, personable with a good weekend tennis game and a firm handshake. I mention this to indicate the kind of man your dean would be meeting." The only appropriate response, after indignation, is sorrow for the student who unknowingly seeks such a recommender. . . .

> The most flagrantly damaging example of fuzzy-headedness occurs when professionals write "He will be a fine teacher," and mean, covertly, that the individual will not publish. There, at the conjunction of two unrelated meanings, many of our professional troubles begin—not in intentional degradation of teaching but in the all too human tendency to balance a known shortcoming with a probable or likely, ability in another field. . . .

> Therefore, as a service at this season, we offer a key to decode the *para*language of recommendations. . . .

> The code:

> Attentive = toady.
> charming = innocuously mindless as opposed to aggressively mindless, usually coded as "forceful, though obscure."
> communicates effectively = repeats common ideas.
> conscientious = frequently means unimaginative.
> devoted to his students = a commendable trait, but the phrase may indicate that the future teacher will avoid peer relationships.
> earnest = humorless.

hard worker = dull, dull, dull.

knowledgeable = knows only what other people know.

a mind which is flashier in seminar than in a sustained research project = the student revealed, in seminar, a fatal flaw in the professor's treatment of his special topic.

perceptive = still a good word.

professionally ambitious, knows what he wants and how to get it = turn your back at your peril.

sensitive young man = perhaps a homosexual (the extent of this coding can be seen in the implications of a frequently used phrase "courteous, though manly").

sensitive young man who prefers an urban environment and really *must* be interviewed = screaming queen.

solid command of his field = probably a marginal or low pass.

thinks on his feet = may indicate a b.s. *artiste*.

thorough class preparation = still good trait.

wife is attractively amiable = ?

workmanlike = uninspired.

(Vic Doyno, "On Recommendations," *Educational Forum* 35 [March 1971]: 390–92; used by permission of Kappa Delta Pi, An Honor Society in Education.)

15. In this regard see Caplow and McGee, *The Academic Marketplace*, pp. 50–51.

16. Ibid., p. 93.

17. In two other letters written on behalf of candidates seeking instructorships while grimly entangled in the process of completing their dissertations, and which did not actually qualify to be used in this study, the specter was raised that since one was sort of a lifeless bore and the other was being done in by his own seriousness of purpose, not much could be expected to come of their projects: unexciting men, unexciting research.

18. Caplow and McGee, *The Academic Marketplace*, p. 165.

19. Bernard Berelson and Gary A. Steiner, *Human Behavior: An Inventory of Scientific Findings* (New York: Harcourt, Brace & World, 1964), pp. 663–64.

CHAPTER 4

1. Caplow and McGee (*The Academic Marketplace*, p. 121) argue that faculty recommendations function primarily to confer disciplinary prestige on individuals and appear to serve little other purpose. It is, of course, not possible to determine the precise influence of letters of recommendation on actual admission to graduate school, particularly since the study does not concern itself with the responses elicited by these letters. Besides the needs of the department, such as the ratio of applicants to vacancies, other documents, such as letters of intention, test scores, and undergraduate transcripts, enter into the decision to accept or reject any particular student. These letters nonetheless dictate careful examination because they reflect what academics consider important for admission to and success in graduate school; they may reflect what a writer feels is germane and/or what he believes others feel is germane. It hardly needs to be said that this assessment is not unrelated to the experiences of the writers, both as students and as faculty, who pass judgment on students.

2. Bernice T. Eiduson, *Scientists: Their Psychological World* (New York: Basic Books, 1962), p. 169. Copyright by Basic Books Publishing Co., Inc.

3. See, for example, the ingenuous (or disingenuous) remarks by Robert Nisbet (in Robert W. Glasgow, "In the Twilight of Authority: The Obsessive Concern with Self," *Psychology Today* 7 [December 1973]: 60), who claims: "on the basis of 34

years in American universities as a faculty member, I've never seen *either* a conservative or radical victimized by colleagues for his political views. I mean in matters of appointment and promotion."

4. This cognate theme of the professor as pitchman is uncommon in the letters, although Eiduson found it in her study of scientists. One of her respondents told her: "The same results will be presented in a journal differently by different people, and salesmanship actually becomes a factor, I feel. You could argue that in the long run the impact on science is the same whether the results are well presented or not. But as far as a man's personal success goes, he can be recognized sooner and promoted faster if, in addition to his innate abilities, he has a sense of salesmanship. . . ." (*Scientists*, p. 187).

5. Ibid., pp. 169–70.

6. Obviously, an obsession with the social ethic could well be dysfunctional to academic ends. As one of Eiduson's scientists admitted: "It is very hard to decide at an early stage about who is the one who is going to originate an idea. Somebody who might be merely a 'screwball' and not get any place afterward might be the person who could do it; yet these 'screwballs' are not the persons who work well in groups—for example, in the lab I have here. The people who work for me have to be a little bit in the category of the bandwagon type; nevertheless you want to encourage them to do work on their own problems as well as on the idea. So far, I haven't had any really creative ones" (*ibid.*, p. 170).

7. Ibid., p. 187.

8. Jencks and Riesman, *The Academic Revolution*, p. 184.

9. Barzun, *The American University*, pp. 229–30.

10. Lewis Coser, "Some Reflections on Academic Freedom Today," *Dissent* 11 (Winter 1964): 77.

11. Jencks and Riesman, *The Academic Revolution*, p. 206.

12. Tawney, *Religion and the Rise of Capitalism*, p. 230.

13. When considered in light of the discussion in chapter 1, which emphasized that the American university tradition is rooted in the English college and the German university, the use of letters from France might seem somewhat peculiar. However, it was not possible to obtain a sufficient number of letters from Germany; and since France also has a long and honorable tradition of scholarship and since it was possible to obtain a sufficient number of letters from France to compare scientists, humanists, and social scientists, it was decided that such an analysis would be illuminating—certainly more so than none at all. Since it was found after the fact that the state of affairs in western European institutions of higher learning with regard to representing candidates does not seem to be bounded by reason any more than it is in the United States, this decision is probably justified. A fellowship awarded by the Committee on Faculty Research Grants of the Social Science Research Council, to whom I am grateful, made it possible to collect these letters and complete this part of the analysis.

14. Eiduson concluded from her in-depth study of scientists:

In science, the "geniuses" and the great men—unconventional as they may be—are honored and revered. But when the craziness or the eccentricity that sometimes accompanies the genius threatens to find embodiment in a colleague or student, there is a great rush to lock the laboratory door.

Every thinker who has revolutionized an area is regarded generally as a man who has been alienated from the values and beliefs of the society of which he has been a part, but today this getting out of the culture is acceptable only if it is so circumscribed that it is confined to the area of scientific thought, and does not spill over into the area of personal behavior. . . .

Scientists do not have a simple time rationalizing this "split." It takes some internal juggling, which tends to go like this: "I have the feeling that very gifted people should be well balanced. I don't like the queer geniuses who are impossible. They grow up sometimes and accomplish great things, but I don't like to have them around. They're too difficult to work with, too hard to fit into the university" (*Scientists*, pp. 165–66).

Or as one of her scientists told her: "these extraordinary people use me up emotionally; extraordinary people are difficult to handle when they are in numbers. The organization can tolerate just so much deviation, and I have to consider how one person's development will affect every one of my people. . . . I like to break through and then I like to have this exploited, so I get people who are plodders to work for me—just to clean up. Do you see my pattern?" (*ibid.*, p. 166).

15. Ibid., p. 172.
16. Robert K. Merton, *Social Theory and Social Structure* (Glencoe, Ill.: The Free Press, 1957), p. 575.
17. Charles Percy Snow, *The Two Cultures and the Scientific Revolution* (Cambridge: Cambridge University Press, 1959) and *The Two Cultures: And a Second Look* (Cambridge: Cambridge University Press, 1964).
Snow's thesis is that intellectuals have been split into two polar groups: the scientists in one camp, the humanists in the other. Over the years, these two bodies have ceased to communicate, and the result has been the development of divergent attitudes and distorted reciprocal images. The humanists often contend that scientists are foolishly optimistic and vainly brash, while the scientists argue that the literary intellectuals lack foresight, are unconcerned with others, and are obsessed with traditional and contemptible social values. Because of common approaches and assumptions, as well as similar standards and patterns of behavior, persons in one camp in a given country are thought to have more in common with their counterparts in other countries than with their opposite numbers at home.
Snow admits that his simple dichotomy is only a crude first approximation. In apparent reference to social science, he sees the development of a new body of intellectual attitudes that has, as its core, a concern with how mankind lives or has lived. He feels that because this group at times communicates with and straddles the two cultures, it is an incipient third culture. He also notes differences between pure and applied science but feels that scientists and engineers have more that unites them than divides them.
The two-cultures situation, Snow argues, has in large part been brought about by extensive educational specialization. He acknowledges that changes in the system of education will not by themselves solve the misunderstandings and problems that are the consequence of divergent cultures but says, nonetheless, that by broadening the primary, secondary, and university educational programs, sufficient changes can accrue to alleviate many difficulties. A climate can be created in which better policy decisions can be made and better conditions in the world can become a reality.
18. Ibid.
19. See, F. R. Leavis, *Two Cultures? The Significance of C. P. Snow*, published with *An Essay on Sir Charles Snow's Rede Lecture* by Michael Yudkin (New York: Pantheon Books, 1963).
20. Cf. Charles Percy Snow, *Public Affairs* (New York: Scribners, 1971).
21. Ibid., p. 58.

CHAPTER 5

1. Caplow and McGee, *The Academic Marketplace*, pp. 224–25.
2. Talcott Parsons, *The Social System* (Glencoe, Ill.: The Free Press, 1951), pp. 184–85.

3. Ralph H. Turner, "Sponsored and Contest Mobility and the School System," *American Sociological Review* 25 (December 1960): 856–57.

4. Ibid., p. 858.

5. A. B. Hollingshead, "Ingroup Membership and Academic Selection," *American Sociological Review* 3 (December 1938): 831.

6. Peter M. Blau, *The Organization of Academic Work* (New York: John Wiley, 1973), p. 273.

7. Wilson, *The Academic Man*, p. 51.

8. Caplow and McGee, *The Academic Marketplace*, p. 109.

9. Ibid.

10. Ibid., p. 225.

11. Ibid., pp. 166 and 132–33, respectively.

12. Cited in ibid., p. 21.

13. Ibid., p. 132.

14. Ibid., pp. 128–29.

15. Ibid., p. 128.

16. Ibid., p. 93.

17. Ibid., p. 248.

18. Brown, *The Market for College Teachers*, p. 63.

19. Jessie Bernard, *Academic Women* (University Park: The Pennsylvania State University Press, 1964), pp. 127–28.

20. Wilson, *The Academic Man*, p. 53.

21. Brown, *The Mobile Professors*, p. 67, n. 4.

22. Ibid., p. 36.

23. Brown, *The Market for College Teachers*, p. 102.

24. Ibid., pp. 103–4.

25. Ibid., p. 119.

26. Ibid., p. 120.

27. Ibid., p. 122.

28. Ibid., p. 137.

29. Brown, *The Mobile Professors*, pp. 97–98.

30. Ibid., p. 101.

31. Ibid., p. 102.

32. Brown, *The Market for College Teachers*, pp. 134–35.

33. Howard D. Marshall, *The Mobility of College Faculties* (New York: Pageant Press, 1964), p. 97.

34. Ibid., p. 85, table 4-5.

35. Albert Somit and Joseph Tanenhaus, *American Political Science: A Profile of a Discipline* (New York: Atherton Press, 1964), p. 114, table 19.

36. Ibid., p. 43.

37. Ibid., p. 44.

38. Ibid., p. 43.

39. Ibid., p. 79, table 13.

40. Ibid., p. 48.

41. Sibley, *The Education of Sociologists in the United States*, p. 72.

42. Berelson, *Graduate Education in the United States*, p. 114.

43. Ibid., p. 113.

44. Ibid., p. 125.

45. Ibid., p. 115.

46. Diana Crane, "Social Class Origin and Academic Success: The Influence of Two Stratification Systems on Academic Careers," *Sociology of Education* 42 (Winter 1969): 8–11.

47. Ibid., p. 12, table 4.

48. Ibid., p. 11.

49. S. Stewart West, "Class Origin of Scientists," *Sociometry* 24 (September 1961): 266.

50. Bernard, *Academic Women*, p. 140.

51. Blau, *The Organization of Academic Work*, p. 95.

52. Ibid., pp. 96–97.

53. Ibid., p. 258. By way of elaboration: "The large amount of research conducted by the faculties at major universities creates an academic climate that stimulates and facilitates the research involvement of new faculty members, at the same time putting normative pressures on them to engage in research . . . and the result is actually higher research productivity. . . . Thus qualified faculty members who are attracted to and can obtain positions at universities with high reputations probably become more productive scholars than they otherwise would be . . ." (ibid., p. 241).

54. Ibid., p. 97.

55. Lowell L. Hargens and Warren O. Hagstrom, "Sponsored and Contest Mobility of American Academic Scientists," *Sociology of Education* 40 (Winter 1967): 24–38.

56. Ibid., p. 34.

57. Ibid., p. 32.

58. Wilson, *The Academic Man*, p. 171.

59. Crane, "The Gatekeepers of Science," p. 199.

60. Ibid., p. 200.

61. Cole, "Patterns of Intellectual Influence in Scientific Research," p. 386.

62. Ibid., p. 392.

63. Ibid., p. 389.

64. In Warren O. Hagstrom, *The Scientific Community* (New York: Basic Books, 1965), p. 24.

65. Diana Crane, "Scientists at Major and Minor Universities: A Study of Productivity and Recognition," *American Sociological Review* 30 (October 1965): 709, 711, 714.

66. Ibid., p. 710.

67. Ibid., pp. 713–14.

68. Philip H. Abelson, "Distribution of Research Funds," *Science*, 25 October 1963, p. 453.

69. Beatrice Dinerman, "Sex Discrimination in Academia," *Journal of Higher Education* 42 (April 1971): 253.

70. Reported in *Newsweek*, 10 December 1973, p. 120, and in *The Chronicle of Higher Education*, 5 August 1974, p. 8. Other studies indicated that these figures, particularly the latter, are somewhat low.

71. Caplow and McGee, *The Academic Marketplace*, p. 226.

72. Ibid., p. 111.

73. Although important first steps, these steps were indeed very small. As Bird has pointed out, the first coeds at Oberlin "were given a watered-down literary course and expected to serve the men students at table and remain silent in mixed classes." Caroline Bird, with S. W. Briller, *Born Female: The High Cost of Keeping Women Down*, rev. ed. (New York: Pocket Books, 1972), p. 22.

74. U.S. Department of Labor, *Trends in Educational Attainment of Women* (Washington, D.C., 1969), p. 16; *Digest of Educational Statistics, 1971*, p. 78.

75. U.S. Department of Labor, *1969 Handbook on Women Workers*, Women's Bureau Bulletin no. 294, (Washington, D.C.: U.S. Government Printing Office, 1969) p. 190; and idem, *Trends in Educational Attainment of Women*, p. 16. The higher the degree, the smaller the proportion of female recipients. For the 1969–70 academic year, the percentages of high-school diplomas, bachelor's degrees, master's degrees, and doctoral degrees received by women were 50.4, 43.0, 39.6, and 13.3, respectively (*Digest of Educational Statistics, 1971*).

76. University of California at Berkeley, "Report of the Subcommittee on the Status of Academic Women on the Berkeley Campus" (Berkeley, May 1970), pp. 69–71, 74–75.

77. Ann Sutherland Harris, "The Second Sex in Academe," *AAUP Bulletin* 56 (Fall 1970): 285.

78. Jo Freeman, "How to Discriminate against Women without Really Trying," mimeographed (Chicago: University of Chicago Department of Political Science, 1971), p. 1.

79. See Michelle Patterson and Lucy Sells, "Women Dropouts from Higher Education," in *Academic Women on the Move*, ed. Alice S. Rossi and Ann Calderwood (New York: Russell Sage Foundation, 1973), pp. 84–89.

80. Ann M. Heiss, *Challenges to Graduate Schools* (San Francisco: Jossey-Bass, 1970), pp. 93–95.

81. The Carnegie Commission on Higher Education reports: "Among the graduate students in the Carnegie Commission Survey of Faculty and Student Opinion, 1969, about 24 percent of the women, as compared with 17 percent of the men, reported an undergraduate grade-point average of A. On the other hand, only 11 percent of the women, as contrasted with 22 percent of the men, reported undergraduate averages of C or less" (*Opportunities for Women in Higher Education* [New York: McGraw-Hill, 1973], p. 92). For students in Ph.D. programs, the American Council on Education reports that the undergraduate grade-point averages for men and women with the best academic records vary as follows (in percent):

Average	Men	Women
A+ or A	9.7	13.8
A−	16.2	23.1
B+	22.6	29.4

(John A. Creager, *The American College Student: A Normative Description*, ACE Research Reports vol. 6(5) [Washington, D.C.: American Council on Education, 1971], p. 45).

82. Lindsey R. Harmon, *High School Ability Patterns: A Backward Look from the Doctorate*, Scientific Manpower Report no. 6 (Washington, D.C.: National Research Council, Office of Scientific Personnel, 1965); and *Careers of Ph.D.'s, Academic v. Nonacademic: A Second Report of Follow-ups of Doctorate Cohorts, 1935–1960* (Washington, D.C.: National Academy of Sciences, 1968).

83. Harmon, *High School Ability Patterns*, esp. pp. 27–28.

84. Bernard, *Academic Women*, p. viii.

85. Helen Berwald, "Attitudes toward Women College Teachers in Institutions of Higher Education Accredited by the North Central Association" (Ph.D. diss., University of Minnesota, 1962).

86. Brown, *The Mobile Professors*, p. 78.

87. Ibid., p. 79.

88. Ibid.

89. University of California, "Report of the Subcommittee," p. 16, table II. In the Spring of 1970, 2 percent of all full professors at Berkeley were women (Harvard University, "Report of the Committee on the Status of Women in the Faculty of Arts and Sciences," mimeographed [Cambridge, Mass., April 1971], p. 1).

90. Ibid., p. 28, table IV-2.

91. Arie Y. Lewin and Linda Duchan, "Women in Academia," *Science*, 3 September 1971, pp. 892–95.

92. Ibid., p. 893. Had the circumstances not been contrived for the purposes of carrying out the experiment, even more discrimination might have been found.

93. Ibid.

94. Ibid., p. 894.

95. Ibid.

96. Ibid.

97. National Education Association, *Salaries Paid and Salary-Related Practices in Higher Education, 1971–72* (Washington, D.C., 1972), p. 13.

98. Reported in *Newsweek*, 10 December 1973, p. 120.

99. U.S. Congress, House, Special Subcommittee on Education of the Committee on Education and Labor, "Preliminary Report of the Status of Women at Harvard," *Discrimination Against Women: Hearings* 91st Cong., 2d sess., June 1970, pp. 183, 185. In 1971 this number had increased to three female professors with tenure, compared with 582 male tenured full professors (*Newsweek*, 17 May 1971, p. 102).

100. Philip H. Abelson, "Women in Academia," *Science*, 14 January 1972, p. 127.

101. Jo Freeman, "Women on the Social Science Faculties Since 1892, University of Chicago." *Discrimination Against Women: Hearings*, pp. 994–97.

102. Harvard University, "Report of the Committee on the Status of Women," p. 1. The situation has not been much better at less prestigious universities. At the University of Illinois (Urbana-Champaign) in 1968, where 11.8 percent of the faculty were women, they were only 3.7 percent of the full professors (Robert C. Carey, *A Study of Academic Salaries at the University of Illinois, Men Compared with Women. Part II: Fall 1968 Salary* [Urbana, Ill.: University Bureau of Institutional Research, 1969]).

103. Helen S. Astin and Alan E. Bayer, "Sex Discrimination in Academe," in *Academic Women on the Move*, ed. Alice S. Rossi and Ann Calderwood (New York: Russell Sage Foundation, 1973), p. 339.

104. Ibid., p. 342.

105. For example, after reviewing eight studies in which the rates of promotion for males and females were compared, Morlock concluded: "Consensus exists among studies in a variety of disciplines that women advance up the academic ladder at a slower rate than their male counterparts. Furthermore, these differences in professional achievement are not merely reflections of differences by sex in degree level, prestige of degree, or rates of productivity" (Laura Morlock, "Discipline Variation in the Status of Academic Women," in *Academic Women on the Move*, ed. Alice S. Rossi and Ann Calderwood [New York: Russell Sage Foundation, 1973], pp. 280–81).

106. Alan E. Bayer and Helen S. Astin, "Sex Differences in Academic Rank and Salary among Science Doctorates in Teaching," *Journal of Human Resources* 3 (Spring 1968): 191–99.

107. U.S. Department of Labor, Women's Bureau, *Fact Sheet on the Earning Gap* (Washington, D.C., 1970), p. 1.

108. Michael A. La Sorte, "Academic Women's Salaries: Equal Pay for Equal Work?" *Journal of Higher Education* 42 (April 1971): 267.

109. Ibid., p. 273.

110. Ibid., p. 274.

111. Ibid., p. 273.

112. Ibid., p. 277. The differences between salaries of males and females remained substantial up through the 1971–72 academic year, the last year for which complete figures were available, in spite of intervention by the federal government to eliminate them. Although meaningful comparisons of the median salaries given below with those of La Sorte can not be made because there is no breakdown according to rank, the magnitude of the differences suggests that there was still considerable disparity in remuneration among the higher ranks:

Median Salaries by Sex, 1971–72, in Dollars

University enrollment	Men	Women	Difference	Percentage of faculty who were women
Public				
10,000 or more	14,342	11,519	2,823	15.6
5,000–9,999	13,112	11,140	1,972	19.7
Less than 5,000	12,887	10,960	1,927	23.5

University enrollment	Men	Women	Difference	Percentage of faculty who were women
Nonpublic				
5,000 or more	14,944	11,367	3,577	13.6
Less than 5,000	13,127	10,787	2,340	15.6

(National Education Association, *Salaries Paid and Salary-Related Practices in Higher Education, 1971–72*, pp. 11 and 62).

113. Astin and Bayer, "Sex Discrimination in Academe," p. 353.
114. Carnegie Commission on Higher Education, *Opportunities for Women in Higher Education*, pp. 199–235.
115. Reported by Pamela Swift, "Keeping Up . . . With Youth," *Parade*, 3 June 1973, p. 22.
116. Helen S. Astin, *The Woman Doctorate in America: Origins, Career, and Family* (New York: Russell Sage Foundation, 1969), pp. 75 and 145.
117. Rita James Simon, Shirley Merritt Clark, and Kathleen Galway, "The Woman Ph.D.: A Recent Profile," *Social Problems* 15 (Fall 1967): 223, table 3.
118. Reported in *Newsweek*, 10 December 1973, p. 123.
119. Bernard, *Academic Women*, p. viii.
120. Alan E. Bayer, *College and University Faculty: A Statistical Description*, ACE Research Reports vol. 5(5) (Washington, D.C.: American Council on Education, 1970), p. 15.
121. Simon, Clark, and Galway, "The Woman Ph.D.," p. 231.
122. Ibid., p. 230.
123. Radcliffe College, *Graduate Education for Women: The Radcliffe Ph.D.* (Cambridge, Mass.: Harvard University Press, 1956), p. 45.
124. Bernard, *Academic Women*, p. 154.
125. Ibid., pp. 270–74.
126. Ibid., pp. 263–67.
127. Brown, *The Mobile Professors*, pp. 80–81.
128. Ibid., p. 75.
129. Ibid., p. 76.
130. Ibid.
131. Brown's ratio is close to what was found in one national study: 24 percent of all faculty were women, but they held only 13.4 percent of the doctor's degrees (Carnegie Commission on Higher Education, *Opportunities for Women in Higher Education*, p. 2, chart 1).
132. Brown, *The Mobile Professors*, p. 77, table 28.
133. Ibid., p. 187.
134. Ibid., p. 80
135. Ibid., p. 78.
136. Ibid., p. 82.
137. Such beliefs, of course, are part of the academic folklore. Over fifty years ago, a survey of faculty found that "while 81% of their male colleagues regard women as equally successful with men in the ordinary college teaching, only 54% think they are as successful with advanced classes, 59% regard them as continuing to advance in their own scholarly life, and only 31% regard them as keeping pace with the men in productive scholarship." And the observations of some of the respondents in this study sound very much like those of Brown. From faculty men:

Equally good. Women usually pay greater attention to details and excel with weak students.

They find the causes for a student's weakness and sympathetically help correct it sooner than a man.

Men as a rule are better able to emphasize the most important topics in a course and accustom students to careful discrimination.

Women are apt to be superior in the technic of teaching and in wholehearted devotion to the pedagogical side of their work, while men excel in independence of judgment, fairness and breadth.

Women are more cautious and conservative, less daring and adventurous, and hence will not give to young people the push and drive they ought to get.

I have no definite facts to adduce; yet, I am of the opinion that the college teaching of men is more vigorous, less colorless, and more original than that of women.

Men have a more comprehensive attitude, are not so nervous. Their emphasis is more on the spirit than the letter. They seem to see more the fundamental importance of their work as related to other things—don't take it so seriously in one way (*i.e.*, the details) more seriously in another (quoted by a faculty man from a senior girl in a woman's college).

And from faculty women and deans of women:

Women are usually more conscientious and give more attention to details. Men on the other hand do not exaggerate trifles.

Women are usually better *teachers*. They are less likely to take to research.

Women are better teachers in all forms of elementary work; men more often give stimulus to independent, creative effort along advanced lines but are not so exacting in their classroom standards for the average student.

In the work of the first two years the woman's work equals or excels work of men instructors. In the last two years the women do not wield the same influence, or have the bigness of view.

Plus ça change . . . ("Second Report of Committee W on the Status of Women in College and University Faculties," *AAUP Bulletin* 10 (November 1924): 66–68, 70).

138. James D. Watson, *The Double Helix* (New York: Atheneum, 1969).

139. Bernard, *Academic Women*, p. 91.

140. Ibid., p. 89.

141. Ibid., p. viii.

142. Ibid., p. 154.

143. Nancy Jo Hoffman, "Sexism in Letters of Recommendation: A Case for Consciousness Raising," *MLA Newsletter* 4 (September 1972): 5–6.

144. In University of California, "Report of the Subcommittee," p. 72.

145. See Robert K. Merton, "The Matthew Effect in Science," *Science*, 5 January 1968, pp. 56–63, esp. pp. 57–58. As Merton points out, "as originally identified, the Matthew effect was construed in terms of enhancement of the position of already eminent scientists who are given disproportionate credit in cases of collaboration or of independent multiple discoveries" (p. 62). But the phenomenon, needless to say, is not so limited.

146. Ibid., p. 59.

CHAPTER 6

1. For another use of this same argument see Merton, *Social Theory and Social Structure*, p. 364.

2. Metzger, *Academic Freedom in the Age of the University*, pp. 217–18. In 1972, two officers (the president and first vice-president) and a former general

counsel of the AAUP affirmed that the Association mediated more than eight hundred cases a year. Moreover, they estimated that approximately two hundred other cases did not arise each year because administrators sought the advice of the AAUP in advance of taking a proposed course of action (Sanford H. Kadish, William W. Van Alstyne, and Robert K. Webb, "The Manifest Unwisdom of the AAUP as a Collective Bargaining Agency: A Dissenting View," *AAUP Bulletin* 58 [Spring 1972]: 57).

3. Wilson, *The Academic Man*, pp. 127–28.

4. David Riesman, *Constraint and Variety in American Education* (Lincoln, Nebr.: University of Nebraska Press, 1956), p. 20.

5. Upton Sinclair, *The Goose-Step* (Pasadena, Calif.: privately published, 1922), p. 437; reprinted in 1970 by AMS Press, New York.

6. This may be a cyclical phenomenon—over fifty years ago it drew some attention in another study of American higher education.

There is one other professor at Columbia who is known to be a Socialist; a very quiet one, who has retired from the Socialist party, and is writing an abstract work on metaphysics. He is useful to Butler and the whole crowd of the interlocking directorate, because whenever the question of academic freedom is raised, they can say: "Look at Montague, he is a Socialist!"

Similarly, in the worst days of reaction in Germany, they used to have in their universities what were called "renommir professoren," that is to say, "boast professors", or, as we should say in vulgar American, "shirt-fronts." In the same way, whenever Bismarck was conducting his campaigns against the Jews, he was always careful to have one Jew in the cabinet. I count over these "renommir professoren" in American universities; two at Columbia, one at Chicago, two at Wisconsin, one at Stanford, and one at Clark, expecting to be fired; a very young man at Johns Hopkins, and two old ladies at Wellesley. That is the complete list, so far as my investigations reveal; ten out of a total of some forty thousand college and university teachers—and that shows how much American colleges and universities have to make a pretense of caring about freedom! (ibid., p. 52).

7. Caplow and McGee, *The Academic Marketplace*, p. 228.

8. Ibid., p. 224.

9. Veblen, *The Higher Learning in America*, p. 129.

10. Ibid., p. 126.

11. Ibid., p. 128.

12. In general there is little in this study to support what has long been an obsession among many academics, intellectuals, and radicals, namely, that the greatest danger to academic freedom and the free exchange of ideas comes from the public and it is therefore best to avoid undue attention in the broader community. Upton Sinclair is one among many who has been convinced that this is the case:

The rub comes when the professor goes outside and lectures to city clubs and chambers of commerce, and gets into the newspapers in favor of the recognition of Soviet Russia. Then all the reactionaries in the state clamor for his scalp.

If you avoid the extremely crucial questions . . . you can get by with this in the majority of institutions, especially if you eschew outside activities and never get into the newspapers (*The Goose-Step*, pp. 231 and 437).

This perhaps overstates the case.

13. This has long been an observation of radical critics of the academic scene. Again, Sinclair has written:

In general, you may be fired if you depart in any way from the beaten track of propriety—and this whether your motives be the lowest or the highest, whether you are subnormal or supernormal, a crank or a genius.

And here is the all-important fact; the decision in this difficult matter lies not in the hands of your colleagues, who know you, but in some autocratic individual who is too important to know you, and too busy" (ibid., p. 401).

14. Robert M. MacIver, *Academic Freedom in Our Time* (New York: Columbia University Press, 1955), p. 73. Robert Presthus holds that many professors accept the definition of being an employee of the university administration, and some probably accept the definition of being an employee of the governing board (see his *The Organizational Society* [New York: Knopf, 1962], pp. 253–54).

15. Charles E. Wyzonski, Jr., "Sentinels and Stewards," *Harvard Alumni Bulletin*, 23 January 1954, p. 316.

16. "What State U Head Must Be: Top Educator, Administrator," *Buffalo Evening News* (Buffalo, N.Y.), 15 January 1964, p. 16.

17. Veblen, *The Higher Learning in America*, p. 51.

18. *Time*, 23 June 1967.

19. Reported in Metzger, *Academic Freedom in the Age of the University*, pp. 153–54.

20. Nicholas Murray Butler, "Commencement Day Address, June 6, 1917," in Columbia University Archives, New York, N.Y.

21. Reported in *Newsweek*, 31 August, 1970, p. 68.

22. Lazarsfeld and Thielens, *The Academic Mind*, p. 179.

23. Veblen, *The Higher Learning in America*, p. 100.

24. MacIver, *Academic Freedom in Our Time*, p. 276.

25. See Caplow and McGee, *The Academic Marketplace*, p. 222.

26. Richard Hofstadter and Walter P. Metzger, *The Development of Academic Freedom in the United States* (New York: Columbia University Press, 1955), esp. chaps. 6 and 7.

27. Ibid., p. 61.

28. The incomplete return, an expectancy for this type of survey, along with the fact that the sample is drawn from one institution, could introduce a bias in the data that must be considered in the interpretation of the findings. Further, because of the anonymity of the respondents, it could not be accurately ascertained who failed to reply. It can be stated with some certainty, however, after comparing the number of returns for each discipline with the number of questionnaires mailed, that those in the humanities had the lowest rate of participation.

29. Lazarsfeld and Thielens, *The Academic Mind*, pp. 148–52.

30. Ibid., p. 113.

31. MacIver, *Academic Freedom in Our Time*, p. 21.

32. Ibid., p. 22.

33. Ibid., p. 94.

34. Lazarsfeld and Thielens, *The Academic Mind*, pp. 88–89, 107–9.

35. Lazarsfeld and Thielens found that subsequent to the McCarthy era, 48 percent of their sample "report neither worry nor caution" about the consequence of both their academic and personal behavior (ibid., p. 80).

36. Clark Kerr, *The Uses of the University* (New York: Harper Torchbook, 1966).

37. Sanford H. Kadish, "The Theory of the Profession and Its Predicament," *AAUP Bulletin* 58 (Summer 1972): 122.

38. "Resolution of Boston State Faculty Federation," AFT Local 1943 (AFL-CIO), 6 February 1970.

39. "Statement on Government of Colleges and Universities," *AAUP Bulletin* 52 (Winter 1966): 375–79, esp. pp. 378–79.

40. City University of New York v. United Federation of College Teachers, AFL-CIO, Local 1460, AAA Case 1330-0286-70 (26 May, 1971).

41. Board of Higher Education of the City of New York v. Legislative Conference, AAA Case 1339-0706-70 (1 December, 1970). The appellate division of the

New York Supreme Court struck down this order of reappointment by a vote of three to two (Legislative Conference v. Board of Higher Education, 330 NYS 2d 688 [App. Div. 1st Dept. 1972]).

42. Board of Higher Education of the City of New York v. United Federation of College Teachers, AFL-CIO, Local 1460, AAA Case 1330-0282-70 (24 June 1972).

43. "PSC Contract Proposals," *Clarion* 2 (October 1972): 5.

44. Malcolm G. Scully and William A. Sievert, "Collective Bargaining Gains Converts among Teachers: Three National Organizations Vie to Represent Faculties," *The Chronicle of Higher Education*, 10 May 1971, p. 6.

45. *Accomplishments in Higher Education*, Association of New Jersey State College Faculties, 1972, p. 4.

46. "Pennsylvania Pact Approved by Profs." *CUPA Voice of the Faculty*, Hawaii, September 1972, p. 1.

47. "Editorial: Where the AFT Stands on Probation," *The Faculty Advocate* 1 (April 1971): 2.

48. Kenneth M. Smythe, "Institutional Differences: Questions and Answers," in *Faculty Power: Collective Bargaining on Campus*, ed. Terrence N. Tice (Ann Arbor, Mich.: The Institute of Continuing Legal Education, 1972), p. 75.

49. *Questions and Answers about AFT*, AFT Item 15, pp. 6–7.

50. Donald H. Wollett, "Issues at Stake," in *Faculty Unions and Collective Bargaining*, ed. E. D. Duryea and Robert S. Fisk (San Francisco: Jossey-Bass, 1973), p. 42.

51. "Bloustein Asks State to Make All 1973–74 Salary Increases 'Merit' Raises," *Rutgers AAUP Newsletter* 4 (December 1972): 12.

52. Kenneth P. Mortimer and G. Gregory Lozier, *Collective Bargaining: Implications for Governance* (University Park, Pa.: Center for the Study of Higher Education, 1972), p. 27.

53. Sumner H. Slichter, James J. Healy, and E. Robert Livernash, *The Impact of Collective Bargaining on Management* (Washington, D.C.: Brookings Institution, 1960), p. 950.

54. "On Implementation of New Academic Salary Structure" (Testimony presented by United Professors of California before the Faculty and Staff Affairs Committee of the CSUC Trustees, 8 December, 1972), p. 1.

55. Walter Oberer, "Faculty Participation in Academic Decision Making: As to What Issues, By What Forms, Using What Means of Persuasion?" in *Employment Relations in Higher Education*, ed. Stanley Elam and Michael H. Moskow (Bloomington, Ind.: Phi Delta Kappa, 1969), p. 143.

56. Samuel P. Capen, *The Management of Universities* (Buffalo: Foster & Stewart, 1953), p. 53.

57. Ibid., p. 54. See also "The Teaching Profession and Labor Unions," in ibid., pp. 55–63. This theme, of course, still informs many academics. In an address at the annual meeting of the American Association of University Professors in 1972, the outgoing president reminded the membership:

Although relying for financial support on private benefactors or the public and justifying our existence in terms of the public good, we make the extraordinary claim that we should be left alone. . . . And all this it asks for the public good and not that of the professor. When asked to explain why private benefactors, governmental agencies, and the public generally should establish for the professor this *imperium in imperio*, free of the controls imposed on other segments of democratic society—business, professional, industrial—our reply and our justification is our special theory of the profession.

The university, we say, is conducted for the common good and not to further the interest of either the individual teacher or the institution as a whole. That common good depends on the free search for truth and its expression by trained specialists in investigation and reflection whose peculiar and necessary service requires that their views and conclusions be their own unquestioned products as people "trained for and dedicated to the quest for truth." It follows therefore that professors must be allowed an academic freedom in their research and teaching in order to be free of restraints from inexpert or not wholly disinterested persons outside their ranks, whether they be governors or legislators, regents or administrators. It follows also that the professor must be provided with security of tenure after a probationary period, in order further to protect this freedom of research and teaching and to assure a degree of economic security, both of which are indispensable to the success of an institution in fulfilling its obligations to its students and to society. And it further follows that the university and the faculty as a collectivity are debarred from identifying with particular causes or particular views of what is true or of what is right—beyond the procedural commitment to freedom—lest an orthodoxy be imposed of greater or lesser extent which subverts the special university role. As Walter Metzger summarized the sense of the framers of the 1915 Declaration of Principles in this respect: "Intellectual inquiry, they insisted, had to be ongoing and individual; organizational fiats defeat it because organizations are mightier than individuals and fiats are inevitably premature. In support of their brief for neutrality they likened the true university to an 'intellectual experiment station' where new ideas might safely germinate, to an 'inviolable refuge' where men of ideas might safely congregate, and—most simply—to a 'home for research' " (Sanford H. Kadish, "The Theory of the Profession," pp. 120–21).

CHAPTER 7

1. Veblen, *The Higher Learning in America*.
2. John H. Crider, *The Bureaucrat* (Philadelphia: J. B. Lippincott, 1944), p. 39.
3. J. M. Juran has referred to duplication as "the common cold of the bureaucratic world" (see his *Bureaucracy: A Challenge to Better Management Effectiveness in the Federal Government* ([New York: Harper & Row, 1944]).
4. This picture may be colored as much by fancy as by fact. The portrait of American institutions of higher learning in the decades prior to the Civil War drawn by Richard Hofstadter would hardly qualify them as meritocracies: "there was no system of rewards for competence; salaries were commonly inflexible, there was no system of raises, no hierarchy of promotion; once installed, the professor was treated much the same whether he was an eminent success or a substantial failure as a teacher. Although a professor usually held office indefinitely on good behavior, his tenure depended upon usage and had no legal status: he could be fired at will by the governing board. . . ." (Richard Hofstadter, *Academic Freedom in the Age of the College* [New York: Columbia University Press, 1961], p. 230).
5. Martin Meyerson, president of the State University of New York at Buffalo, in a statement during the fall semester of 1967 regarding a controversy whether recruiters of the Dow Chemical Corporation and the CIA should be allowed on campus (*Quadrangle*, 16 November 1967, p. 4).
6. Attributed by *Newsweek* to the associate dean of the graduate school at the University of Maryland.
7. Philip E. Jacob, *Changing Values in College* (New York: Harper & Row, 1957).
8. Kenneth A. Feldman and Theodore M. Newcomb, *The Impact of College on Students: An Analysis of Four Decades of Research* (San Francisco: Jossey-Bass, 1967).
9. Kerr, *The Uses of the University*, p. 36.
10. "Who is Running Our Colleges?" in *Columbia College Today*, Winter 1967–68, p. 21.

11. John Henry Cardinal Newman, *The Idea of a University* (Garden City, N.Y.: Image Books, 1959), p. 10.

12. Norman W. Storer, *The Social System of Science* (New York. Holt, Rinehart and Winston, 1966), p. 141.

13. Eiduson, *Scientists*, p. 188.

14. Warren G. Bennis, "Relevant Futures for the Faculty of Social Sciences & Administration," *Colleague* 4 (December 1967): 2.

CHAPTER 8

1. Paul Seabury, "The Idea of Merit," *Commentary* 54 (December 1972): 41.

2. Ibid., p. 43.

3. Correlli Barnett, *The Swordbearers: Supreme Command in the First World War* (New York: William Morrow and Company, 1964), p. 178.

4. Daniel Bell, "On Meritocracy and Equality," *The Public Interest* 29 (Fall 1972): 66.

5. Reprinted with interpretive comments in the *AAUP Bulletin* 56 (Autumn 1970): 323–26, esp. p. 324.

6. Fritz Machlup, "In Defense of Academic Tenure," *AAUP Bulletin* 50 (Summer 1964): 119. Of course, many Tory academic polemicists believe that this argument is utter nonsense. Robert Nisbet, for example, has written: "It is not tenure that significantly undergirds the kind of freedom of research and teaching that is crucial; it is rather the willingness of the institution to defend it when need arises. . . . The report [of the Commission on Tenure, sponsored by the AAUP and the Association of American Colleges] declares tenure justified on the ground of its necessary undergirding of academic freedom. It is all much like the waving of the American flag. In blunt fact it is a non sequitur of high order to derive academic freedom from tenure" ("The Future of Tenure," in *On Learning and Change* [New Rochelle, N.Y.: *Change* Magazine, 1973], pp. 49–50). Curiously, Nisbet sees no relationship between the guarantee of tenure and the "willingness" to defend academic freedom on the part of those who are obligated to do so.

7. Walter P. Metzger, "Academic Freedom in Delocalized Academic Institutions," *Dimensions of Academic Freedom* (Urbana, Ill.: University of Illinois Press, 1969), p. 1.

8. See William J. Goode, "The Protection of the Inept," *American Sociological Review* 32 (February 1967): 5–19, esp. pp. 10–15.

9. Ibid., p. 6.

10. Clark Byse and Louis Joughin, *Tenure in American Higher Education: Plans, Practices, and the Law* (Ithaca, N.Y.: Cornell University Press, 1959), pp. 28–29, 141.

Index

Library of Congress Cataloging in Publication Data

Lewis, Lionel Stanley
    Scaling the ivory tower.

    Includes bibliographical references and index.
    1. College teachers, Rating of. 2. College
teachers—Salaries, pensions, etc. I. Title.
LB2333.L48   378.1'22   75-11358
ISBN 0-8018-1734-x